POPULATION:
THE UNFPA EXPERIENCE

Catherine S. Pierce, *Project Co-ordinator*

Principal Contributors

Hirofumi Ando	Luis Olivos
Roushdi El Heneidi	Jürgen Sacklowski
Mehri Hekmati	O. J. Sikes
Akira Kusukawa	Joseph van Arendonk
Richard Moore	Stephen Viederman
Lamine N'Diaye	Edison Wibmer

Other Contributors: S. Abdul-Hadi, T. Abrams, A. Abu-Nuwar, O. Ajayi, C. Benbow, H. Corvalan, S. Douglas, G. Duce, N. Essan, W. Franco, T. Jafri, S. Jung, D. Langston, L. Le, Y. Lee, S. Looky, U. Luong, A. Marshall, S. Mehra, P. Micou, L. Mubiala, J. Musoke, J. Parsons, E. Ranneberg-Nilsen, J. Rawley, S. Rhodes, A. Sadari, J. Santiago, H. Siddiqui, J. Simonsen, K. Trone, C. Valentine, W. Visser, K. Yamashita, Y. Zenda.

POPULATION:
THE UNFPA EXPERIENCE

NAFIS SADIK, *Editor*

Published for
UNITED NATIONS FUND FOR POPULATION ACTIVITIES
by
NEW YORK UNIVERSITY PRESS
New York *and* London
1984

Library of Congress Cataloging in Publication Data

Main entry under title:
  Population, the UNFPA experience.

  Includes index.
  1. United Nations Fund for Population Activities. 2. Population assistance. I. Sadik, Nafis. II. United Nations Fund for Population Activities. III. Title: Population, the U.N.F.P.A. experience.

HB884.5.P67 1984	304.6'06'01	84-6937

ISBN 0-8147-8170-5
ISBN 0-8147-8171-3 (pbk.)

Manufactured in the United States of America

Foreword

In the spring of 1983, the United Nations Fund for Population Activities reported to its Governing Council the successful transfer of more than a billion dollars of cumulative resources from the developed to developing countries in population assistance. For the Fund, this was a significant acceptance by the developing countries of the relevance of population policies and programmes in their development efforts and the role that multilateral assistance, through the United Nations, has in national programmes.

Up to the last decade, population as part of international development assistance has been a sensitive area for technical co-operation between countries. It was only after the first Asian Population Conference, held in New Delhi in 1963, at which countries requested technical assistance to find satisfactory and effective solutions to population problems, that the attention of the international community focused on this area of collaboration. The United Nations started population assistance in 1969, when UNFPA became operational—then an organization with less than $2.5 million in resources and a staff of five.

The World Population Plan of Action adopted in Bucharest in 1974 confirmed and accelerated global government commitment and support for population programmes in developing countries. The current volume of requests for population assistance to UNFPA far exceeds its capacity to respond despite the substantial increase in its own resources from donor countries.

To have a clearer view of the nature and scope of international population assistance, it is advisable, just before the International Conference on Population, 1984, to examine the programming experiences and management of projects of the Fund. A description of its work can contribute to an understanding of the operational issues likely to arise in the Conference.

It was with the purpose of describing and assessing the Fund's programme activities that I requested Dr. Nafis Sadik, Assistant Executive Director of UNFPA, to convene a task force to record these experiences. The present volume, which she has edited, is the outcome of that endeavour.

This book examines the record of UNFPA in working with countries as they have implemented their population policies with programmes.

v

It recounts how the Fund's mandate has been adapted to the diverse needs and interests of Governments and to the changing demands of the demographic conditions in countries. The book also illustrates how an organization such as UNFPA developed from a conveyor of resources to an innovator in the delivery of population assistance and how its neutrality and sensitivity strengthened the resolve of many countries to address effectively the population issue.

The present volume continues the series of monographs and books that UNFPA has published dealing with the growth and work of the Fund. It is a complement to my volume *Reflections on Population*, which discusses UNFPA policies, published on the occasion of the 1984 International Conference on Population.

New York
February 1984

RAFAEL M. SALAS
Executive Director
United Nations Fund for
Population Activities

CONTENTS

LIST OF TABLES

LIST OF FEATURE PAGES

Definitions

Age-Dependency Ratio—The ratio of persons in the ages defined as dependent (under 15 and over 64 years) to those in the ages defined as economically productive (15–64 years) in a population.

BACHUE—A mathematical tool for development planning which incorporates population variables in equations.

Billion—A billion is 1,000 million.

Dollars—Dollars are U.S. dollars unless otherwise indicated.

General Fertility Rate (also referred to as fertility rate)—The number of live births per 1,000 women aged 15–49 years in a given year.

Gross Reproduction Rate—The average number of daughters that would be born alive to a woman (or group of women) during her lifetime if she passed through her childbearing years conforming to the age-specific fertility rates of a given year.

Growth Rate—The rate at which a population is increasing (or decreasing) in a given year due to natural increase and net migration, expressed as a percentage of the base population.

Infant Mortality Rate—The number of deaths of infants under one year of age in a given year per 1,000 live births in that year.

Multi-bi(lateral) funding—UNFPA uses the system known as multi-bilateral or multi-bi funding to bring together donors and Governments in one of several forms of collaboration. UNFPA may help a Government develop a project and seek assistance from a donor to implement it; it may enlist the help of donors to provide expertise, equipment, supplies or money to support projects; it may create a Trust Fund to manage donors' contributions for the benefit of developing countries; or it may provide for joint financing of population programmes or projects by the Fund and a donor.

Total Fertility Rate (TFR)—The average number of children that would be born alive to a woman (or group of women) during her lifetime if she were to pass through her childbearing years conforming to the age-specific fertility rates of a given year.

Vital Statistics—Demographic data on births, deaths, foetal deaths, marriages and divorces.

Source: Definitions of demographic terms are from Arthur Haupt and Thomas T. Kane, *Population Handbook* (Washington, D.C., Population Reference Bureau, Inc., 1980).

Note on Sources

All population data, unless otherwise indicated, are from the United Nations Department of International Economic and Social Affairs, *World Population Prospects: Estimates and Projections as Assessed in 1982* (New York, United Nations). All economic data, unless otherwise indicated, are from the World Bank, *World Development Report, 1983* (Washington, D.C., The World Bank, 1983). Chapter 7, "Family Planning", draws upon information from *Family Planning in the 1980's: Challenges and Opportunities*, Report of the International Conference on Family Planning in the 1980's, Jakarta, Indonesia, 26-30 April 1981, co-sponsored by the United Nations Fund for Population Activities, the International Planned Parenthood Federation and The Population Council. The text of the World Population Plan of Action, referred to throughout this work, appears in *Report of the United Nations World Population Conference, 1974* (United Nations publication, Sales No. E.75.X-III.3), chapter I.

Glossary of Acronyms and Initials

ACR	Annual Country Review
AHW	Auxiliary health worker
ASEAN	Association of Southeast Asian Nations
CDC	Cairo Demographic Centre, Egypt
CEDOR	Demographic Training and Research Centre, United Nations-Romania
CEDPA	Centre for Development and Population Activities
CELADE	Latin American Demographic Centre
CICRED	Committee for International Co-ordination of National Research in Demography
CONAPO	National Population Council, Mexico
DRSAP	Deputy Representative and Senior Advisor on Population
ECA	United Nations Economic Commission for Africa
ECAFE	Economic Commission for Asia and the Far East

ECE	United Nations Economic Commission for Europe
ECLA	United Nations Economic Commission for Latin America
ECOSOC	United Nations Economic and Social Council
ECWA	United Nations Economic Commission for Western Asia
ESCAP	United Nations Economic and Social Commission for Asia and the Pacific
FAO	Food and Agriculture Organization of the United Nations
FELDA	Federal Land Development Authority, Malaysia
GNP	Gross national product
HRP	Special Programme of Research, Development and Research Training in Human Reproduction, World Health Organization
ICARP	International Committee for Applied Research in Population
ICOMP	International Committee on the Management of Population Programmes
IEC	Information, education and communication
IFORD	Institut de Formation et de Recherche Demographiques, United Republic of Cameroon
IIPS	International Institute for Population Studies, India
ILO	International Labour Organisation
IPPF	International Planned Parenthood Federation
IPS	Inter Press Service
IUD	Intra-uterine device
IUSSP	International Union for the Scientific Study of Population
JOICFP	Japanese Organization for International Cooperation in Family Planning, Inc.
MCH/FP	Maternal and child health/family planning
NGO	Non-governmental organization
PAHO	Pan American Health Organization, World Health Organization
PDP	Population and Development Project, Egypt
PIACT	Program for the Introduction and Adaptation of Contraceptive Technology

PPR	Project Progress Report
PRAC	Programme Review and Allocation Committee
RIPS	Regional Institute for Population Studies, Ghana
SEARO	World Health Organization Regional Office for Southeast Asia
TBA	Traditional birth attendant
TCDC	Technical Co-operation Among Developing Countries
TPR	Tripartite Review
UNDP	United Nations Development Programme
UNDTCD	United Nations Department of Technical Co-operation for Development
UNESCO	United Nations Educational, Scientific and Cultural Organization
UNFPA	United Nations Fund for Population Activities
UNICEF	United Nations Children's Fund
USAID	United States Agency for International Development
WHO	World Health Organization
WHO/AFRO	World Health Organization Regional Office for Africa
WHO/EURO	World Health Organization Regional Office for Europe

PREFACE

The primary concern of UNFPA is to assist Governments in formulating and implementing population policies that have as the ultimate goal the improvement of the quality of life for their people. The Fund also seeks to promote a fuller understanding of the population aspects of development. The aims and purposes of the Fund as specified in Resolution 1763 of the Economic and Social Council (ECOSOC) include the following:

- "To build up, on an international basis, with the assistance of the competent bodies of the United Nations system, the knowledge and the capacity to respond to national, regional, interregional and global needs in the population and family planning fields; to promote co-ordination in planning and programming; and to co-operate with all concerned;
- To promote awareness, both in developed and in developing countries, of the social, economic and environmental implications of national and international population problems; of the human rights aspects of family planning; and of possible strategies to deal with them, in accordance with the plans and priorities of each country;
- To extend systematic and sustained assistance to developing countries at their request in dealing with their population problems; such assistance to be afforded in forms and by means requested by the recipient countries and best suited to meet the individual country's needs; and,
- To play a leading role in the United Nations system in promoting population programmes and to co-ordinate projects supported by the Fund".

The 15 years since UNFPA was established have been critical ones in the population field. Countries in the developing world which were once largely unconcerned about population issues have now taken steps to deal with these matters. Today, about 75 developing countries have population planning units, many of which were initially financed by UNFPA, and more than 90 per cent of the population of the developing world live in countries with population programmes. The progress that has occurred is particularly remarkable in view of the modest resources that have been channelled to population, never more than 2 per cent of all overseas development assistance in any one year. Furthermore, these changes took place despite the world-wide economic recession of the past four years.

Although notable achievements have been recorded, the problems of the population sector are still far from resolved. In view of the considerable challenges that lie ahead, it was felt that it would be useful to compile a volume examining the programming activities of UNFPA. One of the objectives of such a review was to distil from those experiences lessons that might be useful to the Fund and to others working in this sector. The principal sections of this book deal with the Fund's operational experience in the various geographic regions and the development of its programming assistance in the fields of family planning; information, education and communication; basic data collection; population dynamics (research, training and policy formulation); and women's programmes. One of the major tasks of the Fund has been to create an awareness of population issues. Appendix 1 gives some idea of the variety of publications that UNFPA has supported. Although this is a study of operational experience, it was felt that readers might wish some additional population data and thus a summary of demographic indicators has also been included as appendix 2.

Assessing almost 15 years of programming experience, during which UNFPA supported more than 3,500 projects in most countries of the developing world, is a formidable task and could not have been accomplished without the participation and co-operation of many people. I am particularly grateful to Rafael M. Salas, Executive Director of UNFPA, for his constant encouragement and support during the course of this project. A Task Force comprising members of all UNFPA Divisions defined the focus of this study and reviewed its progress at various stages. Senior staff members were most generous in sharing their thoughts on topics discussed in this study. Several UNFPA Representatives and Deputy Representatives and Senior Advisors on Population also made useful suggestions as to the content of this book.

Many staff members were particularly helpful and therefore deserve special mention. I am especially appreciative of the work of Catherine S. Pierce, who made substantial contributions to the entire volume and who responsibly guided the manuscript through the various stages of development. Richard Moore, Sethuramiah L. N. Rao and Jürgen Sacklowski generously offered their insights and comments on several sections. Jyoti S. Singh, Arumugam Thavarajah and Jack Voelpel reviewed the manuscript at different times and made many useful suggestions. The major burden of gathering the information and data for this book fell to the staff of the Programme Division, under the direction of Joseph van Arendonk, and the members of the Technical and Planning Division, under the direction of Jürgen Sacklowski. The Administration and Finance Division, under the direction of Shigeaki Tomita, was most helpful in supplying the required financial data. The contributors are listed at the beginning of this volume.

I would especially like to thank Barbara Ryan, whose superb editorial skills and comprehensive knowledge of UNFPA have contributed substantially to the quality of this book. My thanks also to Gabriela Lampl for her careful proofreading.

All of the contributors to this volume join me in acknowledging the capable assistance furnished by their respective secretaries. In particular, I would like to thank Ethiopia Abraham, Dulce Castillo and Maria Teresa Simpao, who have been primarily involved in the processing of this book.

Nafis Sadik

1. INTRODUCTION

When the Fund began operations in 1969, it was navigating in relatively uncharted seas. Despite considerable experience with multilateral support for development projects, there were few precedents for extending assistance for "soft sector" projects such as education, health and population. The efforts that had been undertaken in population were scattered, poorly documented and had not been evaluated. Also, with the exception of some countries in Asia, there was a limited knowledge of population issues and little perception of their urgency. Population was still regarded as a highly controversial subject, and policy makers, even if convinced of the need for action, were reluctant to become advocates for the cause.

Realizing this situation, the Fund made the creation of awareness a key element in its approach to programming in the population sector. The importance of this function was underscored in ECOSOC Resolution 1763 (1973) which charged the Fund with promoting "awareness, both in developed and in developing countries, of the social, economic and environmental implications of national and international population problems; of the human rights aspects of family planning; and of possible strategies to deal with them, in accordance with the plans and priorities of each country". In implementing this directive, UNFPA has, over the years, supported a wide range of activities. It has opened a dialogue with academics, legislators and non-governmental organizations (NGOs) which has facilitated a continual interchange of information. Its work with parliamentarians has been instrumental in mobilizing the support of government leaders for action in the population sector and other closely related areas.

As the Fund launched its activities, it was apparent that the divergent perceptions of population questions and the various rationales for taking action would significantly shape UNFPA-sponsored undertakings in the regions of the developing world. By the late 1960s, several Asian countries had already identified rapid population growth as a basic constraint to the achievement of their development goals and had initiated family planning programmes as one means of curtailing rapid rates of demographic increase. At the other end of the spectrum were

1

most of the Sub-Saharan African countries, which were largely unaware of their population situations. Many had not conducted a complete census since gaining independence and thus had no firm evidence of the pressures being exerted by high fertility, high mortality and imbalances in population distribution. Falling some place between these two extremes were the countries of Latin America and the Caribbean and those of the Middle East and North Africa. The Latin America and Caribbean region, which had a long tradition of census-taking, was aware of its basic demographic situation, and some countries had already carried out studies of population and development interactions. In addition, a number of Governments were concerned about the high incidence of illegal abortion and were seeking means to reverse this trend. Government inclinations to intervene in the population sector were, however, tempered by the influence and potential opposition of traditional institutions. In the Middle East and North Africa, several countries acknowledged the negative consequences of rapid population growth, but only two—Egypt and Tunisia—had family planning programmes. In other countries in the region, population was too sensitive a political issue, and leaders were wary of antagonizing constituents. Confronted with these widely disparate perceptions, it was clear that the Fund would have to demonstrate that, through appropriate action programmes, trends in the population sector, like those in any other sector, could be modified. Simultaneously, the Fund would have to shape its own institutional development.

FUNDAMENTAL PRINCIPLES

In setting out to accomplish these objectives, the Fund has subscribed to three fundamental principles—neutrality, innovation and flexibility. Because population was a sensitive and complex issue, it realized that any effective international co-operation in this sector would have to be predicated on neutrality. In its dealings with Governments, the Fund, therefore, has always adhered to the principle that every nation has the sovereign right to determine its own population policy, and that individuals have the right to determine freely and voluntarily their family size. UNFPA has never advocated any particular approach to population problems but rather extends assistance to those areas of population that countries themselves deem important. Furthermore, UNFPA has always pursued a multifaceted approach to population. Its primary concern has been to assist countries in identifying and responding to their diverse population needs. Convinced of the Fund's neutrality, Governments that otherwise might have hesitated have sought assistance for whatever they deemed important—population data collection; family planning; information, education and communication (IEC); research on demographic and socio-economic interrelationships; and policy formulation.

The Fund recognized, early on, that flexibility in the application of conventional procedures governing external development assistance and the ability to innovate would be key determinants of its success in keeping pace with the unique and rapidly evolving population sector. The standard forms of technical co-operation—foreign experts, equipment, fellowships and study tours—were inadequate for meeting the considerable and wide-ranging needs in this sector. If action programmes were to take root and expand, other support would be necessary. Therefore, the Fund has covered a variety of local costs; for example, salaries of locally employed personnel, locally manufactured supplies and equipment, the use of national experts and the cost of training conducted locally. It has also financed the provision of transport, supplies and equipment and has funded various types of research —social science, demographic and biomedical—relevant to population. In certain cases, the Fund paid a limited proportion of construction costs if they were judged essential to the success of a project. The Fund has also supported demonstration or pilot projects because interventions of this nature were often pivotal factors in a Government's decision to adopt a population policy.

In order to augment the resources available for population activities, the Fund instituted a multi-bilateral funding arrangement. Under this system UNFPA may pursue any of the following courses: help a Government develop a project for funding by another donor; enlist donors to support specified project components in a UNFPA-funded project; create a Trust Fund to manage donors' contributions for the benefit of developing countries; and provide for joint financing of large-scale population programmes by the Fund and another donor. In selecting executing agencies, UNFPA collaborates with Governments in choosing the most appropriate entity for the task at hand. In the early days, this was usually an agency or organization of the United Nations, but in recent years there has been an increased use of NGOs and universities. Moreover, the Fund has always agreed that certain countries having the requisite technical infrastructure could implement their own projects directly. Initially, only a few countries were in a position to do so, but over the years a considerable number of countries have acquired this capability.

STRATEGIES AND PROCEDURES

As a new organization in a field that was just beginning to accept the validity of action programmes, the Fund was simultaneously faced with the formidable tasks of identifying strategies and of defining operational procedures. The Fund opted to pursue population initiatives at all levels—interregional, regional and country. From the outset, it was apparent that there was an urgent need to strengthen the infrastructure for population activities both in countries and in the United Nations system. According to ECOSOC Resolution 1763 (LIV), the Fund was to build up the capacity of the agencies and organizations of the United Nations system to enable them to respond to national, regional, interregional and global needs in the population field. Thus, the Fund has supported the various United Nations agencies and organizations in amplifying population concerns in their respective areas of competence. Working through their constituencies in labour, agriculture, education and communication, and health, ILO, FAO, UNESCO and WHO have undertaken research and action programmes that have benefited developing countries in all regions. UNFPA has funded special operationally oriented research projects in the United Nations Population Division and has financed posts for population staff in the regional commissions.

As a result of this support, the various parts of the United Nations system were able to undertake a considerable volume of population work—particularly research on methodological issues and the drawing up of training protocols—activities best pursued at the global level not only for reasons of cost-effectiveness but also because most countries lacked the capacity to undertake such tasks. With the exception of countries in Asia, most countries in the other regions were not in a position to absorb large amounts of population assistance; therefore, the interregional and global programme claimed almost half the total of UNFPA assistance during its early years. As countries manifested greater interest in population and as they developed expertise in this field, the share of interregional expenditure declined markedly.

Management of the programme at the field level has always been of great importance to the Fund. In all countries, the UNFPA programme is overseen by the UNDP Resident Representative, who is also the UNFPA Representative. Where the Fund has a large programme, it has established in the UNDP office field units headed by a Deputy Representative and Senior Advisor on Population and composed of national officers and, depending on the magnitude of the programme, an international programme officer. The Deputy Representative, in addition to expediting the UNFPA-assisted programme, often serves as the point of contact for the population activities in a country. On the average, the Fund maintains about 35 field units.

When the Fund began to extend assistance, its approach could best be described as *ad hoc*. Project requests, usually reviewed for soundness by outside technical experts, were approved by the Executive Director. With the rapid expansion of requests, it became obvious that certain jurisdictional rearrangements, greater "in-house" specialization and more systematic procedures were warranted for the Fund to discharge its responsibilities effectively. The General Assembly, in 1972, placed UNFPA under its authority and designated the Governing Council of the United Nations Development Programme to serve as the governing body for the Fund.

Internally, the Fund delineated policy guidelines and procedures for programming, monitoring and evaluation. The programme of assistance was differentiated into various work plan categories—basic data collection; population dynamics (mostly training and research); formulation and evaluation of population policies; family planning; information, education and communication; and special projects and multisectoral activities. Guidelines were drawn up to indicate the kinds of projects and components that UNFPA could finance under each of these headings. In addition, operational guidelines dealing with basic policy matters that cut across all categories were formulated and financial rules and regulations were set up. Periodically, the Fund assesses these procedures to ascertain whether revisions are in order or new areas should be addressed. For example, it was only after the Fund had been programming for some time that it identified the key role women play in the success of population interventions and drew up guidelines dealing specifically with women and population.

The Fund set up two standing committees to handle programme and policy matters. The Programme Review and Allocation Committee (PRAC) is responsible for making recommendations to the Executive Director on programmes and projects and for deciding on allocations; the Policy Committee constitutes the main policy-making body. Gradually, the Fund also began to build up its in-house technical expertise in the population field, leading to the establishment of a Technical Branch.

To promote the successful implementation of projects and maintain accountability for monies it administers, UNFPA instituted a monitoring system having the following objectives: to assess the progress of UNFPA-sponsored activities with reference to the accomplishment of their immediate and long-range objectives; to provide feedback and identify needed adjustments in work plans and budgets in order to

Table 1

UNFPA NEEDS ASSESSMENT MISSIONS BY REGION AND COUNTRY,
1977-1984

Region	Years							
	1977	1978	1979	1980	1981	1982	1983	1984
Africa, Sub-Saharan	*Liberia *Senegal	*Burundi *Gambia *Kenya *Madagascar *Mali *Mauritania *United Republic of Tanzania	*Guinea *Niger *Rwanda United Republic of Cameroon *Upper Volta	*Benin *Comoros *Ethiopia *Malawi *Nigeria Swaziland Togo *Uganda	*Ghana *Sierra Leone *Zambia *Zimbabwe	*Central African Republic	Ivory Coast *Zaire	*Angola Botswana Congo *Lesotho *Mozambique

Asia and the Pacific	Bangladesh	*Afghanistan *India *Indonesia Malaysia Philippines Thailand *Viet Nam	Mongolia *Nepal *Pakistan *Solomon Islands	*Bhutan Kiribati Republic of Korea *Samoa *Sri Lanka Tonga	Fiji *Maldives Thailand *Viet Nam	*Lao People's Democratic Republic	*China
							*Bangladesh *Burma *India *Indonesia *Pakistan *Sri Lanka
Latin America and the Caribbean	Honduras	Paraguay	Cuba El Salvador Guatemala *Haiti Mexico	Ecuador	Peru	Brazil *Haiti	
Middle East and Mediterranean	*Democratic Yemen	*Sudan	Bahrain Jordan Morocco *Somalia Syrian Arab Republic Turkey	*Egypt Tunisia *Yemen	Algeria *Democratic Yemen *Egypt Jordan *Somalia *Sudan		

Source: UNFPA.
Note: Countries that appear twice have had, or are scheduled to have, second needs assessment missions.
*Indicates priority country.

ensure the efficiency and effectiveness of these activities; and to provide information on the nature of future needs for UNFPA assistance. The Project Progress Report (PPR), the Tripartite Review (TPR), Mid-Term Review and the Annual Country Review (ACR) constitute the core elements of the monitoring system. The Government, the executing agency (or agencies) and UNFPA as the funding organization participate in TPRs and ACRs. Because of the varying size and complexity of programmes and projects, not all projects necessitate a TPR and not all countries require an ACR. In general, ACRs are undertaken only in countries having a substantial UNFPA-sponsored multisectoral programme. In addition to continual monitoring and evaluation, the Fund also instituted a system for in-depth, independent evaluations of activities it supported. These evaluations, although co-ordinated by the Fund, are carried out by outside consultants. The reports resulting from such exercises, together with what is known through regular monitoring channels, furnish information that is essential for UNFPA decision-making on the possible extension of the project under review or on funding similar undertakings in the future.

The World Population Conference held in Bucharest, Romania, in 1974 was, in many ways, a turning point in the Fund's operational procedures. The meeting focused world-wide attention on population issues. The document approved at that Conference, the World Population Plan of Action, underscored the urgency of taking action. After 1974, requests to UNFPA increased markedly. It was apparent that the Fund would have to adjust its procedures and, where necessary, institute new ones to handle the growing demand for assistance. UNFPA formalized its country programming process and instituted a system for setting priorities in the allocation of resources among countries. It began to follow a three-stage programming cycle consisting of a needs assessment, which identifies and analyses a country's requirements in the population sector; a programme development stage, during which a programme of assistance is drawn up based on findings from the needs assessment and on discussions with Government; and a programme implementation phase, during which specific projects are formulated and implemented. The needs assessments have been particularly useful for developing countries and the Fund. The needs assessment exercise, in which the Government plays a central role, takes as its point of departure the country's development and population policies. The identification of a country's needs in the population sector helps Governments, UNFPA and other donors to delineate coherent programmes for external assistance in the population field. By the end of the 1983, the Fund had conducted 73 needs assessments. Table 1 lists those countries that have had such assessments.

The Fund, in 1976, devised a priority system, based on selected economic and demographic criteria, to ensure special attention to those countries with the most serious population problems. Initially, 40 countries were designated as priority countries and 14 were identified as borderline countries. In 1982, after reviewing its experience, the Fund revised the selection criteria to include the following: an annual gross national product per capita of $500 or less; annual population increase of 100,000 persons or more; a gross reproduction rate of 2.5 or more; an infant mortality rate of 160 per 1,000 live births or above; and a density of two or more persons per hectare of arable land. A country must be at or below the income threshold and must meet two of the demographic variables mentioned above. The 53 countries now qualifying as priority countries are listed in table 2. In general, about 70 per cent of UNFPA resources for country programming are expended in priority countries.

The Fund's programming procedures, in addition to fulfilling their primary purpose of providing a coherent framework for the disposition of assistance, have also been vehicles for promoting awareness of population issues. By building up a population nucleus in the various United Nations agencies and organizations, UNFPA has brought population concerns to the attention of the United Nations system as a whole. Likewise, the UNFPA-supported network of regional advisers of the United Nations and the specialized agencies has increased country contacts with population experts, a process that has helped to keep population issues in the forefront. The Fund's needs assessment reports have played a key role both in raising national awareness of population questions and in serving as a comprehensive source of information. By placing population in the broad context of development planning, these reports have provided countries with the first systematic account of population-related problems and of the range of policy options to deal with them.

The experience of UNFPA over the years has readily illustrated the interplay between the Fund's approaches and the realities of country programming. Principles, strategies and procedures were essential for responsible programming of resources. The Fund's approach, however, has never been rigid, and its policies have been influenced and modified according to the situation it found in the field and in response to the changing needs in the population sector. Perhaps one of the Fund's most notable achievements is that, as it drew up formal procedures and as precedents were established, it retained its commitment to innovation and its readiness to respond flexibly to ever-changing needs. It is this dynamic quality that has enabled it to work effectively

Table 2

Regional Distribution of UNFPA Priority Countries For Population Assistance

Region/Priority countries

Africa, Sub-Saharan

1. Angola	16. Malawi
2. Benin	17. Mali
3. Burundi	18. Mauritania
4. Central African Republic	19. Mozambique
5. Chad	20. Niger
6. Comoros	21. Rwanda
7. Equatorial Guinea	22. Sao Tome and Principe
8. Ethiopia	23. Senegal
9. Gambia	24. Sierra Leone
10. Ghana	25. Uganda
11. Guinea	26. United Republic of Tanzania
12. Kenya	27. Upper Volta
13. Lesotho	28. Zambia
14. Liberia	29. Zaire
15. Madagascar	30. Zimbabwe

Asia and the Pacific

1. Afghanistan	9. Lao People's Democratic Republic
2. Bangladesh	10. Maldives
3. Bhutan	11. Nepal
4. Burma	12. Pakistan
5. China	13. Samoa
6. Democratic Kampuchea	14. Solomon Islands
7. India	15. Sri Lanka
8. Indonesia	16. Viet Nam

Latin America and the Caribbean

1. Dominica	2. Haiti

Middle East and Mediterranean

1. Democratic Yemen	4. Sudan
2. Egypt	5. Yemen
3. Somalia	

Source: UNFPA.

Note: Criteria for selection as priority country: per capita gross national product of $500 or less and two of the following demographic criteria — annual population increase of 100,000 persons or more; gross reproduction rate of 2.5 or more; infant mortality rate of 160 or more per 1,000 live births; and density of agricultural population on arable land of two or more persons per hectare.

with countries in meeting their diverse population needs.

The chapters that follow recount in detail how the growing awareness of population issues crystallized into action and how UNFPA has worked with Governments in the developing countries and with NGOs in the various regions to help countries implement population programmes consonant with their socio-economic settings and cultural values. The chapters also provide an in-depth look at the principal components of UNFPA programmes and illustrate how UNFPA, together with the countries it serves, has demonstrated that action programmes can be successfully undertaken in the population sector.

PART ONE

REGIONAL OUTLOOKS

Introduction to Part One

Over the past 15 years, the UNFPA programme has developed in response to the changing needs of countries, the growing complexity of working in the population sector and the shifts in available resources. As shown in table 3, from 1969 to 1983, the Fund's programme expenditures totalled more than $1.0 billion, having grown from about $26.5 million in 1969–1972 to a high of $136.4 million in 1980. Funds available for the programme fell off in 1981 and 1982 but increased in 1983.

Most of the Fund's early activities were undertaken on an interregional basis because countries were in the early stages of initiating population activities and possessed limited capacities in this field. The proportion of support going to interregional projects declined over the period as countries acquired the infrastructure necessary to absorb population assistance. Interregional activities, which accounted for about 46 per cent of expenditures in the period 1969–1972 claimed only about 16 per cent in 1983. Many countries in Asia had population activities well under way before the Fund was established; hence, from the earliest years to the present, this region always led other geographic regions in programme expenditures. During the past decade, many African Governments have become more cognizant of the deleterious consequences of rapid growth rates for the well-being of their populations. The increasing propensity to address population concerns is reflected in the increasing proportion of UNFPA programme expenditures in Africa, which rose from about 9 per cent of the total programme in 1969–1972 to 20 per cent of allocations in 1983.

Through careful monitoring and evaluation, the Fund has been able to apply the lessons learned in those early endeavours. This section will review the evolution of the UNFPA programme from the country perspective, showing how approaches were modified to respond to each country's perceptions of its population problems.

Table 3

PERCENTAGE DISTRIBUTION OF UNFPA EXPENDITURES BY REGIONS, 1969–1983

Regions	1969-1972	1973	1974	1975	1976	1977	1978	1979	1980	1981	1982	1983	Total 1969-1983
Sub-Saharan Africa	9.0	9.6	9.9	12.4	13.0	13.2	11.5	14.4	13.9	15.7	16.1	20.4	14.3
Asia and the Pacific	27.5	30.5	29.0	30.7	30.0	33.4	37.0	38.1	37.3	39.2	41.4	38.3	36.1
Latin America and the Caribbean	7.7	11.1	20.3	21.1	25.2	19.8	19.2	16.4	17.2	14.3	13.8	13.2	16.8
Middle East and Mediterranean	9.7	7.0	10.4	10.1	13.2	12.8	11.3	9.9	9.2	9.8	10.1	10.9	10.4
Europe	0.5	0.7	0.3	0.3	0.5	0.6	0.7	1.1	1.1	1.2	1.0	0.9	0.9
Interregional and global	45.6	41.1	30.1	25.3	18.1	20.2	20.3	20.1	21.3	19.8	17.6	16.3	21.5
Total	100.0	100.0	100.0	100.0	100.0	100.0	100.0	100.0	100.0	100.0	100.0	100.0	100.0
(Thousands of US dollars)	(26,501)	(30,067)	(54,103)	(66,673)	(69,368)	(66,551)	(89,230)	(123,624)	(136,357)	(122,543)	(106,244)	(127,165)	(1,018,426)

Source: UNFPA Fact Sheet Number 1.10 (September 1983); UNFPA Fact Sheet Number 1.11 (November 1983).
Note: Figures for 1969 to 1982 are project expenditures; figures for 1983 are project allocations as of 30 November 1983.

2. Sub-Saharan Africa

Compared with countries in other regions, the Sub-Saharan African countries may be considered late arrivals on the population scene, largely because of the paucity of information on basic features of their populations—sizes, rates of growth, distribution and composition—and also because of socio-cultural and religious values that impeded interventions in the population field, such as family planning and even head counts. Until 1970, except for a few efforts to collect demographic statistics, there was almost no population activity in the region.

The barriers to population-related activities began to lift gradually during the 1970s, prompted in part by the initiation of the first World Population and Housing Census Programme by the United Nations in 1970; the activities of UNFPA to create awareness of population issues; and the World Population Conference in Bucharest in 1974. These events helped set in motion the development and expansion of population activities in Africa and spurred policy-making bodies within the countries and within the United Nations system to action. By the end of 1982, most of the African countries had recognized the demographic processes confronting them and had undertaken activities designed either to obtain more detailed information on the causes and consequences of population issues or to change population trends.

OVERVIEW OF THE REGION

Sub-Saharan Africa, according to the UNFPA classification, consists of 42 independent countries, 30 of which have been designated priority countries (see table 2, page 10). The area comprises four subregions: Eastern Africa, consisting of 14 countries and approximately 40 per cent of the region's population; Middle Africa, 9 countries and about 16 per cent of the population; Southern Africa, 3 countries and 1 per cent of the population; and Western Africa, 16 countries and 43 per cent of the population. These countries exhibit extremely diverse economic, social, political and demographic features.

Most of the countries in the region have experienced a range of problems that have exacted a heavy toll on the achievement of development objectives. All have incurred serious economic problems, especially as

16

related to balance of payments, low per capita incomes and diminishing resources for investment. Low levels of productivity characterize almost the entire region. Natural disasters, such as drought and famines, have caused the displacement of millions of persons in the Sahel region and have resulted in widespread starvation and death. The region contains 23 of the 36 countries designated by the United Nations as "least developed countries". Political instability in many countries has often precipitated the movement of people among the African countries. The shortage of skills has been made more acute by the drain of skilled and semi-skilled workers to the more industrialized and stable nations of the North and West. Literacy levels have remained low. In part because of the critical shortage of trained manpower, planning has sometimes been haphazard, a problem compounded by the paucity of data in nearly all sectors. The most crucial issue today—and fortunately one that is receiving increasing attention in both the region and the world as a whole—is population and its pivotal role in relation to land area, growth, fertility and mortality, morbidity, malnutrition and migration.

In this predominantly agricultural continent, there is great population pressure on land. Sub-Saharan Africa comprises 19,096,000 square kilometres of land, and in mid-1984 the region had an estimated population density of 19 persons per square kilometre. There are, however, marked regional variations in population densities, ranging from as low as one person per square kilometre in Botswana to as high as 507 persons per square kilometre in Mauritius, and 159 and 177 persons per square kilometre in Burundi and Rwanda, respectively. On arable land, variations in density become even more pronounced. The extremes are represented by Gabon with 2 persons per square kilometre and 188 persons per square kilometre of arable land, and Kenya, with 27 persons per square kilometre and 884 persons per square kilometre of arable land. In Kenya, which has vast areas of uninhabited land, less than one fifth of the total land area supports more than 80 per cent of the population.

With an estimated annual growth rate of about 3.0 per cent as of mid-1984, the population of Sub-Saharan Africa is growing more rapidly than that of the other major regions of the world. This trend is expected to continue to the year 2000, when projections show a population of about 600 million for the region with approximately the same subregional distribution. Some countries, such as Kenya and Zimbabwe, have registered growth rates as high as 4.1 per cent per annum and 3.5 per cent per annum, respectively. The region also exhibits the highest crude birth and death rates and infant mortality rates. In the period 1975–1980, the crude birth rates averaged 47 per 1,000 live births and the crude death rates 17 per 1,000, as compared with 29 births and 11 deaths per 1,000 population for the world as a whole and an average of 34 births and 12 deaths per 1,000 for developing countries.

Migration, mainly in response to unfavourable climatic and economic conditions, has always been a central feature of African life, but it has now taken on added urgency. Political disruptions have resulted in unprecedented migration streams both internationally and nationally. The number of refugees increases every year, and these movements are putting considerable stress on the meagre goods and services, especially in the urban areas of several countries of the region.

High levels of infant mortality are an urgent concern of all Governments in Africa. Estimates indicate that the infant mortality rate for Africa as a whole, including North Africa, was about 114 deaths per 1,000 live births in 1980–1985. The comparable rate for the world as a whole was 81 per 1,000 and, for developing countries, 92 per 1,000. The average life expectancy at birth in all Africa for the period 1980–1985 —49 years—was considerably below the level of the developing world as a whole—56 years. Mortality declines may have slowed down or ceased in certain parts of Africa, although reliable data to substantiate this observation are lacking.

UNFPA AND SUB-SAHARAN AFRICA

In the decade of the 1970s, the recognition of population-related dislocations in Africa gradually led to the formulation of population policies and programmes. UNFPA played a key role in this process, by working with Governments initially to discover the dimensions of their population situation and, afterwards, to assist them in designing and implementing programmes tailored to their needs and compatible with their cultural ethos. The basic philosophy of UNFPA, its neutrality in population issues and its recognition of the sovereignty of nations and of individual human rights with regard to population matters, made it particularly attractive to African countries embarking on activities in this area. UNFPA, upon receiving requests for assistance from countries in Africa, geared its responses to the prevailing situation. Only after initial efforts in data collection alerted policy makers to the urgency of their population problems were action-oriented policies pursued.

Funding levels

As the data in table 4 illustrate, the highest proportion of UNFPA expenditures in Africa during the period 1969–1983 was for data collection—

Table 4

PERCENTAGE DISTRIBUTION OF UNFPA EXPENDITURES BY WORK PLAN CATEGORIES, SUB-SAHARAN AFRICA, 1969–1983

Work plan categories	Years												Total
	1969-1972	1973	1974	1975	1976	1977	1978	1979	1980	1981	1982	1983	1969-1983
Basic data collection	31.1	42.0	52.1	51.3	50.6	34.1	40.3	38.1	35.1	38.0	33.9	28.4	37.4
Population dynamics	22.2	19.3	11.0	13.2	13.8	14.8	14.0	14.4	18.8	16.7	18.3	15.2	15.9
Formulation and evaluation of population policies and programmes	3.3	4.4	3.7	2.1	1.4	0.4	0.8	1.6	4.0	4.1	3.5	5.8	3.2
Implementation of policies	0.0	0.0	0.0	0.0	0.0	0.0	0.0	0.1	0.0	0.0	0.0	0.0	0.0
Family planning	3.7	10.8	7.2	15.7	16.6	27.4	20.3	22.0	18.1	19.0	23.3	32.8	21.8
Communication and education	22.0	20.0	13.5	12.0	9.4	12.2	13.6	13.1	12.7	9.9	7.6	6.9	10.9
Special programmes	1.0	0.9	1.1	1.0	1.8	3.4	0.4	1.5	1.3	2.0	1.4	0.5	1.3
Multisectoral activities	6.7	2.6	11.4	4.7	6.4	7.7	10.6	9.2	10.0	10.3	12.0	10.4	9.5
Total	100.0	100.0	100.0	100.0	100.0	100.0	100.0	100.0	100.0	100.0	100.0	100.0	100.0
(Thousands of US dollars)	(2,374)	(2,893)	(5,366)	(8,253)	(9,029)	(8,769)	(10,229)	(17,732)	(18,908)	(19,217)	(17,153)	(25,962)	(145,885)

Sources: UNFPA Fact Sheet Number 1.08 (September 1983); UNFPA Fact Sheet Number 1.09 (November 1983).
Note: Figures for 1969 to 1982 are project expenditures; figures for 1983 are project allocations as of 30 November 1983.

an average of 37 per cent, and more than 50 per cent in 1974, 1975 and 1976. The most interesting pattern, however, has been the pronounced increase in the proportion of expenditures for family planning, from 14 per cent in 1969–1972 to 33 per cent in 1983, as awareness of the deleterious effects of population trends prompted Governments to seek external support for remedial actions.

Types of activities

Basic data collection. The lack of basic population data in most countries seriously handicapped effective socio-economic and development planning. Hence, throughout the 1970s, UNFPA provided support to three major types of activity in data collection: population censuses, demographic surveys, and civil registration statistics.

Cumulative expenditures in data collection amounted to $54.6 million; of this amount, approximately 38 per cent was for technical advisory services, 24 per cent for salaries of local personnel, 4 per cent for training, and 34 per cent for equipment and materials. A total of 113 data collection projects were supported.

A major thrust of UNFPA assistance in this sector has been the support for the 1970 and 1980 rounds of population censuses. Under the aegis of the 1970 African Census Programme, 18 national population census projects were assisted in Burundi, Central African Republic, Congo, Gambia, Ivory Coast, Liberia, Madagascar, Malawi, Mali, Mauritania, Mauritius, Nigeria, Rwanda, Senegal, Sierra Leone, Swaziland, United Republic of Cameroon and Upper Volta. Another 24 national census projects have received support in connection with the 1980s census round (Angola, Benin, Botswana, Comoros, Cape Verde, Equatorial Guinea, Ethiopia, Gabon, Gambia, Ghana, Guinea, Guinea-Bissau, Kenya, Lesotho, Liberia, Malawi, Mozambique, Niger, Togo, Uganda, United Republic of Tanzania, Zaire, Zambia and Zimbabwe). Thus, a total of 42 UNFPA-assisted census projects took place during the period 1971–1982. In addition, assistance has been provided to several inter-country activities designed to strengthen and assist national census activities through support to the Economic Commission for Africa (ECA) for regional workshops on census methods and data processing and for the convening of a working group on recommendations for the 1980s round of population and housing censuses in Africa.

As a supplement to the census activities, UNFPA supported demographic surveys designed to provide information on the elements of population change: fertility, mortality and migration. Demographic surveys, in most cases, were conducted simultaneously with the census enumerations. Separate post-census demographic surveys have been assisted in Benin, Central African Republic, Lesotho, Liberia and Rwanda. Furthermore, within the context of the World Fertility Survey, the Fund has supported Benin, Lesotho, Mauritania, Nigeria and Senegal in carrying out nationally representative and internationally comparable sample surveys of fertility. At the intercountry level, resources have also been provided to ECA for the services of a regional adviser in sampling to assist country activities and also for convening a meeting of a working group on the feasibility of a household survey capability in Africa.

As part of an effort to help countries develop and improve their deficient national civil registration systems, assistance has been given for pilot projects to guide methodological development for civil registration systems and training of national personnel in 11 countries (Burundi, Central African Republic, Gabon, Ghana, Kenya, Lesotho, Sierra Leone, Swaziland, Uganda, United Republic of Tanzania and Zaire). To back up these national efforts at the intercountry level, UNFPA supported two regional advisory services at ECA and a meeting of a working group on civil registration systems and vital statistics collection.

Population dynamics. Most African countries in the 1970s lacked the trained personnel and research facilities to conduct activities promoting an understanding of the causes and consequences of their population problems.

An important part of the Fund's assistance has, therefore, been directed towards institution building and improving the knowledge and understanding of demographic phenomena. Resources provided in these two areas totalled approximately $23.2 million, of which 58 per cent was for support of advisory services; 4 per cent for salaries of local personnel; 26 per cent for training; and 12 per cent for equipment.

Although the development of national institutions is a long-term undertaking for which the main responsibility lies with Governments themselves, UNFPA initiated the establishment of several national population training and research institutions. Support was given to 11 countries—Botswana, Burundi, Ivory Coast, Lesotho, Liberia, Mauritania, Nigeria, Sierra Leone, Togo, Uganda and Zaire—to build up the national capability of national middle-level cadres and to undertake research useful to Governments. At the intercountry level, advanced training activities were supported with the Regional Institute for Population Studies (RIPS) at Accra, Ghana, and the Institut de Formation et de Recherche Demographiques (IFORD) at Yaounde, United Republic of Cameroon. These two institutes, supported in part by UNFPA, seek to meet the needs of English- and French-speaking countries in such diverse fields as post-graduate demographic training, research, publications and advisory services in demography and related fields for Governments in the region. By the end of 1983, these two institutes had trained more than 500 students and had undertaken numerous advisory missions to countries in the region.

In research, UNFPA has funded studies on factors affecting fertility, mortality and infant mortality in Botswana, Togo and Zambia. The Fund has supported migration research and labour force surveys to collect data for population and manpower planning in Lesotho and Senegal. At the intercountry level, research studies funded at RIPS, IFORD and at the ECA Population Division have generally addressed concerns related to mortality, infant mortality, fertility, migration and the relationships between population and development. Assistance has been provided to two subregional bodies: the Sahel Institute, for the integration of population studies into the recovery plans of Sahelian countries affected by the drought, and the Regional Centre for Population Studies of the Union Douaniere et Economique de l'Afrique Centrale, for the coordination of research and programme activities among member states of the Union (Central African Republic, the Congo, Gabon and the United Republic of Cameroon).

Population policy formulation and implementation. The initiation of research activities specifically aimed at practical policy issues and the institutionalization of population in the development planning process have constituted two important parts of the Fund's work. By the end of 1983, cumulative expenditures amounted to $4.7 million for support of various project activities.

A study on cultural values and population policy has been supported in Kenya and Upper Volta to obtain information on cultural and social values to be considered in the formulation of national population policies. A research study on the interrelationships of population and development was undertaken in Upper Volta in order to develop research on integrated population and development planning and to prepare population policies. In Nigeria, the Fund has supported research to identify the causes of out-migration and the consequences for rural development. In Senegal, it has supported a study designed to outline viable policy options that the Government might pursue to bring about more satisfactory patterns of population distribution. National seminars have been funded to foster better understanding of population and development among policy makers, political leaders and the public in 11 countries (Congo, Ivory Coast, Kenya, Lesotho, Mali, Mauritius, Nigeria, Senegal, Sierra Leone, Togo and United Republic of Tanzania). At the intercountry level, most of the research assistance supported by the Fund, through ECA, has attempted to clarify the interactions between population and development through comparative studies. In addition, UNFPA has assisted ECA with several meetings including the first and second African Population Conference, the Conference of African Demographers, an Expert Group Meeting on National Population Policies in Africa dealing with policies on urbanization and population distribution and an Expert Group Meeting on Fertility and Mortality Levels and Trends in Africa. The Fund has also supported, in co-operation with the Inter-Parliamentary Union, a regional meeting on population and development for African parliamentarians.

In line with the recommendations of the World Population Plan of Action, six countries—Mali, Rwanda, Senegal, Sierra Leone, United Republic of Cameroon and Upper Volta—have been assisted with the establishment of population units within their development planning ministries. The purpose of these units is to help foster the integration of population factors into national development planning. The Fund has also supported intercountry activities with ECA and ILO, consisting mainly of providing regional advisers in population policy.

Another important contribution of the Fund in this area is the programme "Law and Population", which is designed to identify national laws with provisions that have demographic implications or that are inconsistent with population programme activities. Eight countries have been assisted under this programme (Ethiopia, Ghana, Lesotho, Nigeria, Senegal, Swaziland, Togo and United Republic of Cameroon).

Family planning/child spacing. Since the World Population Conference in 1974 and the World Conference of the International Women's Year in 1975, many Governments have come to recognize family planning as one of several initiatives to improve the welfare of mothers and children and to raise the status of women, enabling them to take a more active part than they have to date in the national development process.

During the period 1969–1971 to 1982, the Fund assisted regional projects and individual projects in 36 countries (Angola, Benin, Botswana, Burundi, Cape Verde, Central African Republic, Comoros, Congo, Ethiopia, Gambia, Ghana, Guinea, Guinea-Bissau, Ivory Coast, Kenya, Lesotho,Liberia, Madagascar, Malawi, Mali, Mauritius, Mozambique, Niger, Nigeria, Rwanda, Senegal, Seychelles, Sierra Leone, Swaziland, Togo, United Republic of Cameroon, United Republic of Tanzania, Upper Volta, Zaire, Zambia and Zimbabwe). UNFPA assistance totalled $31.8 million, of which approximately 45 per cent was for clinical and other equipment; 30 per cent for technical advisory services; 15 per cent for salaries of additional staff; and 10 per cent for the development of an adequate number of trained personnel at all levels.

Governments in the region have endorsed family planning as a means of child spacing and for ameliorating infertility and sterility. Frequent pregnancies at short intervals are detrimental to the health of women and their children and increase the incidence of maternal and infant deaths. Consequently, UNFPA has assisted them in promoting family planning as a means of spacing births and thereby reducing the health hazards associated with frequent child bearing.

The Fund's assistance for family planning and birth-spacing components has usually been within the framework of maternal and child health activities. Recognizing the importance of the need to lengthen life expectancy, several countries have included in their programmes specific measures for mortality reduction. The strengthening of service delivery for the care of pregnant women, lactating mothers, infants and children as well as for family planning has received attention in the UNFPA-assisted programmes. In countries such as Kenya and Mauritius, which have set quantitative objectives for reducing the rate of their population growth, the emphasis of UNFPA support has been more on the provision of family planning activities and less on maternal and child health activities. In three countries, Angola, Malawi and Mauritania, UNFPA assistance has concentrated on strengthening maternal and child health activities as a suitable vehicle for enhancing the acceptance of family planning and child-spacing activities. In Swaziland and Togo, UNFPA assistance for family planning/child spacing has been linked to broader programmes of health and nutrition. The WHO Regional Office for Africa (WHO/AFRO), which has received support for the services of a team of regional advisers on family health, has provided technical back-up to many supported activities. Assistance has also been provided for the establishment and operation of the Regional Training Centre in Family Health, located in Mauritius, to meet the changing needs of African countries in family planning/child spacing. In addition, several regional and subregional meetings on subjects related to MCH/FP have been supported by the Fund.

Population information, education and communication. Over the past few years, as a consequence of the rapid social changes that many African societies are undergoing, population information, education and communication (IEC) activities have become a subject of growing interest. Several Governments, confronted with various social problems such as increased numbers of pregnancies and illegal abortions among schoolgirls, have sought assistance from the Fund.

Cumulative expenditures in this sector to 1983 amounted to $15.9 million. Projects have focused on two major activities: population education, including population studies, family life education, sex education and health education activities aimed at increasing awareness and understanding of the implications of demographic issues and human reproduction among adults and adolescents; and communication activities designed to identify suitable means, methods and training for the delivery of population information to various target groups.

Five countries (Guinea, Kenya, Nigeria, Sierra Leone and Upper Volta) have received assistance for introducing population education into their formal school systems. The focus has generally been on promoting understanding of the implications of population change and designing solutions to problems that ensue. The teaching of human reproduction, family planning and population dynamics within the context of sex education in schools has been supported in four countries: Benin, Cape Verde, Togo and Upper Volta. The Fund has also provided assistance for population education activities integrated with educational programmes having more comprehensive objectives, such as adult literacy, agricultural extension, labour and trade union education, home economics and rural development in 13 countries (Ivory Coast, Kenya, Lesotho, Mali, Mauritius, Senegal, Sierra Leone, Swaziland, Uganda, United Republic of Cameroon, United Republic of Tanzania, Zaire and Zambia).

At the intercountry level, support has been given for a variety of activities. These include assistance to UNESCO and ILO for regional advisers on population education in formal and non-formal education systems and to WHO/AFRO for a health education adviser; a survey by UNESCO on population education curricula in Africa; a subregional demonstration project by FAO on planning for better family life, involving Kenya, Uganda and United Republic of Tanzania; and several workshops, seminars and meetings for educators working with trade union members and co-operative leaders.

Communication activities supported by UNFPA cover a wide range of sectors including census-taking, civil registration and family planning. Most UNFPA-assisted family planning programmes include a built-in communication-information component intended to promote understanding of the health rationale of family planning/child spacing to further the development of responsible attitudes and behaviour leading towards a better quality of family life. Other activities that have benefited from UNFPA funding include the production of films as part of the preparatory activities of the national population censuses in Benin, Gabon, Ivory Coast, Senegal and United Republic of Cameroon and the teaching of population information and communication at the National Institute of Mass Communication in Nigeria. At the intercountry level, funded activities have included regional advisory services in communication to UNESCO; a seminar on family planning communication; the establishment of a population information centre and clearing-house at ECA; and a workshop for English-speaking broadcasters from West Africa.

Special programme: women. It has long been recognized that women's role and status in the community and in the society are of primary importance to the success of population programmes. The well-being of women, including their health, literacy, increased community participation and access to decision-making processes, contributes greatly to women's ability to exercise their "basic right to decide freely and responsibly the number and spacing of their children and to have the information, education and means to do so", as stated in the World Population Plan of Action (14,f).

Over the period 1971–1982, projects costing $1.9 million were approved for women's activities. Women's projects cut across the boundaries of many UNFPA core programme activities, including information, education, communication, research, seminars, training and action programmes.

In the sector of information, education and communication, UNFPA has supported activities aimed at creating and increasing awareness and understanding of population-related matters to improve the quality of life for women. In Mali, UNFPA has funded a project for the advancement of women which provides funds for communication support to a national functional literacy programme, family life education and maternal and child health services. In Senegal, a UNFPA-supported pilot project on education, health, nutrition and population in an urban environment was aimed at women's groups for the enhancement of their health and welfare.

The Fund has also financed research directed at the improvement of knowledge and understanding of population issues related to women. An important study in Mali for which the Fund has provided support is the development of knowledge about the problems of unwed mothers and the relationship between the status of mothers and population. In Congo, a pilot study was undertaken to assess means to improve family well-being and family health and to provide the basis for the formulation of a population policy. The Fund financed a comparative research project on the impact of socio-economic changes on the women of Sub-Saharan Africa, which sought to identify and study the mechanisms by which women are integrated into the development process.

Training activities in home economics have also been financed by UNFPA. Female trainers helped women organize and improve their approach to home-making so that the family's health and welfare would be ameliorated. Support has also been given to the ECA Pan African Women's Centre to introduce population-related issues and concepts into its overall programme.

FUTURE DIRECTIONS

The past few years have witnessed a remarkable change in the perception of population activities in African countries. Efforts in data collection and analysis gave Governments a firmer grasp of various population-related problems and they began to enact policy measures. According to the United Nations Fifth Population Inquiry, all countries in the region are concerned with high levels of mortality and morbidity; most consider the geographical distribution of their populations unacceptable; and the majority considers the fertility level too high. Several countries that, 10 years ago, declared themselves satisfied with the high fertility level have in recent years expressed concern at the continuation of high levels.

Despite the progress made in the perception of population by African Governments and the substantial assistance provided by UNFPA to initiate and implement programme activities, several problems still need action.

Population remains a sensitive issue in many areas, even in countries that launched initiatives in this field. The need for more awareness and better understanding of population matters persists, not only among officials of all branches of Government but also among parliamentarians, local officials, religious leaders, professional groups, community leaders and people at the grass-roots level.

Policy-oriented research on key issues—population distribution and migration, mortality, population growth, fertility and women's participation in development—has been less developed than expected, given the wealth of information amassed in data collection efforts. With a few exceptions, such as Kenya and Mauritius, the countries of the region do not have a well-defined national population policy. Furthermore, an understanding of the process of policy formation and of the role of policies in programme development is completely lacking in most countries. Beyond the mention of population size and growth in national development plans, population is not yet an integral part of the development process. As a consequence, a strong political and financial commitment to population is often absent in many countries despite the growing awareness of Governments of the need to address dislocations resulting from population trends.

Great progress has been made in activities related to family planning and child spacing. In 1973, UNFPA supported family planning projects in only three countries; by the end of 1982, UNFPA had assisted family planning and child-spacing activities in 36 Sub-Saharan countries. Many of these programmes are, however, at an early stage of development, and many people, particularly those in rural areas, are beyond the reach of facilities. As part of their rural development policies, Governments should be mindful of the need to extend maternal and child health and child-spacing activities to these areas for those who wish to space births. Moreover, relatively little research has been conducted on MCH/FP and child spacing in the African context. An effort in this direction is needed to understand attitudes towards family size, family planning and other influences on the design of family planning/child-spacing programmes.

There is still a need to promote census-taking as a regular exercise (once every 10 years as recommended by the United Nations) and a normal Government responsibility, and to reinforce national capabilities for collecting basic population data from censuses and intercensal surveys in order to assess trends in demographic behaviour. Although the data collection activities of the 1970s marked a breakthrough in the accumulation of baseline demographic data, several countries that are due for census-taking in the 1980s have not yet begun preparatory activities.

Subject, of course, to the overall resources available to the Fund, prospects appear good for a substantial increase in resources being channelled to Africa. Africa has the largest number of priority countries, and the absorptive capacity of most African countries is increasing rapidly. Furthermore, the wide range of serious population issues that the region will face in the coming years is of great concern to UNFPA. Given the limited resources available and the magnitude of the needs, UNFPA intends to concentrate efforts on specific area activities to achieve maximum impact.

In accordance with its mandate, UNFPA intends to make an important contribution to increase awareness and understanding of population issues in order to strengthen the Governments' commitment to deal with them. In a rapidly changing region such as Africa, continuous efforts must be made to reach the expanding cohorts of new generations. Support through population education in both formal and nonformal sectors will be aimed at men and women as well as adolescents, who are the future parents and leaders, in order to broaden their under-

standing and improve their decision-making abilities regarding population issues and human reproduction. Wide-scale information and
education campaigns including the use of mass media will be geared
towards the needs of the various target audiences such as government
officials, parliamentarians, community leaders, youth and women.

Efforts will be made to increase access both to information on family
planning/child spacing and to services. In this regard, UNFPA intends
to continue its discussions with African decision makers and planners
concerning the social and economic significance of recognizing the human right to information and the means of determining the number and
spacing of births, as adopted by the World Population Plan of Action
and the United Nations General Assembly resolution 3344 (XXIX) of 17
December 1974. Assistance will be provided to continue to consolidate
and strengthen programmes; to expand coverage of population information, education and family planning/child-spacing services, particularly in the rural areas to fulfil the unmet needs of the rural women; to
develop MCH/FP and child-spacing service statistical systems with appropriate mechanisms to ensure feedback into the service programme
in order to enhance the quality of activities; and to encourage operational and applied research aimed at improving the quality and coverage of services. More attention will be devoted to exploring innovative
approaches through health service programmes, primary health care
approaches, community-based delivery systems and all other means of
reaching the population as well as involving them in the development
of such measures.

In accordance with the needs and perceptions of countries, the Fund
will pay increasing attention to the formulation and implementation of
population policies to enable countries to integrate population measures into their social and economic goals and strategies. Broadening
the technical perspectives of planners and policy makers with respect to
population policies will be a priority action for the Fund in Sub-Saharan
Africa. In this respect, emphasis will be on initiating, developing and
strengthening national capability in population policy and programme
formulation through training, policy-oriented research, and establishing national population commissions to assist Governments in arriving
at informed and consistent decisions on population issues. Concur-
rently, continued efforts will be made to institutionalize population in
the national development process through the establishment, within
the national planning ministries, of population units to deal with the
population aspects of development planning.

As a support activity for the promotion and strengthening of national
population policies, data collection will continue to be financed. Now

that many countries have gained experience in census-taking, the volume of assistance for general activities will be more limited than it was. Support for developing nation-wide vital statistics and civil registration systems will be more selective, and assistance will continue only for pilot projects. The same considerations will apply with regard to surveys; emphasis will be on supporting the development of survey capability on population topics, possibly within the framework of the United Nations National Household Survey Capability Programme.

The development of national personnel trained in population is one of the most important prerequisites both for successfully implementing programmes after external assistance terminates and for fostering national self-reliance in population activities. Therefore, priority will be given to building up national capability at all levels in all programme areas through training, advisory services on programme management, development, execution, evaluation and support for building infrastructure. UNFPA intends to intensify its efforts to encourage and facilitate the strengthening of the African countries' capabilities and self-reliance in population matters.

In connection with UNFPA efforts in the health sector, special attention will be given to ensure the promotion and full participation of women in all aspects of population and development programmes. The full integration of women into all levels of the development process by increasing their access to educational, economic and other opportunities in the community is generally recognized as having a bearing upon economic and social development, as well as influencing fertility behaviour. Women might not be able to improve their living conditions and those of their children unless they have the means to control their fertility and, thereby, can participate in educational programmes, income-generating activities and other measures for their advancement. In this connection, attention will be paid not only to meeting the needs of women through service programmes but also to promoting the role of women as decision makers and participants in population programme activities, because they are the most important target group of population activities.

In addition to supporting country programme activities, the Fund will continue to assist appropriate intercountry activities in Africa.

3. ASIA AND THE PACIFIC

OVERVIEW OF THE REGION

The region of Asia and the Pacific comprises 45 developing countries and territories, 16 of which have been designated by UNFPA as priority countries and territories. Extending from Iran on the fringes of West Asia to the scattered island countries of the Pacific, the region includes a great diversity of economic, cultural, religious and linguistic patterns. This socio-cultural heterogeneity is parallelled by a wide range of demographic conditions. The region is home to the world's most populous nation—China—as well as to some of the smallest—for example, Tuvalu in the South Pacific (with a population of about 8,000).

As a whole, Asia accounts for 56 per cent of the world's population and 75 per cent of the developing world's population. Eleven countries have populations exceeding 25 million—Bangladesh, Burma, China, India, Indonesia, Iran, Pakistan, the Philippines, the Republic of Korea, Thailand and Viet Nam. Whereas almost all countries of the Asian subregion have large populations, the island countries of the Pacific generally have small populations; with the one exception of Papua New Guinea, all are mostly less than one million. Most Asian and Pacific countries have growth rates in excess of 2.0 per cent. The moderate-to-low growth rates of the Pacific Island countries reflect considerable outmigration. A few developing countries of the region—China, Indonesia and Thailand—are on their way towards a transition (low birth and death rates) in population growth patterns.

Notable differences may be observed in birth rates, death rates and income levels. Birth rates in excess of 40 per 1,000 are found in 9 countries. The highest rates are recorded for Afghanistan (49.6) and East Timor (48.0). Lower birth rates, from 28 to 17 per 1,000, prevail in China (18.5), Fiji (27.2), Republic of Korea (21.0) and Singapore (18.0). Levels of fertility as measured by the gross reproduction rate are comparatively high in Afghanistan, Bangladesh, Bhutan, Cook Islands, Iran, Kiribati, Nepal, Pakistan, Papua New Guinea, Samoa, Tonga and Vanuatu. The level of gross reproduction exceeds two daughters per woman in approximately 25 countries of the region. This, in combination with the relatively large population in these countries, points to a continued potentially rapid rate of population growth for several countries of the region.

In many Asian developing countries, the death rates are similar to those in the developed world. Crude death rates below 10 per 1,000 are found in China, Hong Kong, Malaysia, the Philippines, the Republic of Korea, Singapore, Sri Lanka and Thailand, to name but a few. In other countries, the rates remain extremely high. Afghanistan, Bangladesh, Bhutan, Democratic Kampuchea, East Timor, Lao People's Democratic Republic and Nepal—all have rates in excess of 15 per 1,000. In these countries, as would be expected, the average life expectancy at birth is also low, less than 50 years, whereas in China, Hong Kong, Malaysia, Mongolia, the Republic of Korea, and Singapore, among others, life expectancies at birth are in the range of 62-72 years. Although considerable success has been achieved in reducing infant mortality, the rates remain high in Afghanistan (205), Bhutan (144), Democratic Kampuchea (160) and East Timor (183).

Variations in the income levels among the countries of the region are pronounced. The annual GNP per capita is low, less than $600 in about 18 countries. Five countries—Bangladesh, Bhutan, Burma, Lao People's Democratic Republic and Nepal—have an annual GNP per capita of less than $200. On the other hand, Brunei, Cook Islands, Fiji, Hong Kong, Malaysia, Republic of Korea and Singapore have reached per capita levels of more than $1,000 per year.

The countries of Asia led the way in the formulation and implementation of government-supported policies and programmes in the population sector. In the years after the Second World War, public health measures coupled with the use of modern medicines brought about a dramatic reduction in the death rates in many Asian countries. This decline, however, was unaccompanied by a parallel reduction in fertility; thus, rates of population growth reached unprecedented levels. By the late 1950s and early 1960s, Governments in several Asian countries—notably India, Pakistan, and the Republic of Korea—realized that rapid rates of population growth were undercutting the prospects for achieving socio-economic development objectives. They introduced family planning programmes as one means of reducing the prevailing high levels of fertility. Gradually, other countries in the region organized family planning programmes, recognizing both the demographic and the health benefits of such interventions.

Asian countries have also been pioneers in devising measures to deal with unsatisfactory spatial distributions of population. In an effort to redress the imbalance between concentrations of people and availability of resources, the Government of Indonesia initiated the Transmigration

Policy designed to move people from the more crowded islands and to promote the development of unsettled regions. The Mahaweli Project in Sri Lanka and the Federal Land Development Authority (FELDA) scheme in Malaysia are similar initiatives.

In contrast to other parts of the world, the response in the Asia region to designing population policies was relatively positive, possibly reflecting the urgency of population-related problems coupled with, in many countries, a fairly open socio-cultural ethos. That is not to say that, initially, there was not some sensitivity or skepticism in many countries. Even today, the region presents contrasts in this respect, ranging from the far-reaching family planning programmes in China, Indonesia and Thailand to countries such as Burma and the Lao People's Democratic Republic, which are still coming to grips with the population issue.

UNFPA AND ASIA AND THE PACIFIC

Funding levels

In view of the magnitude of its population problems as well as of the propensity of Governments to take action in this sector, the Asia region has always been the principal recipient of UNFPA funds. The data in table 5 reveal something of the evolution of population activities in the region. By the time the Fund began its operational work, several countries had efforts under way in the field of family planning. Thus, from the start, assistance for family planning was the preponderant request from countries in Asia. Consequently, in each year from 1969 to 1980, family planning absorbed at least 60 per cent of UNFPA monies channelled to Asia, and in some years—1973, 1975 and 1976—family planning and the closely linked category of population education and communication accounted for approximately 85 per cent of total UNFPA spending in Asia.

In recent years, the proportion of funds for data collection, population dynamics and policy formulation has risen while the proportion for family planning has taken a downturn. There are several reasons for this shift. In the early 1970s, Asia, unlike other regions, had both the capacity for, and experience with, data collection and population research. In existence since 1957, the International Institute for Population Studies (IIPS) in Bombay, India, had trained many people from the region in basic demography and demographic research. Largely because their planners had an idea of their demographic situations and the consequences of existing population trends, Governments were eager to obtain external assistance for family planning efforts, particularly for action programmes. As these programmes took root and have shown themselves to be effective, countries themselves began to take over a large share of expenditures in this field. This trend accounts to some extent for the decrease in the proportion of the Fund's expenditures for family planning in Asia. For example, according to Government of India figures, that country has doubled the share of its budget committed to family planning between 1974–1979 and 1980–1985. The Fund's increasing amounts for data collection from 1979 to 1982 reflect expenditures incurred in connection with the 1980 round of censuses. The high percentage in 1981 reflects the outlay of $12.7 million for the census in China, which included activities relating to enumeration, data processing and analysis, and dissemination (see feature page in chapter 9 for details on the China census).

The increasing expenditures for population dynamics and policy during the 1980s are to be expected as programmes mature. Population activities have been under way in Asia for more than 20 years. During that time, approaches to this sector have become both more refined and more complex. Since the 1974 World Population Conference, the emphasis has been on the integration of population in the overall development network. As discussed in chapter 10, translating this idea into action is as difficult as it is necessary. Research in Asia is now focused on clarifying with some precision the interrelationship between population trends, resource availability and use, and environmental concerns. New orientations in the population field—for example, integration or community initiatives—require broader and more sophisticated training. All of these issues are a key concern in the region because its long experience in the population sector has brought it, in a sense, to the leading edge of these new directions. For the most part, the countries of Asia are laying the foundations for the programmatic responses that will be adapted for use in many other regions of the world over the coming decades.

Types of activities
Asia has had longer experience than any other developing region with interventions to modify reproductive behaviour. The region had already witnessed the adoption of family planning as a national policy by India in 1950s and in a few other countries such as Pakistan, which then included Bangladesh, and Malaysia in the 1960s. By the time of the World Population Conference in Bucharest in 1974, 17 Asian countries had population policies and almost all countries had family planning programmes. In general, Asian countries have had the least problems in legitimizing family planning as a means of achieving a smaller family size and, consequently, lower fertility rates. The first United Nations

Table 5

PERCENTAGE DISTRIBUTION OF UNFPA EXPENDITURES BY WORK PLAN CATEGORIES, ASIA AND THE PACIFIC, 1969–1983

Work plan categories	Years												Total
	1969-1972	1973	1974	1975	1976	1977	1978	1979	1980	1981	1982	1983	1969-1983
Basic data collection	3.8	5.5	7.7	5.1	4.4	4.1	4.1	9.2	13.7	26.0	12.3	4.9	10.3
Population dynamics	6.4	1.8	2.1	2.3	2.8	2.9	1.4	2.3	2.7	5.0	6.7	8.3	4.1
Formulation and evaluation of population policies and programmes	2.7	0.9	2.1	1.2	2.9	2.4	1.9	1.5	1.9	4.7	4.2	4.1	2.8
Implementation of policies	0.0	0.0	0.0	0.0	0.0	0.2	0.0	7.2	0.6	1.2	0.7	1.8	1.5
Family planning	71.4	68.0	64.9	70.9	73.5	71.2	71.2	61.8	62.7	40.5	56.0	51.7	60.2
Communication and education	11.0	19.1	17.9	15.2	10.8	11.0	8.6	8.6	11.4	13.1	10.4	17.8	12.3
Special programmes	0.7	0.5	0.1	0.2	0.6	0.6	1.3	1.3	0.5	1.3	0.6	0.9	0.8
Multisectoral activities	4.0	4.2	5.2	5.1	5.0	7.6	11.5	8.1	6.5	8.2	9.1	10.5	8.0
Total	100.0	100.0	100.0	100.0	100.0	100.0	100.0	100.0	100.0	100.0	100.0	100.0	100.0
(Thousands of US dollars)	(7,283)	(9,165)	(15,663)	(20,447)	(20,805)	(22,258)	(32,981)	(47,150)	(50,845)	(48,040)	(43,981)	(48,628)	(367,246)

Sources: UNFPA Fact Sheet Number 1.08 (September 1983); UNFPA Fact Sheet Number 1.09 (November 1983).
Note: Figures for 1969 to 1982 are project expenditures; figures for 1983 are project allocations as of 30 November 1983.

meeting on family planning in the region, sponsored by ESCAP (then ECAFE) in 1966, was on the management of family planning rather than on the justification for family planning. Accordingly, UNFPA responded to the needs of the region through extensive support to a wide variety of interventions. By 1983, UNFPA was supporting family planning activities that were integrated into the public health system as well as free-standing family planning programmes. It was assisting the two largest programmes in the world, in China and India, as well as some of the smallest programmes such as those in Samoa and Vanuatu. UNFPA assistance has been extended to a wide range of contraceptive services, including natural family planning.

Population education is essential for increasing awareness of population issues at the individual and societal level. Population information is also necessary to deepen the understanding of socio-economic consequences of demographic conditions, as well as to promote information regarding the availability of family planning services. The UNFPA contribution to the development of population education and information programmes through various channels such as the formal education system and the organized labour sector in Asia has been rather modest in comparison with that for family planning. However, 12.3 per cent of the total resources allocated for the region, or approximately $46 million, was channelled to support IEC activities. Asia has now considerable experience in organizing population education programmes through the school systems or community organizations. The communication strategy and techniques developed for dissemination of population-related information have become increasingly sophisticated. In addition, several countries in the Asia and Pacific region are concerned with specific target audiences for population education, including sex education and population information, such as adolescents. Deliberate efforts have been made to link IEC activities more closely with family planning services or to tailor IEC programmes to contraceptive services.

Support from UNFPA complemented significantly the efforts of countries such as Bangladesh, Burma, Fiji, Lao People's Democratic Republic, Pakistan, Samoa and Tonga to increase their demographic monitoring capability, especially through its assistance for the 1970 round of censuses. In addition to census data collection and analysis, UNFPA funding helped to establish and improve vital registration systems in such countries as Afghanistan, Nepal and the Philippines. The increased demographic monitoring capability has undoubtedly contributed a better appreciation of population factors in the process of development planning and, consequently, facilitated the acceptance of population activities in Asian countries.

As a result of UNFPA support, the region has a considerable capacity, in institutions and personnel resources, to undertake policy research on population and development. This is particularly the case in some East and South-East Asian countries such as the Philippines, the Republic of Korea and Thailand. This increased capacity has contributed to the further appreciation of the measures "beyond family planning" and to the formulation of the so-called second-generation population policies in order to achieve demographic goals.

Recognizing that women's educational attainment and employment prospects significantly influence their fertility behaviour, UNFPA has supported activities designed to help improve the status of women in a number of countries. For example, in Nepal and the South Pacific, efforts include the training of women for income-generating activities as part of population education initiatives. In many cases UNFPA assistance, however modest, has played a key role in increasing women's economic opportunities as well as in promoting their sense of self-confidence in managing their own lives, particularly their fertility behaviour.

Four programmes

Four of the largest programmes of country assistance are in the Asia region; a brief overview of these programmes is perhaps the best way to highlight the variety of activities that the Fund has supported in this region.

China. In June 1980, the Governing Council of UNFPA approved assistance to China, a priority country, in the amount of $50 million for five years. The UNFPA-supported programme emphasizes the introduction of new technologies and equipment not available in China, and the improvement of technical training, research and institutional development.

In view of the importance of improving maternal and perinatal care, and the acceptance of the one-child-family policy, UNFPA provided support for strengthening the capabilities of five maternal and children's hospitals by providing advanced care facilities and special training for their management. The experience gained in these five hospitals in perinatal diagnosis and treatment is disseminated through seminars, training programmes and publications for MCH/obstetrics and gynaecology professionals throughout China.

The National Training Centre for Family Planning Personnel in Nanjing, established with UNFPA assistance, is providing training for the 70,000 full-time family planning workers who staff county and provincial offices. The National Training Centre for MCH/FP Professionals at

Chengdu is providing pre-service and in-service post-graduate training for MCH/FP professionals at the provincial level, to improve the technical quality of family planning work and MCH care and to reduce maternal and infant morbidity and mortality.

UNFPA also assisted in improving the collection and analysis of programme statistics for use in programme evaluation and planning. The findings of a national sample survey conducted in 1982, which revealed, for example, a high rate of intra-uterine device (IUD) failure, will be used as a basis for improvements in the programme.

In line with the Government's goal to provide acceptable, high-quality contraceptives, UNFPA has supported improvements in the manufacture of contraceptives, with the Program for the Introduction and Adaptation of Contraceptive Technology (PIACT) as executing agency. Condom production has been expanded by 25 per cent. The IUD accounts for approximately 50 per cent of contraceptive use (estimates place the number of IUD users at 50-55 million women). UNFPA assistance has been used to renovate a medical instrument plant and introduce technology which will allow production of any existing type of plastic or copper IUD. At the completion of the project, China's total production of IUDs, inserters and measuring devices should meet domestic demand. Equipment and training in the latest manufacturing processes for injectable contraceptives are being provided by UNFPA, which is also assisting the State Pharmaceutical Administration in the development of a new oral contraceptive manufacturing facility within the Beijing Pharmaceutical Factory.

Chinese scientists have been in the forefront of such fields as the development of oral contraceptives. As China manufactures all its own contraceptives, both applied and basic research on contraceptives and reproductive sciences is heavily supported. There are altogether 16 research institutes, of which three are supported by UNFPA and three by WHO. The WHO Special Programme of Research, Development and Research Training in Human Reproduction was designated executing agency for UNFPA-funded projects. Each research institute undertakes scientific research and clinical testing.

Family planning publicity and education has been carried out in China by an extensive network of family planning workers. UNFPA has assisted (through provisions of equipment and materials) in strengthening the publicity divisions of the family planning office, two subcentres, and a network of county-level family planning IEC stations that act as clearing-houses and supply centres for IEC materials and training.

UNFPA assisted the State Family Planning Commission in establishing a Population Information Centre, which has now set up a library and documentation service; translated a large volume of materials into Chinese; and begun publication of several types of population materials.

With financial support from UNFPA and technical assistance from UNESCO, 10 key middle schools and 10 teacher training institutes carried out pilot programmes in population education, in which all students are receiving basic education in demography, biological reproduction, and adolescent hygiene and development.

With respect to population data collection and analysis, UNFPA provided assistance for the preparation, enumeration, analysis and dissemination of the 1982 census. Because of China's population size, the census-taking was important not only for China, but for the rest of the world. The census also marked the introduction in China of electronic data processing for national statistical work. The data processing is planned to be completed by the end of 1984, and analysis will take several years. UNFPA support has been for advisory services, fellowships, training, 21 computers, data entry and other equipment (see feature page 141 for details).

Eleven population institutes at major universities and at the Chinese Academy of Social Sciences were selected in 1980 as members of a core network of population institutes for a programme of demographic research and training assisted by UNFPA. The immediate objective of this programme is the training of personnel to undertake multidisciplinary demographic analyses of various kinds and at different levels of technical sophistication. The support of UNFPA provides inputs for fellowships and study tours to population training programmes abroad; consultants and a resident adviser; books, periodicals and translations of scientific population materials; vehicles; and office, audio-visual and printing equipment. The United Nations Population Centres in Bombay and Cairo are providing additional UNFPA-funded fellowships.

A needs assessment mission visited China in March and April of 1983 and a project formulation mission was subsequently fielded. These two missions have laid the foundation for the Second Country Programme, which will be presented to the Governing Council in June 1984.

India. India was one of the first countries in the world to recognize the relationship between population and development. The importance of population in development planning was emphasized in the third five-year plan, and family planning on a national scale was introduced in 1958. The major association of UNFPA began in 1974, when a small mission from the Fund visited India to have discussions with the Government and to prepare a five-year programme of assistance.

The programme was formulated on the basis of the Government's perception of the population problem and of measures required to cope with this problem. The strategy was based on providing family planning services through the health care system. Because of the health network's limited infrastructure, terminal methods were seen as the most practical. As an interim plan, the infrastructure itself was to be extended by the creation of a national cadre of multipurpose health workers at the field level.

In addition, the Fund was also responsible for developing two innovative programmes. The first was the establishment of a documentation centre, which was to provide a sound data base and statistical base for the planning and implementation of the programme. The other involved enlisting the support of organized labour institutions in promoting the small-family norm. The total package of assistance covered by these proposals was $40 million. Implementation of the programme began in 1975. It soon became evident, however, that this strategy would not achieve the reduction in population growth rates projected in the Government's development plan. The need for spacing methods and for remedies to the deficiencies in communication programmes soon became apparent. In the later days of the First Country Programme, therefore, other activities, such as increasing the supply of pills, increasing the availability of IUDs and designing communication programmes aimed specifically at community leaders in rural areas, were added to the original components.

Several important lessons were learned during the first phase of the programme. It became clear that the allocation to India was insufficient for effective apportionments over the entire national programme. Modifications would, therefore, be needed so that UNFPA funds could have a truly catalytic effect. Second, it became clear that the population problem was not uniform throughout all India. Population growth rates varied widely among the states, and a single uniform national policy was unlikely to produce the required results. Third, it was realized that in certain northern states, growth rates were so high that special measures were required.

To examine this complex situation, a needs assessment mission visited India in 1979 and carried out an in-depth analysis of the principal problem areas. After the mission presented its report and after consultation with Government, UNFPA designed a second programme of assistance that was both selective and comprehensive. Two states in India with very high growth rates were chosen as the principal focuses for UNFPA assistance. Six districts in the State of Bihar with population of 15 million and three districts in the State of Rajasthan with a population of 6 million were to be the principal programme areas. The programme was comprehensive in that, in these nine districts, the Fund agreed to support all the new activities required by a multisectoral programme. The plan was to prepare a programme based on an overall development strategy instead of limiting it to a narrow approach through health care. Special attention was given to programme management, problem solving, interpersonal communication and popular participation, by enlisting voluntary and non-government agencies. Most important, the district administration was given overall responsibility for the programme.

The recommendation of the Fund that special attention should be concentrated on problem states where birth rates were high was reinforced when the 1980 census showed that, despite the nation-wide programme, India had been able in the 10-year period to reduce its rate of population growth by only one-half of 1 per cent annually. The new comprehensive programmes in Bihar and Rajasthan are expected to provide important information and experience which will assist planners in resolving the difficult problems of the northern states. The main task of these programmes will be to introduce a wider framework of administrative responsibilities and improved management and communication systems, designed to make the family planning programme an effort not merely of the Government but of the entire community. These efforts, of course, have to contend with the formidable obstacles of low rural literacy and widespread rural poverty. In addition to these new comprehensive programmes, the Fund continues to support the large programme connected with sterilization and paramedical training on a national scale.

To achieve balance in the programme and to respond to additional needs, other activities have been undertaken including several supply projects (IUDs, condoms, laparoscopes and oral pill raw materials); several projects supported by UNFPA and executed by ILO, aimed at creating information for the introduction of family planning activities and the provision of contraceptive services in the organized sector; and a major national population education programme, in co-operation with UNESCO.

Bangladesh. The UNFPA programme in Bangladesh focuses on the provision of family planning services. The Government, viewing its population programme as an integral part of its overall development strategy, has espoused a multisectoral approach as a means of achieving its target of replacement-level fertility by 1990. To reach this ambitious target, the current level of contraceptive prevalence, which is less than 14 per cent of married women of reproductive age, will have to increase to about 40 per cent. Despite the Government's commitment to delivering family planning and maternal and child health services at the village level, administrative problems, inadequate infrastructure, the shortage of trained staff and weak logistics have all proved formidable obstacles.

In response to some of these difficulties, the Fund has provided extensive assistance for training in the field of health and population, through such initiatives as the training programme for family welfare visitors, who are the key personnel at the village level. Equally important, UNFPA has supported the introduction of a field-based programme for trainers who are posted in the districts and who are responsible for training field staff. UNFPA, with multi-bilateral assistance from the Government of the Netherlands, also provided technical assistance in preparing a comprehensive training plan for health and population manpower in Bangladesh. This multi-bilateral assistance has formed an important part of UNFPA support for training.

Considerable progress has been made in disseminating information to motivate acceptors in family planning, principally through the mass media and the distribution of printed materials. With UNFPA support, the Information, Education and Motivation Unit of the Population Control and Family Planning Division of the Government is undertaking mass dissemination campaigns. The Government has launched population education programmes through the formal school system for students from the fourth grade through secondary school. UNFPA provided technical assistance for the introduction of population education in the curriculum of the schools in 1981 and helped in training schoolteachers at primary and secondary levels. In addition, the Fund supports population education through the organized sector. To date, more than 22,000 teachers and approximately 1,000 labour leaders have been trained in population subjects. UNFPA assistance to Bangladesh through 1984 totalled $28.3 million.

Indonesia. The Fund's First Country Programme Agreement with Indonesia, lasting from 1969 to 1979, included a wide range of projects: health and family planning, information, education and communication; population education; population dynamics; population policy formulation; and a women's participation in development programme. The total allocation under this agreement was $16.8 million of which $13.2 million was allotted to the maternal and child health and family planning project, which was jointly financed by the World Bank, UNFPA and the Government of Indonesia.

Substantial progress has been made on a number of fronts. Nearly all of the 11 outer-island provinces joining the national family planning/ population programme in 1979 have received the vehicles and medical equipment necessary for bringing services to remote areas. The hospital-based family planning effort has been greatly strengthened by a strong commitment from hospital administrators both for increasing the range of services and for expanding the participation of other hospital divisions in the family planning effort. This commitment is largely the result of study tours throughout the Asian region for administrators, the provision of equipment to upgrade the hospitals and the training of staff. The integrated family planning and nutrition project on Sumatra has demonstrated its viability; this and similar projects on the outer islands are increasingly being absorbed into the routine budget of the Government.

The urban project, which has aimed at expanding contraceptive prevalence in five cities by increasing supplies and encouraging demand for such services, is one of the most exciting undertakings in the Second Country Programme, 1980–1984, and has been an ideal experimental project. The project has demonstrated that it is possible for the Government and the private sector to join forces for social service projects and that the resourcefulness of the commercial advertising world can be effectively used on behalf of family planning issues. On the service delivery side, the project has demonstrated the value of the private clinic, with private doctors supplementing the Government's efforts in the cities. The project has also shown that as Government family planning clinics have improved the quality of their services, utilization has increased.

Several seminars and workshops have resulted in strengthening the role of the communications branch within the total programme. The Fund's assistance to the Central Bureau of Statistics, through equipment and training, has strengthened the Bureau's capability in the collection of demographic data. Research and training activities, under way at three demographic research institutes, promise to increase substantially Indonesia's pool of fully qualified demographic analysts. The creation of a Population and Development Research Committee will promote the integration of population and development concerns. The project on women in development is a major innovation; it has greatly boosted the earning power of women participating in the scheme, making them less dependent on traditional money-lenders. Considered a model project, it is being replicated by several other donors.

Other programmes/projects. Since 1971, when UNFPA assistance was first begun in the South Pacific and Papua New Guinea subregion, the programme has grown steadily in numbers of projects and countries involved as well as in the range of substantive areas covered. The first projects were introduced in 1971 in the Gilbert and Ellice Islands (now Kiribati and Tuvalu), Tonga and Samoa. Other countries were rapidly added to this list: Vanuatu (1972), Papua New Guinea (1973) and Solomon Islands, Fiji and Cook Islands (1976). The latest additions were the Trust Territories of the Pacific in 1980 (Marshall Islands, Palau and the Federated States of Micronesia).

The first endeavours were relatively simple projects in family planning and family health, such as funds provided for the purchase of contraceptives. Training components, though included in most projects, concentrated almost solely on the instruction of medical personnel. Emphasis was on clinic-based services, usually for urban areas. The mid-1970s saw a diversification of assistance in response to the request of several countries for help with censuses and related activities. In 1976, five countries held censuses (Cook Islands, Fiji, Samoa, Solomon Islands and Tonga). In these countries and elsewhere, UNFPA provided financing for census operations for analysis of the results. In general, however, the single largest area of UNFPA assistance was, and remains, the family planning and family health area, at present in the range of about 48 per cent of total funds approved for the subregion. Assistance for demographic training and research is now given under the aegis of a subregional project, executed by the South Pacific Commission, that provides technical assistance and training in demography and population statistics to the subregion as a whole.

The next development was a move from the project approach to an integrated programme. Between December 1979 and January 1981, five needs assessment missions were held in Fiji, Kiribati, Samoa, Solomon Islands and Tonga; these provided the basis for four-year programmes for these countries. Generally, family planning and family health projects remain the single largest programme area, but, for the first time, population education projects have been introduced in half a dozen countries. There are also communications projects for increasing population awareness in Fiji and Solomon Islands. In the 1970s, a few projects were organized for the promotion of family welfare through women's and youth organizations in Fiji, Kiribati and Tuvalu.

Not only has the population concept broadened in the South Pacific, but the family planning and family health projects have themselves become increasingly complex. The need for community participation is now recognized, as is the importance of reaching the rural population. Emphasis on the training of medical and paramedical personnel continues but attention is now being focused also on the training of family planning motivators. UNFPA is providing funds in several projects for supervisory visits to outer islands since such visits are vital for an effective functioning of any programme in the South Pacific. Problems such as teen-age pregnancy are being addressed through emphasis on health education for adolescents. In response to requests from the Governments of Kiribati and Tonga, natural family planning projects have been initiated in these countries. Because of the vital role radio plays in communications, funds are being provided for radio broadcasts on population matters.

The increasing number and complexity of the South Pacific projects have required changes in administrative and technical arrangements for monitoring projects. The offices of the two Deputy Representatives and Senior Advisors on Population in Fiji and Samoa have been strengthened in terms of staffing. Three subregional advisers (ILO, UNESCO and WHO) are now stationed in Suva, Fiji, to provide technical back-up and other services to the projects and for programme development. This arrangement has been found to be more feasible than the posting of full-time experts in individual countries at extremely high costs. Cost-effectiveness is a chronic problem in planning projects in the South Pacific, given the small populations and tremendous distances. The Fund's response has been to emphasize subregional activities, such as the projects in demographic analysis and training already mentioned and a project on migration and employment, which deals with issues of key concern to Governments in the area.

Low implementation rates, especially for the family planning and family health projects, are a concern. The lack of infrastructure, unrealistic work plans, communication and travel difficulties, and sometimes, the lukewarm attitude of Governments towards family planning account for this. Several countries do not perceive their high rate of growth as the major problem but are more concerned with migration, unemployment and rapid urbanization.

Intercountry activities. The Fund supports, on a regional or intercountry basis, activities that complement and supplement national undertakings. During the period 1969–1983, the Fund supported more than 280 regional projects totalling approximately $43.0 million. Most of these regional activities were undertaken by organizations of the United Nations system such as the Economic and Social Commission for Asia and the Pacific (ESCAP), ILO, FAO, UNESCO and WHO as well as by many NGOs such as Association of Southeast Asian Nations (ASEAN), International Committee for Applied Research in Population (ICARP), International Committee on the Management of Population Programmes (ICOMP), Japanese Organization for International Cooperation in Family Planning (JOICFP), Press Foundation of Asia and the South Pacific Commission.

The sectoral emphasis of regional activities is markedly different from that of national activities. Whereas family planning has absorbed most of the Fund's support to national activities, population education, communication and population policy activities have dominated the regional programme. Furthermore, the nature of regional activities has shifted over time from its earlier focus on the collection of demographic and family planning data and case studies of population growth to the training of personnel, analysis of demographic data, migration policy research and management of family planning programmes.

The role of training in the development of national and regional self-reliance has always been recognized in UNFPA-supported programmes. In addition to providing assistance for a large array of national training activities and institutional facilities, the Fund has supported activities of regional training and research facilities such as the Statistical Institute for Asia and the Pacific in Tokyo; IIPS in Bombay; and the Asian and Pacific Development Centre in Kuala Lumpur.

FUTURE DIRECTIONS

All but a few countries in the region have now formulated population policies and programmes as integral parts of their development strategies. Although fertility rates in the Asian and Pacific countries have begun to decline, largely because of successful family planning programmes, the population size is expected to increase from 2.5 billion in 1980 to 3.5 billion by the year 2000, even if current decline in the birth rate is sustained. Thus, population growth will continue to be one of the most serious demographic problems for the region. From a programmatic point of view, this means that family planning programmes have to be further strengthened and expanded. Although these programmes have contributed significantly to raising awareness of contraceptive practice, the World Fertility Survey and various contraceptive prevalence surveys show that considerable gaps still exist between the levels of contraceptive knowledge and practice. For example, the Contraceptive Prevalence Survey conducted in 1981 found that more than 90 per cent of the married women of reproductive age in Thailand are aware of the contraceptive need, but only 58 per cent of them are currently practising family planning; the differential is much wider in such countries as Bangladesh, Nepal and Pakistan, where availability and accessibility of services are often extremely limited. In its future support, UNFPA in-

NEPAL'S POPULATION PROGRAMME:
A TEST CASE FOR POPULATION AND DEVELOPMENT
PROGRAMMES

Nepal today faces population and development problems of such magnitude and complexity that development gains, as meagre as they are, are being cancelled by the growing socio-economic demands of an already poor population. The country is characterized by the following:

- A high growth rate (2.3 per cent per annum) and an age structure that could lead to a doubling of the present population of 16 million by the year 2010;
- An already large population relative to land and other natural resources: in 1981, population density was 753 persons per square kilometre of arable land and, in the Hills region, 1,182 per square kilometre of arable land (Bangladesh, with the world's most densely settled rural population, had 990 persons per square kilometre of arable land);
- Poor health of the population, exemplified by a high infant mortality rate (144 per 1,000 live births), which, coupled with "boy preference", has led to an exceptionally high total fertility rate (6.25);
- A predominantly rural and illiterate population with little access to modern communications or services;
- Severe ecological degradation as a consequence of unplanned migration from the Hills to the Terai (lowlands) and the disappearance of commercially exploitable forests.
- A level of contraceptive use (7 per cent in 1981) that is too low to have more than a minimal effect on population growth, despite the considerable development of family planning services.

His Majesty's Government of Nepal and the international donor community concur that concerted and co-ordinated efforts can put Nepal on the road to development. Nepal has a long-standing, comprehensive population policy complemented by policies across the development spectrum. Many national institutions and programmes have been carrying out these policies, and the major multilateral and bilateral donor agencies have collaborated in these efforts.

The Fund's assistance to Nepal, which started in 1972, focused in early years on demographic data collection and analysis. A series of UNFPA-sponsored missions and consultancies were undertaken during the 1970s, including a 1979 needs assessment mission. These efforts reinforced observations that Nepal's population problems cannot be isolated from its development needs. Literacy levels must be raised (especially for women); health and family planning services and support activities should be strengthened and made more widely accessible; infant mortality must be sharply reduced through maternal and child health services; and income-generating activities must be created (especially for women).

The Fund's five-year programme that began in 1980 broke new ground in its breadth, innovations, and integration with the overall development programme and is consistent with the needs and priorities expressed in the country's Sixth Five-year Development Plan (1980-1985). The UNFPA programme includes 30 projects in the fields of basic data collection and analysis (a continuation of earlier work), population planning and policy formulation, research on demographic and related subjects, family planning and maternal and child health services and population education and communication, and in fields designed to develop opportunities for women both socially and economically, as well as integrated rural development to influence fertility and other demographic variables. The programme costs approximately $55 million in total (including Government funds) for the five-year period.

A new five-year (1985-1989) UNFPA-sponsored country programme, now under consideration, will reflect important changes in strategy and emphasis, based on the lessons learned over the past decade. Joint UNFPA-Government reviews have identified several areas for improvement, including the following:

- Better co-ordination and resource-sharing mechanisms between agencies, for example, in logistics and training;
- The standardizing of and improvements in rewards for field supervison activities and outpostings;
- Much greater effort to train top and middle-level programme leadership in management skills;
- Innovative efforts to obtain, purchase and distribute medicines to the village level; and
- The use of more and better qualified technical support agencies.

Through these measures UNFPA and the Government of Nepal anticipate better services and ultimately better health and a more manageable fertility level. The lessons learned in Nepal, because it presents such difficult population and development problems, will be applicable elsewhere as well.

Sources: Data on population density, density on arable land and contraceptive usage in Nepal are from The World Bank, Nepal: Report on Population Strategy (Washington, D.C., The World Bank, 1982), p. 34; the figure for population density in Bangladesh is from The World Bank, Bangladesh: Current Economic Situation—Review of Second Five-year Plan (Washington, D.C., The World Bank, 1981). Other demographic data are from the United Nations Department of International Economic and Social Affairs, Demographic Indicators of Countries: Estimates and Projections as assessed in 1982.

tends to work with the Asian and Pacific countries to respond to the problem of a large unmet need for family planning.

To increase the efficiency and effectiveness of the Asian family planning programmes, more attention should be focused on management issues. Over the past years many countries have identified similar stumbling blocks: cumbersome logistical systems; lack of co-ordination between various entities involved in the programme; lack of a proper chain of supervision; and poor management information systems which thwart programme monitoring and evaluation. UNFPA will support countries and work with them to improve the management aspects of their programmes.

In addition, a number of Asian countries are increasingly concerned with the continuous availability of contraceptives to meet the need. UNFPA will extend its assistance to countries requesting help in order to facilitate the local production of contraceptives whenever it is technically and economically feasible. UNFPA has already successfully assisted China in the local production of various types of contraceptives.

There is also a need to shift the IEC strategy from emphasis on the value of the small family to emphasis on how family planning services can be obtained. Messages should promote more information about the location, time and types of family planning available rather than simply the normative message that "a small family is a happy one".

The countries in the region, while continuing to address the perennial question of population growth, will also have to recognize other emerging demographic issues—population distribution and migration, the aging of populations, and problems of other special groups such as the adolescent. According to the United Nations Fifth Inquiry on Population, most of the Asian countries responding listed their dissatisfaction with prevailing patterns of population distribution. Rapid population growth has compounded the imbalance between population settlements and the availability of resources and employment. Heavy rural-urban migration has accelerated the pace of urbanization. At present, UNFPA assistance in this regard has been confined to small-scale studies on the interrelationship between population distribution and development. In the future, the Asian region will require more comprehensive support from UNFPA to develop the capacity not only to monitor the population distribution and migration pattern but also to formulate and implement viable population distribution policies.

The improvement of general health conditions has resulted in a greater proportion of people surviving until older ages. For instance, the life expectancy of Chinese males increased from about 45 years in 1950 to 66 years in 1980–1985. By 2000, China will have more than 200 million people over 60 years old compared with 80 million currently. Many Governments in the region are now realizing that increases in life expectancy will alter age dependency patterns and will necessitate the implementation of special programmes geared to the needs of older persons. UNFPA is expected to assist the Asian countries in building up their research on issues related to aging population structures and in strengthening their capacities to undertake innovative activities in this area.

Although the major emphasis of UNFPA assistance to the region will continue to be on family planning programmes through the MCH systems and other channels, emerging population issues will also require action. The experience of Asian countries in population policy formulation and programme implementation over the last decade has produced invaluable expertise, making Asia a principal source of technical co-operation among developing countries (TCDC). Future UNFPA assistance will be more oriented to facilitating TCDC by deploying such expertise within and outside the region. For this purpose, emphasis should be given to subregional activities for countries with geographical or cultural affinities. Emphasis should also be given to clearing-house activities for the exchange of technical knowledge and experience among the countries of the region and with other regions as appropriate. Moreover, the relative success of the Asian population programmes has sometimes masked the necessity of training technical personnel in new techniques and new approaches in demographic monitoring and programmatic research. There is already a growing shortage of trained personnel for the rapidly expanding population programmes in the Asia and the Pacific region. For this purpose, a commitment of additional resources is required for the future training of Asian social scientists, especially in programme research, and of programme managers so that the critical mass necessary for the efficient functioning of programmes will be available. In the past, emphasis has been on short-term training and on applied research. The situation in the region, however, requires more long-term training of personnel and attention to basic research, if UNFPA and other donors are to respond to these needs.

The Third Asian and Pacific Population Conference meeting in Colombo in 1982 reaffirmed that closer co-operation and collaboration among the countries of the region are needed in dealing with population and related socio-economic and health problems, so that all people of the region can enjoy a desirable and sustainable standard of living. UNFPA is committed to working with the countries of the region in reaching these goals.

4. Latin America and the Caribbean

OVERVIEW OF THE REGION

Spanning the vast territories from Tierra del Fuego to the Rio Grande and the Caribbean Sea, the region of Latin America and the Caribbean displays a wide variety of geographical, socio-political and cultural characteristics.

Latin America

In the last several decades, the population of the Latin American region as a whole has exhibited considerable demographic change. Latin America's population more than doubled over the course of the decades since 1950. At present, the rate of population growth for the region is estimated at 2.3 per cent. There are, however, great variations between the subregions, which include three major Spanish-speaking areas in temperate and tropical zone countries.

The three principal Spanish-speaking subregions, located on the continental mainland, vary considerably in their demographic profiles. The temperate zone countries—Argentina, Chile and Uruguay—exhibit demographic characteristics remarkably similar to those of developed countries. With a total population of approximately 45 million and an average density of 16 persons per square kilometre, their annual growth rate, on average, is 1.6 per cent, and life expectancy at birth is 68 years.

In contrast, the regions of Middle America and tropical South America show markedly higher growth rates, 2.7 and 2.4 per cent, respectively. With fertility levels of 4.8 per woman and 4.1 per woman as well as a lower expectation of life—about 65 and 63 years, respectively—those regions have much in common with other developing areas of the world.

Grouping Latin American countries by fertility rates, along with other indicators of development such as life expectancy at birth, produces clusters roughly similar to those within the aforementioned subregions. Temperate South America has a total fertility rate of 3.2. Cuba has a total fertility rate of less than 2, placing it in the advanced stages of the demographic transition.

Some tropical South American countries—Brazil, Colombia, and

51

Venezuela—as well as Costa Rica and Panama have entered into an early stage of the transition, that is, the beginning of a significant decline in fertility (between 3.5 and 4.5) and sharp declines in mortality rates, coupled with life expectancies ranging between 63 and 71 years. Mexico has also experienced a marked decline in fertility and improved life expectancy. Fertility has not significantly decreased in Middle America, nor in Bolivia, the Dominican Republic and Haiti. Fertility rates for these countries range between 4.5 and 6.7, and life expectancies are between 53 and 66 years of age.

Today's high growth rates are a result of changes in mortality trends in the region. As health conditions have improved over the past decades, death rates have plummeted to unparalleled lows, and substantial gains have been made in life expectancy. Malnutrition remains a problem, however. A study of national nutrition patterns indicates that 35 per cent of the population of nine large countries in the region— Argentina, Brazil, Chile, Colombia, Ecuador, Honduras, Mexico, Peru and Venezuela—have average family incomes that do not permit regular balanced diets. As a result, malnutrition among children under five years of age is one of Latin America's most serious problems, especially in Central America. Infant mortality rates ranged from 20 per 1,000 (Costa Rica) to 120 per 1,000 (Bolivia) recording an average of 67 per 1,000 for the whole region. Primarily these rates were highest among children living in rural households and the urban marginal communities where scarcities of all sorts are typical.

Despite an overall low population density for the region as a whole, Latin America is one of the most crowded areas in the world. The urban population of the region, which in 1950 numbered a little more than 40 million, or 25 per cent of the total, had increased by 1980 to more than 200 million, or 63 per cent of the total. In the period 1950–1975, the urban population grew more than three and a half times faster than the rural population. In several countries the urban population increased at an average annual rate of more than 5 per cent, doubling in less than 15 years.

The urban population is concentrated in the capitals and other large cities. Today, Latin America has 20 cities with more than one million in population: among the largest are Sao Paulo, with a population of 12.5 million (1980 census); Mexico City, 10.2 million (1980 United Nations estimate); Rio de Janeiro, 9.0 million (1980 census); Bogota, 4.3 million (1980 estimate); and Buenos Aires, 3.6 million (1980 United Nations estimate). If present demographic trends hold, the region will have a population of 619 million in the year 2000, of which the urban population will constitute 75 per cent, 466.2 million people.

Migratory flows between the countries of the region have been increasing, in some countries significantly affecting population growth, especially in frontier zones. Emigration of skilled personnel to the developed countries is still a serious problem for many Latin American countries. In addition, undocumented migration, which has deep economic, social and political repercussions in both the countries of origin and those of destination, is a major source of concern to several countries in the region.

The Caribbean

The Caribbean, an integral part of the Americas, differs markedly in its ethnic and linguistic composition from the three Hispanic-American subregions. Historical events have produced a pluralistic Caribbean, with several languages and different races, institutions and customs. The region was conquered and colonized by the British, the Spanish, the French, and the Dutch; subsequently, slaves were imported from Africa and, later, indentured workers from Asia. Except for Guyana and Trinidad and Tobago, where half to two thirds of the population are of East Indian descent, the population of the Caribbean region is predominantly of African descent. Mainland countries bordering on its tropical waters—Belize in Central America and French Guiana, Guyana, and Suriname in South America—share the cultural characteristics of the Caribbean Islands, although for reporting purposes these countries are grouped under Middle America and tropical South America.

The estimated population of the region was 31.3 million in 1984, ranging from fewer than a half million inhabitants on some islands to more than 6 million in Cuba, Haiti and Dominican Republic. Population growth has remained fairly steady since 1950, averaging approximately 2 per cent during the 20-year period 1950–1970. Crude birth rates for the region as a whole decreased in the last decade and were estimated at 27.0 per 1,000 population in 1980–1985. The total fertility rate fell from 5.2 in the five-year period 1950–1955 to 3.4 in 1980–1985. The spread of family planning programmes is one of the causes for the decline in fertility.

Improvements in sanitation, housing and nutrition, and control of endemic and parasitic diseases have contributed to a sharp decline in death rates to 8.4 per 1,000 population in 1980–1985. The age group most affected by this decline in mortality has been children under one year of age. Infant mortality was halved during the 20-year period 1950–1970, and is now estimated at 58 deaths per 1,000 live births. Life expectancy at birth in the Caribbean has risen to 64 years in the region as a whole, and to more than 70 years in Barbados, Guadeloupe, Jamaica,

Martinique, and Trinidad and Tobago. Despite improved health-care services and nutrition, the major causes of mortality are still the easily treatable communicable diseases, although the importance of chronic diseases as causes of death is beginning to increase.

More than half the population of the Caribbean is under age 20, and this broad-based age pyramid tends to put a great strain on the provision of health, education and social services; it also calls for a rate of job-creation that most countries will not be able to meet.

In the past, most of the population of the Caribbean lived in rural areas, but there has been a persistent and heavy exodus towards the towns. In Trinidad, 22 per cent of the population are urban; in Barbados, 39 per cent; and in the Caribbean as a whole, 51 per cent of the population are located in urban areas.

The search for educational and employment opportunities motivates young people and their families to migrate abroad, either to other countries in the Caribbean or outside the region. In this century there has been a steady outflow to Panama, Venezuela, United States of America and the United Kingdom as well as the movement of people between the islands. Although migration has relieved population pressures, it is mostly the skilled people who leave. The Caribbean has lost a great many of its highly trained and skilled workers to developed countries.

Population policies

Government views and policies on population issues match the diversity of the region's demographic mosaic. Toward the mid-1970s, however, most Governments had come to accept the view that demographic factors played a significant role in the process of socio-economic planning. This view gradually evolved into today's widely held consensus that population policies constitute an integral part of development policies.

Seven Latin American countries—Costa Rica, Dominican Republic, El Salvador, Guatemala, Mexico, Nicaragua and Peru—perceive their rates of growth as being too high and pursue policies to alter spatial distribution and international migration patterns, and directly or indirectly to lower fertility. Brazil, Colombia, Cuba, Ecuador, Haiti, Honduras, Panama and Venezuela perceive their rates of growth and fertility rates as satisfactory. Nonetheless, they all provide some form of government support for family planning. Sometimes support is provided directly through the public health structure; infrequently, by tacit endorsement of a non-governmental group.

Argentina, Bolivia, and Chile desire higher rates of growth. Argentina and Bolivia do not limit access to family planning services but do not provide government-subsidized services, whereas Chile provides some direct support for family planning.

Most Caribbean Governments have at least an implicit policy to slow down the rate of population growth and many have enacted measures to achieve this objective. Barbados, Dominica, Grenada, Jamaica, and Trinidad and Tobago have implemented family planning programmes. Although the Bahamas, St. Lucia and St. Vincent do not have government-supported interventions for this purpose, access to contraceptives is not restricted. Guyana and Suriname regard their growth and fertility rates as acceptable.

All Latin American and Caribbean countries perceive their present mortality rates as being too high, and some have set targets to further mortality reductions.

As for international migration, many Latin American countries have established policies to prevent the departure of their professional and highly trained workers seeking better employment conditions elsewhere in the region. Similarly, the immigration of unskilled workers has been the subject of legal restrictions imposed by almost all countries. In this respect, some Caribbean nations have actively prevented such labour migration from neighbouring countries. However, it remains a fact that some countries do encourage the departure of their excess workforce as a sure way of reducing population growth and ameliorating their unemployment problems.

UNFPA AND LATIN AMERICA AND THE CARIBBEAN

Funding levels

From 1969 through 1983, UNFPA contributed $171 million or approximately 17 per cent of its total programme to population activities in Latin America and the Caribbean. This support has been directed to projects mostly in the fields of basic data collection, family planning, and population education and communication. Action programmes have absorbed about 75 per cent of all allocations to the region, with training accounting for an additional 15 per cent. Expenditures on research averaged about 10 per cent over the 1969–1983 period, having increased from 5 per cent in 1969–1972 to a high of about 16 per cent in 1977. Since 1973, the bulk of all monies slated for the region has been expended at the country level; before then, regional activities absorbed more than half of the funds.

As shown in table 6, in the early years data collection, policy formulation and demographic research accounted for approximately 70 per cent of UNFPA expenditure in the region. The year 1973 marked the beginning of a shift in funding towards the family planning category. In 1973, expenditures in this sector totalled about $890,000; in 1978, they amounted to about $11,000,000. Over the 1969–1983 period, family planning accounted for 50 per cent of the Fund's expenditures in Latin America and the Caribbean; population dynamics and policy formulation ranked second, having absorbed about 22 per cent of programme allocations.

Types of activities

Basic data collection. Since 1969, UNFPA has funded 30 censuses, 11 demographic surveys and 4 projects for the improvement of civil registration systems in the region. Countries have obtained UNFPA assistance for updating cartography, designing sample frames, training enumerators and other census personnel, carrying out two experimental censuses and implementing a communication campaign to enlist public co-operation in census operations.

Several innovations have resulted from UNFPA assistance. In Peru, for example, recent advances in sampling theory and methodology were introduced to expedite data collection; not only were these cost-effective but they permitted more rapid data processing. A second innovation was the use of graphic materials and audio-visual techniques in the training of many enumerators. The effectiveness of these relatively inexpensive training methods has led to their adoption in basic data collection projects elsewhere in the region.

Population dynamics and population policy formulation and implementation. The preponderant share of UNFPA resources for population dynamics and policy formulation has been channelled to activities at the regional rather than the country level. Most projects funded during the 1969–1976 period concentrated on training national personnel in the analysis of population data: 43 per cent of regional activities have been for training. These regional projects were implemented mostly by the Latin American Demographic Centre (CELADE). UNFPA funding was also instrumental in the creation of population planning units in 11 countries. These units have analysed census and survey data and have undertaken research to facilitate the incorporation of population variables into development planning.

Much research conducted at the country level has dealt with the issue of population distribution and with the causes and consequences of migration. UNFPA has funded 16 such country projects and has supported the ILO Regional Employment Programme Advisory Team for Latin America and the Caribbean. The Team has helped develop several

Table 6

PERCENTAGE DISTRIBUTION OF UNFPA EXPENDITURES BY WORK PLAN CATEGORIES, LATIN AMERICA AND THE CARIBBEAN, 1969–1983

Work plan categories	Years												Total
	1969-1972	1973	1974	1975	1976	1977	1978	1979	1980	1981	1982	1983	1969-1983
Basic data collection	28.7	17.7	18.2	13.6	15.8	8.1	4.6	11.3	18.5	19.9	12.3	6.8	13.3
Population dynamics	8.7	7.4	3.4	1.9	9.5	11.1	10.6	11.7	15.0	13.5	11.9	9.6	10.3
Formulation and evaluation of population policies and programmes	32.7	27.4	18.5	16.9	4.7	7.3	7.6	8.5	7.3	12.3	15.7	14.0	11.3
Implementation of policies	0.0	0.0	0.0	0.0	0.0	0.0	0.0	0.0	0.0	0.0	0.0	0.0	0.0
Family planning	14.3	27.8	47.3	56.4	57.9	62.0	66.3	54.0	45.0	37.3	42.5	50.4	50.8
Communication and education	13.9	14.4	9.1	8.3	8.5	7.4	7.7	8.8	9.4	9.0	8.6	10.1	8.9
Special programmes	1.6	0.0	0.0	0.3	0.0	0.1	0.1	1.2	0.4	0.6	1.0	2.2	0.6
Multisectoral activities	0.1	5.3	3.5	2.6	3.6	4.0	3.1	4.5	4.4	7.4	8.0	6.9	4.8
Total	100.0	100.0	100.0	100.0	100.0	100.0	100.0	100.0	100.0	100.0	100.0	100.0	100.0
(Thousands of US dollars)	(2.054)	(3,339)	(10,983)	(14,147)	(17,443)	(13,163)	(17,171)	(20,318)	(23,465)	(17,570)	(14,608)	(16,808)	(171,069)

Sources: UNFPA Fact Sheet Number 1.08 (September 1983); UNFPA Fact Sheet Number 1.09 (November 1983).
Note: Figures for 1969 to 1982 are project expenditures; figures for 1983 are project allocations as of 30 November 1983.

country projects on the issue of labour migration and has provided the necessary technical back-up. The projects summarized below afford a more detailed idea of the range of undertakings the Fund has supported in this area.

UNFPA has assisted Bolivia in undertaking basic research on its population and in creating population groups in various sectoral ministries to serve as counterparts to the Population Department of the Ministry of Planning. One detailed study, *Bolivia: Outline for the Definition of a Population Policy*, presents a prognosis for population-related concerns over the next 25 years. Important technical back-up for this project was provided by CELADE. The experience gained from this project demonstrated that the process of including population components in national development plans and in the plans of sectoral ministries cannot stop with the creation of a population department. It is equally important to design a strategy for awareness-creation in the sectoral ministries and to establish channels of communication among institutions.

The population and development project in Panama is another example of how UNFPA assistance has furthered the incorporation of population concerns in macro planning. High-level staff attended courses on this topic, and the results of operational research on trends in fertility, mortality, internal migration and spatial distribution in Panama were subsequently used for planning purposes. A population documentation centre was established to provide information to government officials and others on population publications. Personnel from the documentation centre assisted in setting up a similar centre in El Salvador, thus adding a dimension of TCDC not originally anticipated. Interest generated by this project sparked the reactivation of the national committee on political demography.

Today, Mexico is the only country in Latin America with a population policy that includes explicit and comprehensive demographic targets for growth and distribution, disaggregated to the subnational level. The UNFPA project with Mexico's National Population Council (CONAPO) has provided institutional and methodological bases for integrating population and development programmes by setting up formal working groups composed of personnel from CONAPO and each of the sectors involved. These groups are analysing demographic data and facilitating their use by state and federal planning agencies; analysing population policy and sectoral plans; and identifying relevant areas for integration. The Government has selected 12 priority states for project activities. A special co-ordinating body oversees the interaction among six sectors—education, labour, human settlement, health and social security, industry and agriculture—examining the programmes of each to ensure compatibility with demographic goals (see feature page 61).

Family planning. Family planning projects in the region are generally comprehensive and provide services as an integral part of existing maternal and child health programmes. These programmes were started in the late 1950s as a result of the medical profession's growing concern with the high incidence of induced abortion and high rates of foetal and maternal mortality. Family planning was a sensitive subject and thus early initiatives were undertaken, under the pioneering leadership of the health profession, by national family planning associations which were usually affiliated with the International Planned Parenthood Federation (IPPF).

The success of the early programmes convinced government policy makers that a considerable market for family planning services did exist. Gradually Governments began to see the merit of providing these family planning services through their own public health network. Because the provision of contraceptive services was not tied to a demographic objective but rather was implemented to reduce maternal and infant mortality, services were offered in the framework of the health system. Countries requested UNFPA funding and, with the assistance of the Pan American Health Organization (PAHO), they developed integrated programmes for family planning combined with maternal and child care services. This approach not only enhanced the availability of family planning services but also contributed to the strengthening of the health network. UNFPA also extended support for training personnel and for building up the administrative system needed to monitor the incipient MCH/FP programmes.

Regional projects have played an important part in strengthening country-level MCH/FP activities. Of the $9.7 million for regional MCH/FP regional projects, 60 per cent went for administration, management and the evaluation of country family planning programmes, with almost 30 per cent channelled towards improved training of MCH/FP personnel. PAHO, the major international organization responsible for MCH/FP regional activities in Latin America and the Caribbean, has contributed, with UNFPA funding, to the development of standards for the delivery of services; the development of evaluation models; the preparation of training manuals for health personnel at different levels; the collection, analysis and dissemination of technical and scientific material on issues related to demography and family planning; the establishment of systems for collecting service statistics and for monitoring and supervisory activities; and the undertaking of research to assist in improving service delivery.

In 1975, the Government of Mexico and UNFPA agreed on an expanded programme of medical services for MCH/FP. Under this programme, contraceptive and maternal and child health services were provided throughout the country's health structure, involving 1,500 health centres in 1975. Two years later, a National Family Planning Plan was adopted in order to provide the coverage necessary to reduce population growth to the targets enunciated by CONAPO, namely to 2.5 per cent by 1982 and 1 per cent by 2000. Special attention was directed towards the needs of marginal groups in urban and rural areas. By 1979, the programme covered almost the entire country. By 1980, the programme had reached all localities of 500 to 2,500 inhabitants—a goal originally scheduled to be met in 1982.

Several countries in the region have emphasized the importance of community support for family planning activities. In Ecuador, the Fund supported a pilot project in two remote rural areas to test a community-oriented system for the delivery of services. Traditional birth attendants, valued as trusted members of the community, were trained in basic MCH/FP skills. In the Dominican Republic, the Fund financed the community-based distribution of contraceptives.

Cuba's family planning programme, one of the most extensive in the region, has three principal components: family planning, sex education and maternal and child health care. The family planning programme, which has received UNFPA support since 1974, has extended services so as to minimize regional differences, resulting in a significant increase in the utilization of contraceptive methods supplied by the Government.

Certain technical elements of the MCH programme in Cuba make it a model project, for example, the location of service units according to population density and proximity to rural agglomerations. Other elements are community participation, central planning, mass organization, medical and social rural services and monitoring and supervision. The Cuban model, which is centred around the trained medical specialist and the physician, uses an extensive network of polyclinics, rural hospitals, rural health posts and a large urban infrastructure of hospitals. However, the essential element is the commitment of sufficient resources to health as a pillar of economic and social development.

UNFPA has supported natural family planning in Chile, Ecuador and Haiti, where limited-scale projects oriented towards direct training of couples in the use of natural methods for controlling their fertility are under way. The results of these projects will probably be influential in national policy decisions on whether to apply training in natural methods on a wider scale. In Colombia, a recently initiated communication

MEXICO: EVOLUTION OF A POPULATION POLICY

In the early 1970s, the Government of Mexico undertook a broad population and development programme containing demographic objectives. A New General Population Law passed in 1973 included provision for a government-sponsored family planning programme and created the National Population Council (CONAPO) to be responsible for demographic planning and population programmes. In 1974, the Constitution specified the right of all persons to decide on the number and spacing of their children.

These steps were in response to several interlinked population problems: rapid growth, uneven distribution with massive interregional, interstate and rural-urban migration, and rising unemployment, among others. Mexico is one of the most populous nations of Latin America, with a population of 77 million in 1984.

UNFPA assistance to Mexico began with a 1972 grant to the Foundation for Population Studies and, in 1973, to the Government's maternal and child health and family planning programme. Assistance continued throughout the 1970s and, in 1980, following a needs assessment mission, UNFPA and the Government undertook a comprehensive programme that included attention to population and development planning, migration and employment policy, projects in population dynamics, maternal and child health and family planning, education and communication, and the integration of women into development. Linked to a sex education project supported by a Swedish Trust Fund, the programme constituted a complete population programme.

One project was designed to assist CONAPO in establishing the methodological and institutional bases and co-ordinating mechanisms for the integration of population policy into socio-economic development plans carried out by the governmental institutions at the national and state levels. Among project activities were the preparation of a demographic diagnosis and population policy for 15 states and the sponsoring of a Latin America Regional Seminar on the integration of population policies into development strategy, held in Mexico City in November 1982. One result of the project was the signing of agreements with 21 states interested in the integration of population policies into their development and the preparation of 21 monographs on demography for these states.

Among the many activities undertaken, UNFPA is currently collaborating with CONAPO on a project that aims at complementing the training of rural women with the provision of population information. The educational facets of the project deal with family planning and sex education, health and nutrition, demography, environment and family life.

UNFPA is also supporting a variety of regional and interregional activities that will contribute to the national projects. For example, the UNFPA-assisted Latin American Demographic Centre (CELADE) has trained a number of demographers who are working in the Mexican Government, has collaborated with CONAPO in designing and implementing special training courses and has undertaken research on population policy that draws upon Mexican data. UNFPA also supported the policy-oriented research that led to the publication of *State Policies and Migration: Studies in Latin America and the Caribbean*, edited by Peter Peek and Guy Standing (London, Croom Helm, 1982), which included a chapter on Mexico, "Industrialisation and Migration in Mexico".

UNFPA assistance to Mexico totalled $22 million between 1973 and 1983. The Government of Mexico, because of the success of the MCH/FP programme in improving health services and extending services to rural communities, expanded it greatly and assumed expenditures for local staff. Thus, UNFPA support was instrumental in moving the programme towards self-reliance.

technique (couple-to-couple method) is imparting wider knowledge of natural family planning. In addition, UNFPA has supported regional meetings to disseminate the concepts and training techniques required for natural family planning programmes.

Population education and communication. The total of UNFPA assistance to population education and communication between 1969 and 1983 was $15 million, in support of 30 regional projects and 23 country projects. As a result of the promotional activities of the UNESCO Regional Team, Governments began to recognize the importance of introducing population components in school curricula, giving rise to a series of country projects. UNFPA has provided support for the analysis of curricula, elaboration of training manuals and training of teachers in six countries of the region. Population education activities for out-of-school adult populations have been supported in four countries. A number of innovative projects on responsible parenthood for adolescents have been supported in some countries of the English-speaking Caribbean. On the whole, there are relatively few projects in population communication *per se* in the region since population communication is considered a support activity for programmes; for example, some form of population communication is a feature of most MCH/FP projects.

Regional projects in this sector have been instrumental in providing technical assistance for the elaboration, execution and evaluation of country activities. The printing, editing and dissemination of textbooks, manuals, technical reports and monographs in population at Economic Commission for Latin America (ECLA)/CELADE constitute an important aspect of the UNFPA-funded programme in this field. UNFPA supports the Latin America Population Documentation System, which collects, abstracts and stores population documentation for distribution upon request. Regional activities have received 62.6 per cent of total allocations to the sector.

Since 1979, UNFPA has supported the Ministry of Education in Paraguay in the implementation of a national family education and population programme which, in many respects, has come to be seen as a model project. Initial activities concentrated on incorporating population components into the formal sector of the education system by the development of a curriculum based on a well-defined conceptual framework for family education in Paraguay, the production of teaching materials and the training of local personnel to work in the Ministry of Education as well as to teach in the classroom. In the second phase of the project, emphasis shifted to a massive training programme in population and family-life education for primary and secondary school directors, professors and teachers on the basis of the revised curricula. The relative ease with which it has been possible to revise curricula and train supervisors and teachers in population issues resulted from the conscientious planning initiated at the various pre-project seminars as well as from a study of the knowledge, attitudes, practices and values of the Paraguayan family, which produced the information necessary for the revision of curricula.

The project has also served as a technical resource for the incorporation of population content in larger scale education activities funded by USAID and the World Bank, thereby multiplying the effectiveness of UNFPA funding.

UNFPA assistance to the Dominican Republic for family planning has a history almost as long as that of the Fund itself. A relatively new component of that co-operation, however, touches upon an essential complement to successful family planning programmes and public education on population matters. In 1979, the Government requested support in integrating population as a field of study into the curricula of the primary schools. UNFPA agreed to help set up a small team of professionals to revise curricula and design teaching materials appropriate for various grade levels. For many children, especially in the rural areas, primary school would constitute their only formal education.

Along with the design and distribution of these materials, a training programme carried out between 1979 and 1982 familiarized district school supervisors and school principals with population matters. The Government is now embarking, with UNFPA assistance, on a second phase of the project to consolidate this successful beginning. The current phase will extend the curriculum revision into the secondary school levels and direct training of teachers in selected areas of the country will get under way.

In a majority of the English-speaking countries of the Caribbean, UNFPA has financed family life education programmes aimed at youth. Teenagers who have already left school and those who remain in school constitute the two principal target groups. In the out-of-school programmes, counselling and services have typically been offered through youth centres, which combine recreation and informal education with the acquisition of productive skills. More recently, health authorities have recognized the need for separate clinics to supply teenagers with family planning advice and methods in a congenial atmosphere.

UNFPA assistance to this region will continue to emphasize education and services for youth.

Special programmes: women. UNFPA has contributed to the regional-level activities related to the status of women and youth of ECLA and other United Nations bodies. These have included assessments of information about women in censuses and surveys, identification of research needs concerning the female labour force, and meetings for youth to deal with health-related issues. UNFPA assistance to this sector has been in the form of funds for courses, seminars and workshops, and for the provision of technical expertise.

In Mexico, CONAPO has received UNFPA funding for an extensive training project aimed at rural and marginal urban women, to assist them in co-operative economic enterprise and, simultaneously, to provide them with information about their family roles and control of their own fertility.

A recent innovative approach in the region has been the mobilization of influential women to discuss population and development programmes and their relation to women (see chapter 11 for details).

FUTURE DIRECTIONS

Family planning has been and will continue to be the central element of UNFPA support. Whether these services are delivered as part of broader maternal and child health programmes, or as independent elements, is primarily a matter to be decided by Governments. If the recent trend continues, the majority of programmes will be more refined versions of the integrated approach to service delivery. The number of requests for assistance to family planning has increased while simultaneously evidence has mounted of significant improvements being made in countries' capabilities to deliver such services effectively. Hence, there is an increasing need to diversify such support not only to encompass the delivery of the means of fertility regulation, but also to extend the coverage and improve the quality of programmes. Consequently, UNFPA will be funding activities aimed at improving programme management and at evaluating service statistics, coupled with training assistance for medical, paramedical and support personnel.

Also, in this region, research on the social and psychological aspects of reproductive behaviour will be encouraged to strengthen existing family planning programmes. At the institutional level, initiatives are now under way to strengthen the collaboration between UNFPA, PAHO and other related health organizations, to address these issues and to foster the development of integrated family planning programmes. In keeping with its commitment to support the provision of contraceptive methods considered technically safe and effective by WHO and acceptable to recipient Governments, the Fund will continue to consider requests for natural family planning services.

Education and communication programmes in support of MCH/FP strategies also constitute important areas that are likely to receive continued support from UNFPA. Projects leading to the incorporation of population components into school curricula as well as broad family life education programmes aimed at out-of-school audiences, and projects educating adolescents in responsible parenthood, are the types of projects that will be pursued. Moreover, in specific country contexts, where communication media can be marshalled to disseminate balanced information on population problems and the existing means to correct these, project requests will be considered. The Fund will be specially interested in communication projects directed at public opinion leaders and those exploring new modalities of service delivery. In short, both education and communication programmes will continue to be viewed as significant elements supporting population programmes and family planning services.

Censuses have been conducted in almost all countries of the region, in most cases more than once; thus, in the future UNFPA will place more emphasis on supporting analyses of data already collected. Strengthening data-processing capabilities where needed will also require support. Development plans need to be based on careful assessments of demographic data examining the relationship between demographic variables and indices of socio-economic development, which are viewed by many countries as essential components of their long-range national goals. Thus, the Fund envisages sustained, perhaps even strengthened, support for this subject and for the creation within planning ministries of population units entrusted with such responsibilities.

Population policies may be seen as the overarching frameworks for all the above-mentioned areas and programmes. The Fund's assistance for policy formulation, whether in the form of technical advice, feasibility and impact studies, or training, will continue. In Latin America and the Caribbean, such support must inevitably embrace projects dealing with spatial distribution, urbanization and employment. These population-related issues are of great concern to most countries in the region, now suffering the effects of economic stagnation and profound social transformations. Consequently, the Fund is likely to favour projects that address these issues.

Women play an important role in all population programmes. In the past, projects have tended to view women as passive recipients of services or as marginal actors in the development process. The Fund's 1983 seminar for women leaders in the Caribbean and similar efforts aim at redressing such shortcomings. UNFPA-funded projects are also taking account of the role women should play in the management and active implementation of population projects.

It is useful to reiterate that UNFPA is fundamentally a supplier of financial resources for population programmes, and, therefore, the involvement of institutions capable of implementing large and complex projects in the field is necessary. Despite a significant proportion of UNFPA-supported programmes implemented directly by self-reliant governmental institutions, in the majority of cases an executing agency at the international level will continue to be useful. In particular, innovative subject areas and exploratory small-scale projects may be most effectively handled by NGOs with the appropriate expertise acceptable to both the Fund and the recipient nation.

5. MIDDLE EAST AND MEDITERRANEAN

OVERVIEW OF THE REGION

Stretching from the Arabian Gulf in Asia to the Atlantic coast in Africa, the Middle East and Mediterranean region, in the UNFPA classification, includes 23 states and covers approximately 15 million square kilometres. Twenty countries have predominantly Arab populations: the three non-Arab nations in the UNFPA regional classification are Cyprus, Malta and Turkey. The population numbers about 230 million at present, located in four major areas: North Africa, including Algeria, Libyan Arab Jamahiriya, Morocco and Tunisia; the Nile Valley and the African Horn—Djibouti, Egypt, Somalia and the Sudan; the eastern Mediterranean, including Cyprus, Turkey and the Fertile Crescent—Iraq, Jordan, Lebanon and Syrian Arab Republic; and the Arabian Peninsula and Arabian Gulf region, including Bahrain, Democratic Yemen, Kuwait, Oman, Qatar, Saudi Arabia, the United Arab Emirates and Yemen.

Socially and demographically, most countries of the region are similar. They have high rates of population growth, a young population structure, high rates of marriage, early age at marriage, large family size, and an agrarian, rural-oriented community life, although most also display high rates of urban expansion and city growth. Childhood and maternal mortality rates are generally high and life expectancy is moderate, 55 to 60 years, in most countries. Economically, however, there are marked differences in the region. For example, GNP per capita (in 1981 dollars) ranged from $280 in Somalia to $20,900 in Kuwait and $24,660 in United Arab Emirates.

A mosaic of population problems

The region is characterized by a wide range of population problems. In addition to excessive population growth in countries with limited resources, which remains one of the most pressing problems, unbalanced

---

Much of the material in the first section of this chapter is excerpted from Abdel-Rahim Omran, *Population in the Arab World: Problems and Prospects* (New York and London, United Nations Fund for Population Activities and Croom Helm Ltd., 1980).

population distribution in the region as a whole and within each country, unplanned urbanization and explosive growth of cities, poor manpower distribution and, in a few countries, underpopulation—all loom as urgent concerns. Furthermore, the dislocations attendant on such trends—the pressure to provide for the health, housing and educational needs of growing populations; the burden on urban infrastructure; and the economic and social imbalances associated with migration, particularly international migration—pose serious problems for Governments in the region.

Many countries in the region suffer from high population growth rates and limited availability of resources. Taken as a whole, the region has a population growth rate of about 3 per cent per annum compared with 2 per cent annually for the developing world as a whole. Growing at this rate, the region will double its population in less than 25 years. Fertility has been and still is extremely high. The women in this region are likely to bear six or seven children during their reproductive spans, as opposed to two children per woman in the more developed regions and four children per woman as a global average. High fertility in this region stems from early age at marriage, universality of marriage, pronatalist cultural attitudes, and the high correlation between a woman's fertility and her family's prestige in the community. Children are still regarded as assets rather than as liabilities. Contraception is not yet widely accepted. As fertility is high at almost all levels of income, literacy, electricity consumption, and other indicators of social and economic development, development alone will probably not reduce fertility in the region, unless and until appropriate family planning programmes as well as development activities are operating. Even if rates of growth begin to fall, the population of the region will continue to increase for several decades because of the previous high rates of population growth and the momentum inherent in a young age structure.

As a whole, the region is sparsely populated, with 11 inhabitants per square kilometre. However, population density differs from one country to another and within various regions of each country. Many small communities consisting of only a few hundred to a few thousand people are widely scattered, and the routes to supply these settlements are generally inadequate and isolated from resource centres. This isolation creates many hindrances to the distribution of services, social and cultural development, and security, and has prompted substantial out-migration.

In the cities and urban centres population is growing at a rate at least twice as fast as that of the total population–6 per cent per annum. Indeed, the so-called city states, such as Qatar and Kuwait, are becoming urbanized at phenomenal rates of 10 and 15 per cent annually. The cities of Kuwait and Doha will double their population in less than 10 years. Decreasing per capita agricultural area in some countries, notably Egypt, has made it more difficult to sustain people in rural areas. Therefore, the rural inhabitants are being pushed to the cities to seek a livelihood. Another component of urban growth in this region is the migration of people across borders to take advantage of life in countries having greater resources and more employment opportunities. Finally, a temporary factor in urban growth is the urban relocation of populations displaced by war. The great number of Palestinians who have settled mainly in Jordan, Lebanon and Syrian Arab Republic also constitute a unique population problem in the region.

In all cases, the expansion of urban centres has been unguided, uncontrolled and unplanned. Population growth aggravates the burden on already inadequate housing, sanitary installations, schools, hospitals, roads, transportation, energy sources and other public utilities. Furthermore, it contributes to the deterioration of the environment and may also exacerbate the problems of real unemployment or unemployment that is disguised by the hiring of more than one person to perform the duties of one job.

The age structure of the population in many of these countries—both rich and poor—poses great social and economic problems. Because more children now survive infancy and because high fertility has been sustained, children under age 15 often constitute close to 50 per cent of the total population. Such high percentages of dependent young people place considerable constraints on economic development in the region.

Underpopulation is a concern in Kuwait, Libyan Arab Jamahiriya, Saudi Arabia and, to a lesser extent, in the Gulf States and the Sudan. In some of these countries, the problem is compounded by inadequate development of agricultural and mineral resource industries. These problems stem from uneven population distribution and poor use of modern technology and mechanization. A situation common to most countries is the small size of the labour force, a result of the high proportion of the population below 15 years and inadequate technical training. Another reason for small labour forces is the low participation of women: it has been estimated that less than 8 per cent of the region's labour force is composed of women.

Rapid population growth has been overtaxing the economy of the Middle East and Mediterranean and has impeded the process of development in the non-oil-producing countries. A sizeable share of total investment in these countries is absorbed in what is termed "demographic investment", activities to prevent the prevailing standard of living from deteriorating because of increasing population. In many countries, this demographic investment may be as high as 30 to 50 per cent of the total investment compared with only 10 to 15 per cent in European countries, where population growth is slow.

Education systems are inadequate because the rate of growth of facilities and staff is much slower than that of the population. In the wealthier countries, despite the availability of substantial funds for education and the ability to construct a large number of schools quickly, a major constraint lies in the development of an adequate pool of trained teachers. Classes are conducted in Arabic and thus the allocation of funds to import teachers would serve no purpose; there are simply not enough Arabic-speaking teachers to meet the needs of the growing student enrolments.

Health systems, already less than adequate in many countries, have also been overtaxed by rapid population growth. Most countries have shortages of physicians, nurses and paramedical workers. Although rich countries can afford to import physicians and paramedical personnel, these foreigners are seldom accepted by the conservative population in the countries of the region, especially by the women.

Population policies

There is wide variation among the countries in the region in the perception of their population problems and their readiness to adopt population policies. The Governments of Egypt and Tunisia have launched national programmes for population activities designed to accomplish explicit demographic objectives of reductions in fertility and population growth. The Governments of Algeria and Morocco have, to a lesser extent, defined the magnitude of their population problems and have initiated programmes to provide their populations with information and services about family planning as part of basic health services. With the exception of Libyan Arab Jamahiriya, the countries of North Africa have similar population problems and Governments that have adopted population programmes.

The countries of Western Asia can be classified into two groups. Some, including Democratic Yemen, Jordan, Syrian Arab Republic and Yemen, have proceeded to integrate family planning with maternal and child health services as part of the basic health services provided to the people. Somalia and the Sudan have similar activities. Other countries, the Gulf States and Iraq, have no stated population policy and no direct national population programme except for policies regulating immigration of the exogenous labour force.

By and large, almost all the countries of the region lack adequate infrastructure for population data collection and analysis; generally, they have weak or no civil registration systems. Their development plans generally do not take demographic variables sufficiently into account.

UNFPA AND THE MIDDLE EAST
AND MEDITERRANEAN

When the Fund was established in 1969, it found it necessary to initiate an extensive programme to create awareness of population issues at all levels of decision-making. Several seminars, workshops and conferences addressing various aspects of the population problem were conducted. Countries were encouraged to request the services of a population scientist who could draw on the expertise of professionals in a variety of fields to assist in analysing the impact of population on employment, health services, agriculture and food availability, education and other sectors. Within one or two years, this information alerted decision makers to population problems and fostered their interest in finding solutions.

Types of activities
Basic data collection. As table 7 shows, assistance to data collection activities in the region has been important throughout the 1970s and into the 1980s. The first step towards creating awareness among officials of the importance of population was an assessment of the infrastructure and capacities of various countries in population data collection and analysis and their experience, if any, with periodic censuses. Before 1970, Democratic Yemen, Djibouti, Somalia, Sudan and Yemen (which had not yet gained independence) had never had population censuses; they derived estimates from incomplete demographic surveys that rarely covered the whole country but were limited instead to rough head counts in industrial or coastal zones, areas of interest to the colonial power. Other countries, for economic or political reasons, avoided conducting population censuses.

Population data collection is basic to any modern development planning effort. Therefore, the countries of the region received UNFPA financing to conduct national censuses so that Governments would have at their disposal correct information about the size, structure and distribution of their populations. It was a difficult undertaking: most countries had no cartographic maps delineating urban and rural zones or designating administrative units. In fact, most countries did not even have a system of street naming and house numbering in their main

Table 7

Percentage Distribution of UNFPA Expenditures by Work Plan Categories, Middle East and Mediterranean, 1969–1983

Work plan categories	Years												Total
	1969-1972	1973	1974	1975	1976	1977	1978	1979	1980	1981	1982	1983	1969-1983
Basic data collection	8.4	42.0	26.1	35.2	24.4	33.2	14.6	23.7	26.7	29.5	29.7	13.3	24.8
Population dynamics	3.1	2.8	2.5	1.8	3.0	4.2	15.0	12.7	16.6	12.0	13.2	19.0	11.0
Formulation and evaluation of population policies and programmes	2.6	4.8	3.7	2.4	0.8	0.6	3.2	1.4	3.0	4.1	3.5	4.3	2.8
Implementation of policies	0.0	0.0	0.0	0.0	0.0	0.0	0.6	0.5	0.4	0.4	0.1	0.4	0.3
Family planning	78.8	32.2	54.1	47.0	55.4	46.6	46.9	41.7	29.7	26.4	26.6	31.4	39.4
Communication and education	6.1	5.4	0.7	5.0	7.5	6.0	9.7	8.2	10.2	13.9	13.8	20.0	10.4
Special programmes	0.0	0.0	0.0	0.0	0.1	0.6	0.9	0.7	1.2	0.8	0.2	1.2	0.6
Multisectoral activities	1.0	12.8	12.9	8.6	8.8	8.8	9.1	11.1	12.2	12.9	12.9	10.4	10.7
Total	100.0	100.0	100.0	100.0	100.0	100.0	100.0	100.0	100.0	100.0	100.0	100.0	100.0
(Thousands of US dollars)	(2,561)	(2,112)	(5,605)	(6,736)	(9,187)	(8,487)	(10,075)	(12,180)	(12,513)	(11,947)	(10,739)	(13,888)	(106,030)

Sources: UNFPA Fact Sheet Number 1.08 (September 1983); UNFPA Fact Sheet Number 1.09 (November 1983).
Note: Figures for 1969 to 1982 are project expenditures; figures for 1983 are project allocations as of 30 November 1983.

cities. Therefore, census preparations were extensive. UNFPA co-operated with the Governments in conducting the first nation-wide censuses in Democratic Yemen, Djibouti, Somalia, Sudan and Yemen. UNFPA financed local costs for enumerators and provided the necessary vehicles for transport. In some countries, it was necessary to buy donkeys and camels for enumerators to reach remote areas. In this connection, a curious cable was received in New York Headquarters. It read in part:

"Reference National Population Census Project. Regret advise UN donkey number one died while on duty due to excessive heat and rough terrain. According to UN bidding procedures have located young, energetic substitute. Please authorize $430 immediately repeat immediately".

Such a cable was necessary because equipment and vehicles provided by UNFPA remain the property of UNFPA until the end of the approved duration of a project.

It was also difficult to count nomadic populations. Most census questionnaires assume that a person is enumerated at a place of residence. In Sudan, with an area equal in size to nine countries in Europe, the Government contracted with a Swiss commercial airline company to take aerial photographs of nomadic populations and arrive at estimates of their numbers by photo-interpretation. Cultural taboos also affected the accuracy of data collection. For example, many male heads of households in Yemen live and work in the surrounding Gulf States. When census enumerators visited households presided over by the wife, she was not able to answer the door because in Yemen the voice of a woman is considered as a form of "nakedness" and a man not known to the family should not hear that voice. Once identified, this situation led to a decision to recruit women as enumerators to conduct a follow-up demographic survey, which was financed by UNFPA.

For countries with experience in census-taking, UNFPA assistance was still immensely important to improve and strengthen the capability of the central statistical offices by providing electronic data processing equipment. Such was the major component financed in, for example, Algeria, Egypt, Jordan and Syrian Arab Republic. In Egypt, the project included the establishment of a computer terminal in each of the 26 governorates linked to Central Agency for Public Mobilization and Statistics. This improved infrastructure was subsequently used, *inter alia*, for improvement of civil registration and the recording of vital events. The Fund's assistance to several Arab countries for electronic data processing equipment ensured the accuracy of data generated and greatly strengthened their institutional capacity. The modernized infrastructure in the central statistical offices of various Middle Eastern countries is largely a result of UNFPA support.

Population planning and policy research. With the completion of the initial round of population and housing censuses in the early 1970s, countries requested UNFPA assistance for data analysis and policy formulation. UNFPA support was extended for the creation, usually in the ministry of planning, of population planning and policy research units that would examine population issues in the context of, *inter alia*, human resource availability and development, employment, labour markets, women's role and participation in the labour force, internal and international migration, income distribution and poverty. These projects were designed to enhance the knowledge and understanding of the complex interrelationships between population and development so as to contribute to national policy design, analysis and implementation. In the early stages, these programmes, by necessity, had to be "promotional", creating an awareness among policy makers and technical officials of the importance of the interrelationships between population and development. The primary focus of policy research has been on manpower planning and migration.

Manpower planning. In most countries of the region interest in the population question is not necessarily sparked by over-population *per se* but by a concern for better management of human resources and manpower planning. Thus, in its work in the Middle East and Mediterranean, UNFPA collaborated closely with ILO to advance policy-oriented research intended to lead to the adoption of national population policies. Initially, UNFPA financed a large number of national and regional seminars on population, employment and development, which enhanced the knowledge and analytical skills of national planners and technicians. UNFPA has supported projects in manpower planning in Democratic Yemen, Egypt, Iraq, Jordan, Syrian Arab Republic and Yemen. The basic objectives of such undertakings are to help design comprehensive population policies and measures covering all the important aspects of population and human resources in a particular country; to identify data gaps and promote and assist in carrying out policy research studies; to help produce co-ordination and collaboration with the other units in the planning organization so that population activities mesh with economic growth and social development goals, targets and programmes; to make the necessary technical contribution to the work of the planning organization; to supply other units in the planning organization with the data and analyses they need for planning, programming and monitoring; and to draw up, in collaboration with research and training institutions, universities and Government bodies, intermediate and advanced multidisciplinary training programmes for national cadres in order to generate a continuous supply of well-trained specialists in population dynamics and development. To upgrade the present professional staff of Government agencies, the unit should also contribute to the design and organization of short-term in-service training courses on population, human resources and development planning.

A comprehensive project for population and employment planning in Jordan was one of the most successful of such projects (see feature page 77).

UNFPA has also supported the Government of Cyprus in the fields of basic population data collection and the study of the interrelationship between population, employment and labour force mobility. The Government sought to increase the registration of vital events, obtain an estimate of the economically active population and formulate a population research programme that would further understanding of population dynamics. Based on this information, the Government could formulate a model for a system of manpower planning in order to estimate labour demand and supply by sectoral and occupational categories; it would also be able to formulate educational and manpower training policies to match estimates of labour force demand with those of supply. These two projects, initially under the direction of UNDTCD and ILO, respectively, were taken over by the Government in 1982.

Migration. Internal and international migration is an urgent issue to most Governments in the Middle East. Officials have been most interested in research on the determinants of migration and the consequences of migratory movements for receiving and sending areas; the effects of migration from rural to urban areas on infrastructure needs, both public and private; the demographic consequences of migration, including effects on fertility behaviour, marriage patterns and mortality; the effects of migration on the socio-economic status of those left behind; and extent and effects of circular (temporary) migration and commuting; the role of return migration in rural development; and the design of policies aimed at a better spatial distribution of employment opportunities. UNFPA has funded policy research addressing such issues in Democratic Yemen, Egypt, Jordan and Syrian Arab Republic.

Recent research has addressed the growing phenomenon of international "contract" migration, especially from the developing countries of South and East Asia and other Middle Eastern countries to the oil-rich Gulf States. Studies have found that the labour-sending countries expe-

POPULATION AND EMPLOYMENT PLANNING IN JORDAN

A comprehensive project for employment planning was initiated in Jordan in 1980. This project, based in the Human Resources Department of the National Planning Council, was instrumental in creating a self-reliant national institutional capacity for population and development planning. In the short span of two years, the project had succeeded in completing
- A review of population and labour force data;
- A compendium of population and manpower statistics;
- Studies of the labour force, including female participation and industrial and occupational structure;
- The development of manpower planning methodologies, taking into consideration demographic variables and labour force characteristics in terms of their industrial, occupational, functional and institutional dimensions;
- Projections of manpower demand and supply;
- A survey of the manpower implications of plan projects; and
- Guidelines for population and manpower policies, which included, *inter alia*, regulating population growth, raising female labour force participation, ensuring better spatial distribution, curtailing rural-urban migration, regulating international migration, raising wage levels and attracting foreign capital.

A work plan for the Human Resources Department was also prepared for the two-year period following project completion. The services of the UNFPA/ILO regional adviser on population and human resources planning were made available as needed for accomplishing this work plan.

The project has thus provided a tool for Jordan's development, particularly for its population and manpower policies, and for dealing with the anticipated increased participation of women in the labour force and the regulation of migration of skilled labour from Jordan to various countries.

rience significant short-term benefits, especially the alleviation of domestic labour over-supply and the opportunity to earn scarce foreign exchange through workers' remittances home. However, the sending countries, particularly those in the Middle East, are becoming concerned over the longer term and perhaps less desirable effects of these flows. Careful studies of the demographic, social and economic effects in the sending countries are overdue. Even if the measurable gains from the process continue to accrue, the costs in social and economic disruption are likely to increase. The priority need of these countries is for policies and programmes that will stem the adverse consequences for the migrants' families, their communities and the society.

In Malta, the heavy emigration of young persons, the return of emigrants at older ages and a decline in the birth rate have resulted in an age structure in which about 13 per cent of the population is more than 60 years of age. Realizing the need for appropriate policies, the Government requested that UNFPA provide an expert on aging to develop a comprehensive community health service for the elderly. An assessment was conducted and targets were defined for implementing a plan involving the communities. The project, which was executed by the Regional Office for Europe of WHO (WHO/EURO), ended in 1982 with the establishment of a model day-care programme for the elderly in association with St. Vincent de Paul Hospital.

Family planning. Considerable strides have been made in the region in introducing action programmes in MCH/FP and in population education and communication as well as in the pursuit of operational research to buttress such endeavours.

In the mid-1970s, assistance was rendered to Algeria and Jordan for strengthening MCH and introducing family planning and child-spacing programmes in selected health centres. The plan for the project in Jordan called for trained staff and equipment for the delivery of family planning services to be made available in six centres each year over the three-year project period. Once the demand for family planning became apparent, the Government on its own initiative enlarged the appropriations for this programme, increasing the number of centres covered to 10 a year. The Minister of Health in July 1979 instructed that all health centres under the Ministry should be staffed and equipped to deliver family planning services upon request. This programme started with a component of approximately $10,000 for contraceptive supplies; through the Government's arrangements with other donors for a progressive increase, this component now exceeds $800,000 per annum, thus making contraceptive methods widely available at low prices. Similar evolutions in family planning services took place in Democratic Yemen, Somalia, Sudan, Syrian Arab Republic and Yemen.

In countries where Governments had adopted a well-designed population policy designed to curtail population growth, the UNFPA programme concentrated on financing efforts to increase the availability of family planning services throughout the country. When UNFPA began its assistance to Egypt in 1971, the principal commitment was to increase the number of health centres and strengthen their staffing. In 1971, the country had approximately 400 family planning clinics; by 1975, there were 4,350 centres with trained staff and adequate equipment for the delivery of family planning services and the distribution of various methods of contraception. In support of this programme, UNFPA continued to finance, at an average of $1 million per annum, the purchase of raw materials for the local manufacture of contraceptive oral pills, supplementing Government imports; today oral pills are available at the equivalent of 10 cents a monthly cycle. At present, more than 25 per cent of Egyptian women in the reproductive age group are practising family planning.

In 1975, the population policy in Egypt was further refined and called for addressing population within the overall context of social and economic development efforts, which were to be directed at raising the socio-economic standard of the family; revising the educational system so as to relate education to employment; promoting women's employment in the modern sector; mechanizing agriculture and promoting agro-industries to mitigate rural-urban migration; increasing social provisions; reducing infant mortality with special attention to sanitation, nutrition and environmental factors; providing information and communication; and increasing the availability of family planning services.

Reflecting this shift in policy direction, the UNFPA/Government of Egypt's Second Country Programme Agreement, 1975–1980, included projects for the creation of employment opportunites for women, literacy classes and other community-based activities to motivate the population for accepting family planning. The broadened scope of this policy orientation was based on the findings of surveys and studies conducted between 1965 and 1975 which indicated that the "direct" family planning approach did not by itself sufficiently or effectively achieve the Government's population objectives. Elaborations of policy after 1975 addressed the four interrelated aspects of population growth, distribution, characteristics and structure. As they evolved, these policies have not neglected, but rather have reinforced, family planning services by giving rise to measures addressing socio-economic concerns.

In 1976, as part of the Egyptian Government's decentralization, governors were given the responsibility for preparing development plans most appropriate for their respective governorates. On the basis of the 1976 population census carried out with UNFPA support, each governor was advised of the number of women in the reproductive age group in the governorate so that a target could be set for increasing the number of family planning acceptors.

The Population and Development Project (PDP), initiated in 1977, was a significant step in amplifying the new, broader approach to population issues. With assistance from UNFPA and subsequently from other donors, this project has financed, through a fund that awards interest-free loans, projects of importance to communities as a reward for achieving a specified number of family planning acceptors. A trained population co-ordinator advised on the priority to be given projects bearing on fertility behaviour, such as women's employment projects or literacy classes for women. Parallel to this effort, each participating governorate inaugurated a programme for service statistics and established demographic units to improve the availability of statistical information and to assess the impact of the project. (Cornell University's International Population Department is responsible for an objective assessment of the project's impact on fertility behaviour.) By 1983, the project was operational in 12 of 26 governorates, serving some 14.5 million people. The Federal Republic of Germany, the Netherlands and the United States Agency for International Development (USAID) have all substantially contributed to expanding this programme nation-wide.

The Government of Tunisia and UNFPA in 1975 signed an agreement under which the Fund, over a three-and-a-half-year period, would assist the Tunisian family planning programme in projects covering a range of population activities: support for clinical services, population education in schools and in the rural and labour sectors, equipment, training and a law and population project for reviewing laws bearing on population and family planning. The second phase of UNFPA support to the national family planning programme provided for the refinement of ongoing activities and for research and evaluation of the family planning programme. By the end of 1981, UNFPA had provided Tunisia with $8.3 million to support its population programme.

Needs assessment and project formulation missions were conducted in 1980, and a new programme was approved by the Fund's Governing Council in 1981. It placed renewed emphasis on expanding family planning activities in rural areas, both in the provision of services and in education and communication efforts. Plans were also made to introduce population studies in the final years of primary schools, particularly for students not continuing on to secondary school.

In countries such as Democratic Yemen, Jordan, Somalia, Sudan, Syrian Arab Republic and Yemen, which have considerable family planning efforts primarily for health reasons, UNFPA funding has supported the training of medical and paramedical personnel, particularly traditional birth attendants, in various family planning methods. Assistance has also been given to strengthen the infrastructure of ministries of health to permit the delivery of family planning services integrated in MCH as part of ongoing primary health care programmes.

Population education and communication. In support of the above-mentioned family planning efforts and in the interest of promoting knowledge about population and development interrelationships, a number of countries in the region have introduced population education into curricula of various levels of schooling as well as into national programmes of non-formal education and campaigns to eradicate illiteracy. Through UNESCO's participation as executing agency, population education for teacher training commenced in the early 1970s, resulting in the development of teacher training manuals in Arabic for civics, biology, history and other courses that would include attention to population issues. Projects for population education exist in all countries of the region where UNFPA now has a programme, and population education is gradually becoming part of the curriculum for secondary schools and, in some cases, for that in institutions of higher learning. To complement this effort, population education in the out-of-school programmes has also been important. In Morocco, building upon a national programme covering 360 women's centres in rural areas and urban slums under the auspices of the Ministry of Youth and Sports, UNFPA has supported the training of all centre supervisors *(monatrices)* in nutrition, hygiene, home economics, child spacing and its importance for the well-being of the family. This project also included components to strengthen the training capability of the women's centres in skills that can help a woman join the wage-earning labour force such as typing, bookkeeping and accounting.

With ILO as executing agency, UNFPA has supported population education and family welfare programmes designed to institutionalize a population education component in the work-place of labourers in the organized sector, trade unions and employer organizations. This programme was extended to include co-operatives and rural institutions. UNFPA assisted countries in the establishment of demographic training centres, usually within the central statistical offices, to give middle-management employees of various ministries courses on population and its consequences for various sectors. In order to meet Governments' long-term demand for personnel who are knowledgeable about population, UNFPA has financed population study centres within the universities in Bahrain, Iraq and Jordan.

Regional assistance

UNFPA regional projects in the Middle East and West Asia are executed by the United Nations, UNDP, ILO, FAO, UNESCO, WHO, UNICEF, UN/DTCD and UNFPA itself. These projects provide assistance to conferences and seminars, to regional institutions for research, training, communication infrastructure and other programmes as well as to international institutions.

The United Nations Economic Commission for Western Asia (ECWA), through its Population Division, assists Governments and regional institutions in collecting demographic and related socio-economic data; conducting demographic analyses, including estimates, projections and demographic studies; undertaking research and studies in population development; monitoring population policies; and disseminating population education and information.

Between 1980 and 1983, UNFPA budgeted almost $4 million for this programme. With UNFPA support, ECWA provides two regional advisers, one in population statistics and one in demography. The research agenda of the Population Division of ECWA has focused on population data collection and analysis, including the study of interregional migration, growth trends in major cities and mortality characteristics; population and development, the study of the relationship between population, socio-economic trends and economic development; and population policies, including research activities and seminars leading to the development of guidelines for the elaboration of national population policies.

ECWA has also planned meetings and seminars on population problems such as migration and urbanization in the region and has published papers and bulletins on research findings and population topics.

The ILO Labour and Population Programme in the Middle East region came into existence in 1972 with the appointment of a regional adviser on workers' population education. Since 1976, the ILO Population and Labour Policy and Research Programme has developed training programmes in population, employment and development planning for national policy makers and planners in order to promote the integration of population factors into development planning. The services of two regional advisers, in population and labour policy and in population and employment research, and headquarters staff from the Population and Labour Policies Branch are available on an *ad hoc* basis to government agencies for technical collaboration in population and employment-related areas.

The Regional Population Communication and Education Programme of UNESCO, established in the early 1970s, is funded by UNFPA to provide all the countries of the region with population education and communication services. The UNESCO Regional Advisor for Curriculum Development in Population Education in the Arab States has assisted interested countries in the development of in-school and out-of-school programmes, has worked with university faculties of communication, in Egypt, for example, to develop guidelines for programmes of higher studies, and has extended technical assistance to country projects like those in Bahrain and Syrian Arab Republic. At the regional level, under the Fund's regional programme with UNESCO, the following training activities have been undertaken: workshops on curriculum development; seminars on evaluation of population education activities; seminars on methodologies in non-formal population education; seminars on sex education; and workshops on training, including teacher training by correspondence.

The World Health Organization's Eastern Mediterranean Regional Office in Alexandria, Egypt, focuses principally on the improvement, development and delivery of health services integrated with maternal and child health care and family planning services. Emphasis has been placed on the training of medical and paramedical personnel and on collaboration with countries' health services and medical schools. The Regional Advisor on Family Health (medical officer) provides advisory services to UNFPA-supported projects and the WHO Regional Office, as a whole, is available for collaboration, especially through regional advisers on MCH, health statistics, health personnel education and nurse/ midwifery. The Regional Advisor on Health Statistics works with countries' in the development of vital and health statistics systems. Advisory services also address methodological issues in connection with collecting field data and training.

Interregional activities

UNFPA support to the Cairo Demographic Training and Research Centre (see feature page 153) and to the International Islamic Research and Study Centre at Al-Azhar University constitutes the principal interregional activity in the Middle East. The project at Al-Azhar is of tremendous significance throughout the Muslim world. In 1971, when the project was being prepared, the student body at Al-Azhar University was 38,000. The project's objectives are to introduce a programme of higher studies for students of various faculties in the University dealing with demographic changes and their socio-economic impact on Islamic societies; to establish a link with all institutions of research and higher learning in the Muslim world to co-ordinate their activities and ensure the flow of information between them; to co-ordinate socio-economic and demographic research conducted in various countries; and to disseminate the findings of relevant research work in all appropriate languages for consideration in the preparation of socio-economic development policies.

The International Islamic Research and Study Centre currently receives substantial support from several donors in addition to UNFPA, including many Governments. Courses on population are now being offered by the various faculties. Through the Centre, schools have published works discussing Islamic views on family planning and the rights and responsibilities of women and children, as well as findings of research projects conducted in Egypt and elsewhere on such topics as population in relation to health, development, social change and ethical values. A programme for publishing scholarly works on population issues in Arabic and English is already under way. The Centre also annually convenes an international symposium addressing subjects of population and social change.

FUTURE DIRECTIONS

UNFPA programmes in the Middle East and Mediterranean have worked for the most part with traditional clinical fixed-point services that rely on trained nurses and physicians to consult with patients and provide for their needs. When introduced by these means, family planning services generally gain immediate acceptance and are integrated into the services already provided. However, a large proportion of the population in the region is rural, and clinics are few and far between. Some other means of reaching non-urban communities must be found if reductions in crude birth rates are to be achieved. Only a handful of countries in the region has birth rates under 40 per 1,000, and a dozen or so have rates that are among the highest in the world.

Some countries, already aware of these problems, have taken steps to deal with them. There are the efforts to train village motivators in Egypt, rural health workers in Morocco, mobile teams in Tunisia and traditional birth attendants in Syrian Arab Republic. Possibly, all of these programmes or a combination of any of them will be necessary to provide services for those who wish to lengthen birth intervals or to limit the size of their families. At any rate, given the reluctance of highly trained professionals to leave urban areas, it is essential that emphasis be placed on training paramedical personnel and traditional birth attendants in their own communities. They will have to be counted on, not only for family planning services but also for providing nutritional information and simple remedies, such as oral rehydration salts, that have demonstrated effectiveness in reducing infant and child malnutrition and mortality. In rural areas, the death toll on infants and children still remains unacceptably high. Without a reduction in this burden, the possibility of wide acceptance of family planning methods in these areas remains slim.

The last decade or so has witnessed an increase in a number of population problems in the region accompanied by an increased awareness of them at the national policy-making levels. Because of differential growth among the countries of the region, relatively large numbers of migrants have moved, and continue to move, across national boundaries, particularly from the non-oil-producing countries of Democratic Yemen, Jordan, Lebanon, Syrian Arab Republic and Yemen to the oil-exporting countries of Kuwait, Qatar, Saudi Arabia and United Arab Emirates. These major population movements have resulted in unique situations in both receiving and sending countries. In most of the receiving countries, between 50 and 90 per cent of the labour force is now non-national, whereas in most of the sending countries, one third or more of the labour force works abroad, creating manpower shortages that constrain development efforts.

Major population movements are also taking place within many countries of the region. The concentration of economic activities in the capital cities caused by many factors, including the nature of the development process itself, has resulted in mass movements from rural areas to the cities, often overburdening them while draining the countryside of much needed manpower resources. Even problems related to fertility and population growth have begun to appear in this region. Outside Egypt, where such problems have long been present and widely recognized, a number of countries in the region have begun to recognize that the very high fertility levels are having harmful effects on the health of mothers and children and on the welfare of families. These emerging population problems in the Middle East and Mediterranean require purposeful policies for their solution, and the formulation of these policies requires policy-relevant research identifying the socio-economic determinants and consequences of trends and shedding light on the policy options available for their modification. The expertise required is not in formal demography but in the broader interdisciplinary area of population studies, particularly in population and development, manpower planning and migration.

6. EUROPE

OVERVIEW OF THE REGION

Europe has had a long history of involvement in population activities. European universities have provided a wide range of training in demography. Since 1927, four major population conferences have been held in Europe: Geneva in 1927; Rome in 1954; Belgrade in 1965; and Bucharest in 1974. In 1980, the Conference on Population and the Urban Future was held in Rome. In addition, in the early 1970s, several European countries, such as Bulgaria, Byelorussian Soviet Socialist Republic, Czechoslovakia, Norway, Poland and Romania, established commissions or agencies responsible for population matters.

Of 34 countries that are members of the United Nations Economic Commission for Europe (ECE), 11 developing countries have programmes supported by UNFPA: Albania, Bulgaria, Cyprus, Czechoslovakia, Greece, Hungary, Poland, Portugal, Romania, Turkey and Yugoslavia. UNFPA support to these countries is, for the most part, limited to technical assistance. A great deal of emphasis has been placed on training, and these countries have come to serve as a training ground for personnel from developing countries of all regions.

In terms of population, these countries are characterized by low rates of growth resulting, in some countries, in labour shortages; infertility; increasing adolescent sexual activity; changing marital patterns; and populations with ever greater proportions of the aged. Albania and Turkey are two exceptions to this pattern: they have high rates of population growth and, consequently, populations with a young age structure. Migration, internal and international, is also considered a problem in many of the developing, as well as developed, countries in the region.

UNFPA AND EUROPE

UNFPA has responded to the needs of developing countries in Europe by providing financial support to help them carry out their population and development programmes. Because of the relatively higher socio-economic level in these developing countries compared with those elsewhere, UNFPA support has not been designed on the findings of needs assessment missions as in the case of other countries; rather it has been part of an ongoing effort to help Governments bridge gaps in the population and development plans they have drawn up.

Funding levels

Of the $8.8 million the Fund has spent in this region, 60 per cent was expended for country projects, the balance for intercountry projects. As shown in table 8, the bulk of UNFPA funding has gone to family planning; population dynamics and data collection also account for a substantial share. The intercountry activities were mainly in connection with data gathering and analysis, the World Fertility Survey, and the interregional demographic training programmes in the United Nations Demographic Training and Research Centre (CEDOR) in Romania and, in Moscow, the Demographic Training and Research Programme in Population and Development Planning.

The majority of the projects in these countries has been executed by organizations of the United Nations system. In several cases, however, because of the relatively well-established administrative capabilities of the European developing countries, country projects have been directly executed by Government agencies alone, occasionally with an international consultant. NGOs have executed a number of projects, with prompt recruitment of experts and flexible responses to shifts in demands in the projects.

Types of activities

Requests from the developing countries in Europe fall into two broad groups: support to develop a family planning programme, including components addressed to infertility and sterility programmes, and support for work in the area of population dynamics and policy formulation, particularly policies to integrate demographic, economic and social data into development planning.

Family planning and related activities. In the countries that have requested UNFPA assistance for family planning—Greece, Portugal and Yugoslavia—the birth rates are low and thus family planning is viewed not so much as a fertility regulator as a health and human right. Governments wishing to reduce the reliance on abortion as a major method of child spacing by promoting contraception have asked UNFPA for a variety of support. Approximately 43.4 per cent of UNFPA allocations in Europe between 1969 and 1982 went for family planning. Funds were allocated mainly for project personnel, equipment and contraceptives, the major emphasis being on training. Family planning was delivered almost exclusively through health-related systems. These projects were not, however, developed in isolation.

Table 8

PERCENTAGE DISTRIBUTION OF UNFPA EXPENDITURES BY WORK PLAN CATEGORIES, EUROPE, 1969–1983

Work plan categories	Years											Total	
	1969-1972	1973	1974	1975	1976	1977	1978	1979	1980	1981	1982	1983	1969-1983
Basic data collection	0.0	2.3	0.0	0.8	0.8	0.7	16.8	20.0	23.4	17.3	23.7	0.1	14.5
Population dynamics	62.6	53.3	41.9	22.7	37.8	31.3	15.1	10.3	24.9	20.0	24.0	18.3	22.6
Formulation and evaluation of population policies and programmes	0.0	0.0	6.5	5.5	0.0	2.6	0.0	0.0	0.0	2.2	4.3	2.7	1.7
Implementation of policies	0.0	0.0	0.0	0.0	0.0	0.0	0.0	3.5	2.2	0.5	0.1	1.8	1.3
Family planning	37.4	44.4	51.6	46.2	36.7	45.4	52.7	52.1	37.1	45.1	25.7	26.3	40.3
Communication and education	0.0	0.0	0.0	0.0	0.0	0.0	0.0	1.6	3.4	3.1	4.3	1.7	2.0
Special programmes	0.0	0.0	0.0	0.0	0.0	0.0	0.0	4.9	1.9	1.0	0.1	27.7	4.7
Multisectoral activities	0.0	0.0	0.0	24.8	24.7	20.0	15.4	7.6	7.1	10.8	17.8	21.4	12.9
Total	100.0	100.0	100.0	100.0	100.0	100.0	100.0	100.0	100.0	100.0	100.0	100.0	100.0
(Thousands of US dollars)	(147)	(214)	(184)	(238)	(357)	(425)	(615)	(1,361)	(1,588)	(1,484)	(1,062)	(1,096)	(8,771)

Source: UNFPA Fact Sheet Number 1.08 (September 1983); UNFPA Fact Sheet Number 1.09 (November 1983).
Note: Figures for 1969 to 1982 are project expenditures; figures for 1983 are project allocations as of 30 November 1983.

In Portugal, for instance, where family planning first became legal under the 1976 Constitution, an integrated programme of six projects was developed in 1977. The goals were to investigate possible cultural constraints to accepting family planning, train public health personnel in family planning counselling and services, start a mass media information campaign on family planning, incorporate family planning into the Lisbon Medical School curricula (see chapter 7) and institute services at the school's teaching hospital, work with a rural community to interest it in family planning and expand the community work of the Family Planning Association.

In the project for the training of medical and paramedical personnel in the public health sector, curricula were developed for different types of personnel providing family planning counselling and services, with the help of the Regional Office for Europe of the World Health Organization (WHO/EURO), following which the Directorate General of Health of Portugal itself undertook the training. It was more difficult, however, to incorporate family planning theory and practice into the medical school curriculum. Although UNFPA supported a project for this purpose, as well as to provide family planning clinic experience for fifth-year students and interns in the university hospital, only after the project had been in operation for about four years was more emphasis placed upon family planning in the regular medical curriculum. The reluctance of the medical school faculty to include family planning was unanticipated, so that much education of the faculty had to take place through consultants and seminars before this goal could be accomplished.

One effective support communication project using mass media and carried out by the Commission on the Status of Women between 1978 and 1981 was a survey to discover how much Portuguese people knew about family planning. This survey was followed by an inquiry into psychological or cultural attitudes that would hinder or facilitate the practice of family planning. Based on this information the Commission placed articles on family planning along with related information in a weekly women's magazine. At the end of each article, women were encouraged to write or to telephone for more information.

The problem of lack of information on family planning in urban areas was tackled through the community outreach programme of the Family Planning Association of Portugal and in rural areas through a model grass-roots programme carried out by the Commission on the Status of Women. In the latter, an international team comprising a public health nurse, an audio-visual specialist, a social worker and a communications specialist went to the northern Portuguese village of Faraginhas, a remote hamlet with no electricity or running water, to bring family planning services to the inhabitants and to assist them in improving their health and living conditions. The team trained a local team and helped establish various village improvement groups (including a women's health group and a youth group) which discussed family planning, nutrition and sanitation. As a result, sanitation improved, the local clinic is now fully committed to family planning and the villagers seem to be more confident in their ability to effect improvements.

In Greece, few family planning services have been available except through private physicians. In 1982, the Government requested UNFPA support to establish a network of family planning clinics in 20 government-assisted hospitals. Ten teams, one from each of the health districts in the country, were trained in family planning and counselling methods and in clinic administration. These teams will, in turn, be training others in their home districts. Women from two national women's organizations were given training in family planning communication in order to set up a women's information network to promote family planning. Conducted by one of the project directors of the successful Portuguese mass communication project, the training programme is an excellent example of technical co-operation among developing countries.

Yugoslavia's Constitution refers to family planning as a basic human right. UNFPA began to assist the Government in 1977. Courses in fertility-regulating methods were held for physicians, nurses and midwives. On the basis of a comparative survey of fertility and family planning services by the Yugoslav Demographic Research Centre, family planning programme projects for UNFPA assistance were developed by the Socialist Republics of Macedonia and Serbia with support from the Federal Council of Family Planning.

Pursuant to a law passed by the Yugoslav Federal Assembly in 1969 emphasizing the importance of educating the population on the need for better understanding and more equal status between the sexes as well as for responsible parenthood, the Governments of two socialist republics, Bosnia-Herzegovina and Montenegro, requested UNFPA support for training in sex education and for improving the status of women. Since 1980, the Fund has supported training in responsible parenthood at the post-graduate level in the University of Sarajevo for professional personnel, lawyers, social workers and educators. Students attend classes about 10 days a month; assignments are designed to be done after working hours. Lectures include biology, medicine, law, sociology, demography, psychology and pedagogy. An enrolment of 40 was envisaged, but many times that number applied.

In 1982, the Government of Albania requested the co-operation of UNFPA in a project on maternal and child health that commenced in 1984. This is one of the few externally assisted projects in the country.

UNFPA has also supported family planning research in developing countries in Europe. Bulgaria obtained assistance with the implementation of its population policy to increase the fertility level by reducing infertility and sterility, which affect about 10 to 15 per cent of the population. A research centre was established in 1979 at the Institute of Obstetrics and Gynaecology of the Medical Academy in Sofia. More than 40,000 couples were registered and the number requesting assistance has been rising dramatically. In 1980, 5,250 clients were examined; during the first six months of 1982, the number was 4,300. This project has been extended through 1986 so that work in this important field could be expanded.

The Government also sought UNFPA help in establishing a family planning counselling and research centre for couples at risk of bearing children with birth disorders. Training and equipment were needed to carry out the 1979 decision of the Parliamentary Commission on Social Policy to reduce infant and child morbidity and mortality through counselling and services for chronically sick and handicapped children and for their parents. As a result of this project, a Laboratory of Metabolic Diseases in Childhood was established at the Institute of Paediatrics of the Medical Academy in Sofia, and an information, registration and family planning counselling system for at-risk families designed.

Most of the UNFPA-supported initiatives in Europe have emphasized training, and several projects have placed special emphasis on training candidates from other developing countries. For example, the Ministry of Health in Czechoslovakia in co-operation with UNFPA in 1981 organized a seminar on primary health care during infancy and early childhood for participants from developing countries. Emphasis was placed on family health implications and the importance of family planning. It was executed by WHO/EURO.

In Hungary, UNFPA has been supporting a training programme on fertility-regulation methods, including clinic management, for physicians from other developing countries, again under WHO/EURO. Two courses had been held as of July 1983. About 40 doctors have been trained from countries such as China, Greece, Lesotho, Malawi and Mexico. The University Hospital at Debrecen has built special classrooms in which to conduct these courses, and clients come from the surrounding area so that partcipating physicians can acquire ample practical experience. UNFPA supports such an intercountry approach because it facilitates exchanges of experience that participants might not have in their home countries. In addition, bringing a number of people to a central training point is more economical than setting up separate training centres in each developing country.

In Poland, 5 three-week courses were conducted in English between 1977 and1981 for teachers of nurses and midwives. Held under the direction of WHO/EURO and the National Institute of Mother and Child, Warsaw, the courses covered fertility-regulation methods; family counselling, including sexual and genetic counselling and sex education; education and training of nurses and midwives in family planning; and psychosocial aspects of family planning. Similar courses took place at the International Children's Centre in Paris and at the Free University of Brussels for French-speaking participants from developing countries. To date, some 500 medical and paramedical personnel from more than 30 developing countries have been trained in such courses.

Population dynamics. The other principal field that UNFPA has supported in the developing countries of Europe is population dynamics, particularly the interaction of demographic and socio-economic variables. The largest proportion of UNFPA expenditures has been for training, and most support has been at the intercountry level. Programmes have been organized at Sussex University in England (which no longer requires UNFPA support), Moscow State University, and CEDOR in Romania (see feature page 153).

The formulation of appropriate population policies has been a concern to many of the developing countries in Europe. Bulgaria, which views its rate of population growth as too low, received UNFPA support in 1978 for a series of studies on manpower capabilities, projections and planning needs. It also obtained support to integrate its social and demographic statistics into one computerized system to permit better planning of economic and social development.

The Governments of several developing countries in Europe have been concerned with increasing urbanization and its environmental impact on population. The problem was addressed at a seminar on population, supported by UNFPA, which took place in Hungary in September 1983. Five principal topics were covered: population and its impact on urban environment; damage to the urban and rural environment; effects of urban environment on population; similarities and differences in urban and rural environmental problems in more and less developed countries and the relevance of the European experience; and the measurability of environmental effects on population. The final report in English and French will serve as a guide to Governments in environmental planning in urban areas.

The Economic Commission for Europe's co-operation with UNFPA has been substantial. UNFPA funding began in 1971 to enable ECE to collect and analyse demographic statistics for Europe as part of its research for the Economic Survey of Europe. A comparative study of fertility and family planning in 12 European countries was published in 1976 in English, French, Spanish and Russian with UNFPA support. As a follow-up to this work, the Commission, with UNFPA funding, co-operated with the World Fertility Survey in the study of comparative fertility in 18 low-fertility countries in Europe. In addition, ECE updated its 1974 study on the determinants of fertility trends in Europe.

More recently, the Commission has been working with UNFPA support on migration and aging problems, which concern many countries in the region. These studies, based on a model developed by working groups composed of participating states, will be carried out by national institutions, an approach growing out of UNFPA recommendations that regional projects focus more directly on national problems.

UNFPA has also given peripheral support to a number of conferences which have been held in Europe on population matters. For example, in 1979 the Academy of Sciences of the Union of Soviet Socialist Republics in co-operation with the Pacific Science Congress organized in Khabarovsk a seminar for scholars from the Pacific Basin countries to discuss demographic issues related to the development of this area; UNFPA financed the travel expenses of participants from the developing countries. In 1982, the Swiss Government hosted a European seminar, organized by WHO/EURO and funded by UNFPA, to consider the health aspects of European population problems.

FUTURE DIRECTIONS

The need for UNFPA co-operation with developing countries in Europe will continue, but the emphasis will change slightly. Once basic family planning services have been established and are being used, it is anticipated that UNFPA support will be requested for other population problems facing these countries: the status of women, sex education both in and out of school, aging, migration, and demographic factors in development planning.

PART TWO

THE MULTIFACETED PROGRAMME

INTRODUCTION TO PART TWO

The Fund has adopted a work plan system that comprises eight categories as shown in table 9. Although this system is a useful management tool, the actual projects seldom conform to such neat categorization; frequently, they contain elements of more than one work plan category, but for convenience are placed in the slot that best reflects their principal direction. The data in table 9 indicate that, in each year since 1969, family planning has absorbed the largest share of the Fund's resources. Assistance for family planning totalled $444 million, or about 43 per cent of the total over the period 1969–1983. The real figure is probably higher because activities listed under the headings of special programmes (which include women's activities) and communication and education often have elements directly or indirectly related to family planning.

In recent years, there has been an increase in the share of the programme for communication and education and a decline in the proportion for data collection. As countries become more cognizant of the consequences of population trends and as more of them adopt comprehensive family planning programmes, population communication and education activities have taken on increased importance. On the other hand, as a result of the extensive data collection activities undertaken during the 1970s, most countries now have some capacity in this field and the volume of requests has, on the whole, declined. The sharp increase in data collection activities in 1981 reflects the large expenditure in support of China's first complete census since 1964. This, however, was a one-time expenditure. In the coming years, it is likely that the category of population dynamics will continue to account for about 10 to 12 per cent of programme expenditures, as the Fund encourages countries to analyse existing data files, to undertake appropriate research and to disseminate research findings. In the category of special programmes, the amount devoted to women's activities has been steadily increasing as countries have come to recognize the importance of women's role in population issues. In its overall programming, the Fund ensures that, to the extent possible, all projects pay special attention to the needs of women.

The sections that follow discuss the kinds of projects supported in the principal work plan categories, assessing how and why certain approaches have worked in various settings; they also explore some

Table 9

Percentage Distribution of UNFPA Expenditures by Work Plan Categories, 1969–1983

Work plan categories	Years												Total
	1969-1972	1973	1974	1975	1976	1977	1978	1979	1980	1981	1982	1983	1969-1983
Family planning	51.7	41.0	39.8	49.3	50.0	50.4	51.1	44.5	41.3	31.8	39.8	40.5	43.0
Communication and education	7.5	11.5	10.8	10.5	9.7	10.7	10.5	10.7	11.7	12.3	10.8	14.2	11.3
Basic data collection	7.4	12.6	15.9	16.5	17.3	14.5	12.1	15.8	18.6	24.3	17.1	11.5	16.2
Population dynamics	8.4	7.8	7.4	6.8	9.0	9.1	8.8	9.6	11.3	10.7	12.4	13.0	10.2
Formulation and evaluation of population policies and programmes	4.9	4.7	6.0	5.6	3.4	3.7	4.2	4.4	5.6	6.0	6.4	6.0	5.2
Implementation of policies	0.0	0.0	0.0	0.0	0.0	0.1	0.1	2.9	0.7	1.1	0.8	1.2	0.8
Special programmes	1.4	2.8	2.5	2.0	1.3	1.3	1.7	2.0	1.5	1.9	1.2	1.4	1.7
Multisectoral activities	18.7	19.6	17.6	9.3	9.3	10.2	11.5	10.1	9.3	11.9	11.5	12.2	11.6
Total	100.0	100.0	100.0	100.0	100.0	100.0	100.0	100.0	100.0	100.0	100.0	100.0	100.0
(Thousands of US dollars)	(26,501)	(30.067)	(54,103)	(66,673)	(69,368)	(66,551)	(89,230)	(123,624)	(136,357)	(122,543)	(106,244)	(127,165)	(1,018,426)

Sources: UNFPA Fact Sheet Number 1.06 (September 1983); UNFPA Fact Sheet Number 1.07 (November 1983).
Note: Figures for 1969 to 1982 are project expenditures; figures for 1983 are project allocations as of 30 November 1983.

thoughts on future directions. In all programme areas, the Fund finances projects at both the country and intercountry (regional and global) level; training, research, action programmes and support communications are the principal types of activities funded. In recent years, there has been a considerable shift in emphasis from intercountry, particularly global, activities to country-level projects as Governments have built up their capacity to absorb such assistance.

7. Family Planning

The 1974 World Population Plan of Action acknowledged the basic right of "all couples and individuals . . . to decide freely and responsibly the number and spacing of their children and to have the information, education and means to do so" (paragraph 14[f]). The provision of family planning information, services and contraceptives facilitates the achievement of those goals. Over the past 15 years, UNFPA has worked with Governments, helping them to design family planning programmes that are financially feasible and appropriate to the particular culture. In extending assistance for family planning, UNFPA supports all methods of fertility regulation, including natural family planning, that are considered technically safe and effective by WHO and that are in accordance with the policies of requesting countries. UNFPA recognizes that countries implement family planning programmes for a variety of reasons, ranging from child spacing to limiting population growth, from curtailing illegal abortions to dealing with problems of infertility.

FUNDING LEVELS

From 1969 to 1983, the Fund's assistance to family planning totalled $444 million, of which $364 million was expended at the country level and $80.0 million at the interregional and global level. In all years, the Asia and Pacific region has led the way in expenditures, accounting for a total of $228 million or 51 per cent of UNFPA assistance to family planning over the period.

Differences in the levels of expenditures between one region and another usually reflect the timing and level of commitment with which countries have accepted family planning. Asia lays claim to the earliest developed and largest family planning programmes in the world, whereas in most African countries, interest in family planning activities began to crystallize only in the mid-1970s. Variations within and between regions may also be the result of budgetary adjustments in UNFPA programming rephasals, as well as intensified support to periodic activities, such as a national census.

As a result of the growing propensity and capability of Governments to initiate and pursue family planning activities at the country level,

UNFPA assistance to the country level has grown in relation to its assistance for activities at the interregional and global level, which declined from 42 per cent of expenditures in 1969–1972 to 8 per cent in 1983.

Among the functional categories, service delivery programmes have claimed 69 per cent of the Fund's total outlay for family planning; training has accounted for 15 per cent; support communication, 9 per cent; and research, 7 per cent. In all categories except research, spending at the country level has run considerably ahead of intercountry expenditures; by contrast, 73 per cent of the Fund's support to research has been at the intercountry level, whereas 27 per cent has been for country research endeavours. Several factors account for this pattern. Economic and practical considerations made it advisable to undertake early efforts in social research related to family planning acceptance on an intercountry basis; for the same reasons, biomedical research continues to be pursued at the global level. As countries increase their research capabilities and as more resources are channelled towards testing the safety of contraceptives and towards programme-related research, the gap between intercountry and country research expenditures is likely to narrow.

Governments, WHO, UNICEF and NGOs have executed most UNFPA assistance for family planning. Expenditures for projects directly executed by Governments amounted to approximately $136 million or 31 per cent of the total. By 1983, expenditures on WHO-executed projects had amounted to $156 million, or 35 per cent of the total family planning expenditures. Expenditures on projects delivered by UNICEF totalled $55 million or 12 per cent of the total, whereas expenditures on projects executed by NGOs totalled $61 million or 14 per cent. The balance of assistance was executed by universities.

Most family planning and health projects executed by WHO were integrated, with the family planning services fitted into a pattern of care that included other aspects of maternal and child health care, such as nutrition, immunization and health education. WHO personnel and consultants provided the technical and managerial support required for the planning, programming, implementation and evaluation of programmes at the country level. Family planning projects executed by UNICEF included those designated as joint programmes and those in which UNICEF executed only the equipment component of the project, undertaking reimbursable procurement of contraceptives, medical equipment and vehicles.

TYPES OF ACTIVITIES

Delivery of family planning services

Assistance for the delivery of family planning services—action programmes and communication support—made up 78 per cent of all UNFPA expenditures in family planning from 1969 to 1983. Delivery of services accounted for 83 per cent of all country-level expenditures for family planning and 44 per cent of intercountry monies in this area. Over the past 20 years, the validity of family planning as a health and demographic policy, as well as a basic human right, has been widely acknowledged. UNFPA has worked with countries representing all levels of commitment to family planning, from those espousing family planning primarily for demographic purposes—such as China, Egypt, India, Indonesia, Mexico, the Republic of Korea and Tunisia—to those that have adopted family planning for health benefits—such as Algeria, Ethiopia and United Republic of Tanzania. Over the same period, delivery systems have evolved from clinic-based models to programmes incorporating outreach, wide use of paramedical personnel and community-oriented strategies, such as using community networks for motivating acceptors, distributing contraceptives and involving the private sector. The earliest national programmes were often "vertical" or free-standing efforts, largely because in many countries the health infrastructure was not strong enough to sustain an additional service. Also, it was felt that the creation of a family planning programme as a distinct entity called attention to the importance of the endeavour. Gradually, however, increased emphasis has been put on establishing community-oriented family planning delivery systems within the context of primary health care and ongoing local development efforts. Most of the action programmes UNFPA supports are of such an integrated nature. The integrated approach not only facilitates the provision of closely related services—for example, pre- and post-natal care, nutrition and immunizations—but also helps to blunt some of the sensitivity still attached to family planning.

Reaching underserved groups. Once Governments have fielded family planning programmes, they all face the formidable problems of getting quality services to the target population and managing the programme efficiently and effectively. UNFPA has funded a number of projects designed to make family planning services more available to groups that are usually underserved—for example, dispersed rural populations, marginal urban groups, migrants and adolescents. For some services, such as sterilization, men may also be considered underserved.

In Colombia, Ecuador and Mexico, UNFPA support made it possible to extend service to rural areas, thus increasing the level of contraceptive prevalence. In Bangladesh, Malaysia and Sri Lanka, UNFPA assistance has been used to bring family planning services to those on the plantation estates. In the Middle East and North Africa, UNFPA has assisted several countries in extending the benefits of maternal and child health and family planning services to populations in outlying areas. The density of service points has been increased, outreach workers are being used and traditional health workers are being trained in modern methods. With UNFPA support, Haceteppe University and The Population Council set up a pilot project in Yozgat, Turkey, which provided MCH/FP to areas not previously served. In rural areas of the Tunisian province of El Kef, UNFPA and the Royal Dutch Institute of Tropical Medicine set up a clinic staffed by two physicians and by four nurse-midwives. In addition to improving services, this project trained village women as outreach workers. Both the Yozgat and El Kef projects demonstrated that greater availability of services improves health levels and acceptance of family planning. Such projects, however, require intensive infusions of both trained staff and financial resources, which make them difficult to replicate on a nation-wide basis.

UNFPA has encouraged countries to focus attention on population groups who are hard to reach. It has supported, for example, the Government of Thailand's efforts to develop a low-cost programme of primary health, maternal and child health and family planning services for the minority groups of the hill tribe villages in the northern part of the country. Not only has this project brought services to those whose needs were previously unmet, but it has also engendered enthusiastic community participation: young men and women recruited from the villages serve as auxiliary health workers (AHWs), and villagers have contributed building materials for the construction of health facilities and have assisted AHWs on their periodic visits (see feature page 103).

A long-standing, difficult task of family planning service providers is to improve the acceptability and demand for these services. The basic family planning task in improving acceptability is sensitively to modify technology and programmes to fit people, rather than attempting to modify people to fit technology and programmes. The Fund and other agencies have sponsored research attempting to create a better understanding of what has been called the "user perspective". The demand for services, the family size that couples desire, the socio-cultural values regarding fertility limitation and overall levels of development and modernization are closely related to the actual practice of contraception. Of the twin variables that govern family planning success—supply and demand for services—demand remains the most problematic in its resistance to intervention. The principal intervention strategies now employed are information, education and communication programmes, which are described elsewhere in this volume. Other efforts to understand and influence demand include the underwriting of research and data gathering on social and demographic issues related to fertility behaviour, and to the integration of family planning information and services across the widest possible development spectrum.

THAILAND: A SUCCESSFUL FAMILY PLANNING EFFORT

Thailand's population grew rapidly during this century, from approximately 8 million at the time of the first census in 1911 to more than 47 million in 1980. The effects of high fertility were accentuated by the falling mortality rate. Despite rapid population growth, Thailand maintained an essentially pro-natalist population policy through the 1960s. However, beginning in 1963, the interest of several key health officials led to a series of national population seminars conducted by the National Research Council. By the mid-1960s, regular activity in family planning had been initiated at clinics in four Government hospitals in Bangkok. In 1968, the Ministry of Public Health established a family planning section and initiated a three-year family health project, utilizing existing health personnel and facilities. This undertaking has since become a major feature of Thailand's health services.

Thailand is currently in the midst of a major decline in fertility. Between 1969 and 1979, marital fertility appears to have declined by close to 40 per cent. Contraceptive knowledge has increased rapidly and is now almost universal among women. The practice of contraception has increased dramatically as well. As of 1981, more than 58 per cent of women in the reproductive ages were practising some method, compared with less than 15 per cent 10 years ago.

Although an increase in age at marriage may have reduced the birth rate in the years before 1960, since then changes in patterns of nuptiality have not been important in reducing the birth rate. The mean age at marriage for women is now about 22 years. Changes in the age structure also have not contributed significantly to declining birth rates. The recent decline in fertility is thus largely a product of changing reproductive behaviour within marriage. The reduction of fertility has occurred despite a trend towards shorter duration of breast-feeding in both rural and urban areas.

The decline in fertility and increase in contraceptive use are pronounced in the rural sector. The urban-rural gap in fertility decline has almost disappeared. Women of all educational backgrounds, including the least educated women, have participated in the changes taking place.

The growth rates in the early 1960s ranged from 3.2 to 3.4 per cent, falling to between 2.6 and 2.9 per cent by 1970, and continuing to fall to between 2.3 and 2.6 per cent by 1975. The most recent Government estimate of growth rate is 1.95 per cent in 1981; thus, the goal of reaching a 2.1 per cent growth rate by the end of 1981 was achieved. By the end of 1986, the Government expects to reduce the growth rate to 1.5 per cent.

The explanation for Thailand's "reproductive revolution", most observers conclude, lies in a combination of socio-cultural factors and the relative accessibility of contraceptive information and services.

The Thai people have been receptive to the idea and practice of fertility regulation, including sterilization. One important supporting factor is the nature of Thai Buddhism, which encourages personal responsibility for behaviour and individual autonomy; these principles carry over into social and family relationships, shielding couples from pro-natalist family influences and providing higher status for women. Thai women tend to act independently of their husbands with regard to contraception. The high literacy rate for both sexes further contributes to informed decision-making and the advanced status of women.

The Thai people have relatively good access to contraceptives. The credit for providing services to most Thais can be attributed to the activities of the National Family Planning Programme of the Ministry of Public Health. It is estimated that, overall, at least 80 per cent of all contraceptive users receive their supply of contraceptives from programme sources.

The number of family planning acceptors attributed to the programme grew steadily from an average of about 60,000 new acceptors annually during 1965–1968 to 1,000,000 by 1980. The success of the programme in reaching a large number of acceptors is the result of a variety of factors. Of particular importance is the involvement of health personnel at all levels in family planning activities and especially the delegation of family planning tasks to non-physicians. The 1971 decision to allow auxiliary midwives and nurses to provide contraceptive pills, and the 1976 decision to provide pills free of charge, increased dramatically the acceptance of the pill, which is the main contraceptive used in Thailand. Women obtain the pill mostly from Government sources (73 per cent), although pharmacies provide pills to another 21 per cent of users. Another factor in the success of the National Family Planning Programme is the wide variety of methods available, including injectables.

UNFPA has been assisting population activities in Thailand since 1971. During this period, more than $20 million has been provided through three country programmes. More than 90 per cent of this amount has gone to support the National Family Planning Programme in its service delivery activities; training; and information, education and communication activities.

The current UNFPA programme includes projects for improving the delivery of family planning services and management; formulation of a manpower development plan and training of personnel for MCH/FP services, improving and designing population information, education and communication strategies; in-school and non-formal population education; operations research; policy and programme formulation and evaluation; and special programmes for particular target groups of the population. Attention is being given to innovative strategies in communication and motivation, and to community participation and the provision of comprehensive MCH/FP for minority groups in the northern and southern regions of the country. UNFPA assistance also provides international and local consultants and experts as necessary; training, including fellowships and study tours within the country and abroad; expendable and non-expendable equipment and supplies; and some local personnel payments.

Although Thailand's National Family Planning Programme still has important and difficult tasks ahead, it is now a mature undertaking. As the programme has evolved, UNFPA assistance has also changed in order to remain of maximum use and relevance. The Thai-UNFPA cooperation now emphasizes assistance only for specific inputs that well-advanced programmes need. This collaboration is also aimed at making the Thailand programme self-reliant in human resources, supplies and financing as soon as possible.

Sources: Information and data on the family planning programme in Thailand are from Allan Rosenfield, et al., "Thailand's Family Planning Programme: An Asian Success Story", in *International Family Planning Perspectives*, VIII, 2 (June 1982). The Government's target for the 1986 growth rate is from "Evaluation Report of UNFPA Assistance to the National Family Planning Programme in Thailand" (New York, UNFPA, April 1982).

Contrary to popular perception, it is often difficult to maintain high levels of family planning acceptance among urban populations, particularly among low-income groups, recent migrants and teenagers. The primary reasons for this are that problems of low demand and poor access to services are often as bad in urban as in rural settings, especially among new urban migrants and slum dwellers. Realizing this, several countries have sought UNFPA assistance for designing service delivery systems tailored to the needs of urban populations. Following a UNFPA-supported evaluation of its national family planning programme in low-income areas, the Republic of Korea requested UNFPA financing to strengthen its urban family planning delivery system. Subsequently, the Ministry of Health and Social Affairs opened additional family planning clinics in Seoul and Pusan in order to make services more readily available and to train community volunteer leaders in communicating family planning messages. Under the auspices of a UNFPA project, the Government of Indonesia intensified its service network in five cities, building up both government and private channels of contraceptive distribution. One innovation was the use of advertising to stimulate demand for family planning and to attract private physicians and midwives to the national programme. Indonesia also introduced a system for monitoring contraceptive prevalence in urban areas.

The dispersed populations of the island countries of the Pacific may also be considered in the "hard-to-reach" category. UNFPA has assisted these countries in providing information and services for all methods of family planning, including natural family planning efforts in Kiribati and Tonga since 1978, and by providing assistance to various aspects of family planning programmes in Cook Islands, Fiji, Papua New Guinea, Solomon Islands and Vanuatu.

Promoting integrated services. There is an increasing conviction that family planning is most effective when delivered in relation to other social and development activities. A major context for delivering family planning services is now seen to be the primary health care network pioneered by WHO and UNICEF. This strategy emphasizes the delivery of basic health care, particularly the key preventive services such as maternal and child health and family planning. The role of the community is considered basic to the success of this approach. In line with this strategy, UNFPA has supported activities to improve integrated services and to link family planning with broader development initiatives. In Bohol Province in the Philippines, UNFPA, using The Population Council and WHO as executing agencies, supported an experimental project to determine the impact of an intensive MCH/FP project on the levels of infant mortality and morbidity and on contraceptive practices in this predominantly rural area. In Indonesia, UNFPA, in co-operation with UNICEF, assisted in implementing a programme for the delivery of family planning, nutrition and primary health services to the outer islands.

One of the most innovative integration schemes supported by UNFPA has been Egypt's Population and Development Project (see the description in chapter 5). Initiated as an experimental project in 1977, this undertaking sought to increase the acceptance of family planning by linking population activities to development efforts at the community level. By 1982, more than 525 village councils in 12 governorates were implementing this approach, and the project was serving about 15 million persons.

To bring about a more balanced distribution between population, resources and economic opportunities, several countries have embarked upon population resettlement programmes, for example, transmigration in Indonesia and the FELDA programme in Malaysia. UNFPA encourages Governments to ensure that family planning services are available in newly settled areas. In this connection, UNFPA has worked with the Government of Sri Lanka to provide family planning services as a part of all relevant national development schemes.

UNFPA has channelled extensive support to integrated family welfare projects in selected districts of Rajasthan and Bihar as part of the Indian Government's intensification of efforts in 46 districts throughout the country. The fundamental objective is to improve living standards by accelerating socio-economic development and by broadening the use of family planning as a means of reducing birth rates and improving health. The intermediate goal is to build up the health infrastructure, and thus construction components are prominent. In Rajasthan, 70 sub-centres have been built and numerous other facilities have been refurbished. Construction of local and district-level health facilities has taken place in Bihar. Information and education campaigns have also been mounted in connection with these programmes. Because of the magnitude and innovative nature of these interventions, special attention is being paid to monitoring and to evaluating impact. Baseline surveys as well as ongoing data collection over the life of the project will enable programme managers to assess progress.

UNFPA has also worked with the Japanese Organization for International Cooperation in Family Planning (JOICFP) in its programmes combining family planning with basic health services, nutrition and parasite control. Programmes along these lines have been implemented in several countries including Colombia, Malaysia, Mexico and Nepal.

Ensuring contraceptive supplies. An adequate supply of appropriate contraceptives is essential to the success of any family planning delivery system. UNFPA has assisted countries both through the outright provision of contraceptives and by financing efforts designed to make countries more self-reliant in contraceptive production and supply. UNFPA has supplied contraceptives to many countries including Bangladesh, Cuba, Indonesia and Zambia. Support for the local production or processing of contraceptives and for upgrading the logistics of contraceptive supply is a notable feature of the UNFPA programme in Asia and the Pacific. With UNFPA assistance, India is producing oral pills and IUDs; in Indonesia, UNFPA has financed the purchase of raw materials for the production of 14.2 million oral-contraceptive cycles by a government pharmaceutical company. A feasibility study, financed by multibilateral funds from Norway, was conducted in Bangladesh to assess the capacity to undertake local production of contraceptives. The results of a similar study have prompted the Government of Viet Nam to request UNFPA assistance for the local manufacture of condoms. UNFPA has also encouraged countries to conduct "demand surveys", like ones done in Sri Lanka and Thailand, in order to identify contraceptive needs and work out plans for meeting them.

Support for contraceptive production constitutes 15 per cent of UNFPA assistance to China's family planning programme. UNFPA has financed the technology and equipment, particularly new packaging machinery, necessary to improve the quality of condoms and to increase their acceptability and shelf life. UNFPA has also supported the design and installation of a new factory in Shanghai for the production of injectables and the establishment of a facility in Beijing for the manufacture of oral contraceptives. UNFPA assistance for new equipment and for upgrading plant sites has made it possible for the Chinese to manufacture the newer plastic and copper IUDs. All these projects are implemented by the Program for the Introduction and Adaptation of Contraceptive Technology (PIACT), an NGO. In addition to increasing China's production of contraceptives, the projects have had the desirable side-effect of updating China's infrastructure and training workers in modern production and management techniques.

Training

When countries decide either to initiate or to expand family planning programmes, one of the first difficulties they encounter is the shortage of trained personnel. By assisting countries in building up their institutional strength in the training field and by financing in-country courses, fellowships and study tours abroad, and in-service training for health professionals, traditional midwives and paramedicals, UNFPA has helped countries build up a corps of trained workers. Training accounts for 15 per cent of the Fund's expenditures in the family planning field. UNFPA has also supported internationally recruited family planning experts to work with national authorities in managing, supervising and evaluating programmes. The tenure of their assignments—long-term (two to four years) and short-term (less than one year)—depends on the expertise available in the country. In some cases, the international specialist fills a regular post left vacant by a national who has gone abroad for training. International specialists have often worked together with a national counterpart, giving on-the-job training and advice in health management, in public health, health statistics and family planning techniques. UNFPA also finances WHO regional advisory teams, which have helped to compensate for the shortage of trained family planning personnel. These teams back up country-level activities and serve as important links in family planning sector activities in each region. The efforts of these regional teams are supplemented by the UNFPA-supported interregional teams in Geneva.

The scarcity of trained personnel continues to be Africa's most pressing problem in the family planning sector. UNFPA has responded by setting up regional and national training programmes and has, on occasion, provided funds for payment of local costs for training courses, for example, stipends for trainees, honoraria for teachers and various operational costs. Refresher courses or specialized courses in MCH/FP for health personnel are usually conducted by national training staff, sometimes with technical assistance in training techniques and curricula from international specialists.

To strengthen the national capacity of African countries, UNFPA supported the establishment of a Regional Training Centre in Family Health in Mauritius. The Centre trains managers and country training personnel in aspects of maternal and child health and family planning. In November–December 1982, the first group of 18 family health personnel from French-speaking African countries attended a six-week course at the regional training centre. The second such course, in May–June 1983, was attended by 21 participants, also from French-speaking Africa, and later in the year a third training course was conducted for English-speaking health personnel. The Centre is supported jointly by the Government of Mauritius and UNFPA. In conjunction with WHO/AFRO, UNFPA has supported an MCH/FP project to provide training for family health personnel along with advisory services. A team consisting of four members is located in Benin and covers all countries in the region. Its main objectives are to assist in the organization of initial and in-service training of personnel in family health, and to assist Governments in the planning, execution and evaluation of family health programmes. To permit the Benin team to concentrate on French-speaking Africa, it was decided, as part of the UNFPA 1984–1987 programme, to base a second team in Zimbabwe to serve the English-speaking countries.

The training of traditional health workers to promote the acceptance of family planning and to deliver services has been one of the most successful ways of extending coverage to rural areas. In Pakistan, UNFPA has financed education programmes for *hakeems* (traditional healers), equipping them to provide counselling and motivation for family planning and to distribute contraceptives. The Fund has assisted the Indian Ministry of Health and Family Welfare in training *dais* (traditional birth attendants) in modern midwifery techniques and in techniques for motivating couples to accept family planning. Similarly in Nepal, trained *dhammi jhankris* (faith healers) now serve as promoters of health and family planning services.

The Government of the Syrian Arab Republic, realizing that lack of health services in rural areas was a strong contributor to the high level of infant mortality, requested UNFPA assistance for training TBAs in aseptic delivery techniques, in nutrition education for mothers and in delivering certain family planning methods. One of the first steps taken was to explain to the medical community the need to enlist TBAs in such a project, given that these women already deliver the majority of Syrian babies. Even in urban areas, approximately 40 per cent of births are attended by TBAs. (According to one estimate there are 250 TBAs for every 1,000 people, an indication of their potential impact.) Moreover, the nation has difficulty attracting trained medical and other health personnel to rural areas, a gap that trained TBAs could easily fill for the short term. UNFPA, with WHO assistance, has been able to interest trained nurse-midwives in assisting the Ministry of Health in this project. Project activities have been under way since 1981.

The training of health and community workers has been one of the mainstays of UNFPA-assisted programmes in Latin America and the Caribbean. In Haiti, trained rural motivators and community workers have increased the coverage of the MCH/FP programme. Likewise in Colombia, Ecuador and Honduras, UNFPA has supported the training of paramedicals and community health workers in order to extend MCH/FP services to rural and marginal urban populations.

UNFPA has also supported training efforts directed at physicians and nurses. Programmes in human reproduction and family planning were offered in Sri Lanka at the Colombo Medical School, the Galle Medical

School and the Pervadeniya Medical School. Such activities have sought to increase the awareness of family planning among medical students and to develop the necessary skills for extending such services. In Pakistan, UNFPA, in co-operation with The Johns Hopkins Program for International Education in Gynecology and Obstetrics, has financed a programme for physicians to improve their contraceptive surgery techniques. Six leading medical institutions have participated in this undertaking, which has incorporated training in the use of laparoscopic and mini-lap techniques. Upgrading the family planning skills among village doctors was the objective of a recent project in Bangladesh. In a number of low-income European countries—Bulgaria, Greece and Portugal—UNFPA has sponsored training endeavours aimed at health professionals. Physicians at the Institute of Obstetrics and Gynaecology of the Medical Academy of Sofia have received special training in human reproduction and family planning to enable them to deal more effectively with problems of infertility. The University of Lisbon Medical School now offers family planning as part of its curriculum, and since 1976 more than 1,300 physicians and nurses in Portugal have been trained to offer family planning counselling and services. Before such courses began, only 78 public health clinics throughout Portugal provided family planning services; now more than 300 do so.

Research

In family planning research, UNFPA has supported the study of socioeconomic and cultural factors that influence fertility and the practice of family planning, as well as programme-related operational questions and biomedical work in connection with methods of fertility regulation. Over the period 1969–1983, research accounted for approximately $32.0 million or 7 per cent of the Fund's spending in family planning; of this amount, $9.0 million was spent at the country level and $23.0 million at the intercountry level. Although this distribution appears to be rather lopsided, it is often more economical to conduct research, particularly contraceptive research, at the regional or global level; moreover, this research was largely concerned with devising methodologies or strategies for use at the country level.

Most of the family planning research supported by UNFPA has been undertaken in conjunction with WHO. Since the mid-1960s, WHO has had a broad mandate and an active programme of research in family planning and related institution strengthening for such research in developing countries. Interested in accelerating work in these areas, WHO in 1972 established the Special Programme of Research, Development and Research Training in Human Reproduction (HRP). One major goal of HRP is, through programme research, to devise improved approaches to the delivery of family planning care in the primary health care context, including psychosocial aspects. Major current lines of research include the use, training and supervision of community workers and health personnel; community participation; integration of family planning with other services; service and psychosocial factors affecting family planning practice; field trials of family planning methods new to a programme; and needs for services in countries considering setting up family planning services, including services for infertility.

The prevention and treatment of infertility are integral parts of family planning care. In some developing countries, up to one third of either family planning or other gynaecological consultations relate to complaints of infertility. Epidemiological research in this field attempts to determine more precisely the magnitude of the problem of infertility and the distribution of causes in different communities in developing countries. Research is addressed to these questions and is also directed at devising simpler methods of diagnosis and better methods of cure, suited to primary health care.

Research on infertility is funded at a lower level than research on methods of birth control and is conducted by fewer agencies. About $4 million out of the $6 million spent in 1982 by the public sector was devoted to research into unexplained causes of infertility, and most of that was conducted by the Center for Population Research in the United States. WHO expenditures on infertility research amounted to about $900,000 in 1982. Industries are interested in developing diagnostic procedures for infertility and in conducting research on new drugs for treatment of this problem.

Greatest demand for increased research on infertility has come from Sub-Saharan African countries. Higher priority in this region was given to infertility research than to research on other aspects of fertility-regulation at a WHO consultative meeting on research in human reproduction at Yaounde, United Republic of Cameroon, in December 1978. A number of countries in the Middle East, such as Kuwait and Saudi Arabia, and in Latin America, such as Argentina, also ascribe high importance to it.

The research activities mentioned above are extended by other programmes in WHO, namely by the WHO Division of Family Health in certain specific areas of social, programme and biomedical research. The risk approach for MCH/FP care has been developed as a managerial tool in programme research to develop locally suited strategies for increased coverage and efficiency of family planning services. Studies are also under way on adolescent fertility, reproductive health and contraception, and on the relationship among breast-feeding, lactation and fertility and the implications of these for programmes promoting breast-feeding and other fertility-regulating practices. Other projects are concerned with community participation in family health care and with health education aspects of family planning.

Efforts to develop new contraceptive techniques and to adapt known methods have claimed over one third of all UNFPA support for research. To date, the WHO Special Programme (HRP) has received $12.1 million to study and develop the safety of birth control methods among different populations. The Fund also supports the work of PIACT to improve the availability, acceptance and expanded use of fertility-regulating products in developing countries by modifying and adapting contraceptive products to fit the preferences and cultural values of the environment in which they are to be used. Through the project, PIACT has helped a number of countries in Asia and Latin America and has also carried out research at the global level. By 1983, UNFPA assistance to PIACT had totalled about $2.4 million. UNFPA is also prepared to assist other organizations in an effort to improve and accelerate the contraceptive development process.

FUTURE DIRECTIONS

At present, there is a consensus that most family planning programmes are in critical need of better management systems. This view is borne out by the findings of UNFPA evaluations of family planning projects in Botswana, Colombia, Egypt, Swaziland and Thailand. Overly optimistic project objectives in view of institutional capacity or resources have sometimes jeopardized project performance. Supervision of personnel is another weak link in the management chain; evaluations have underscored the need to train personnel to fill supervisory functions. In addition, data collection and analysis for programme monitoring and evaluation need to be strengthened.

In light of such findings, UNFPA has been working with countries to strengthen their programme management capabilities and is providing technical assistance, through projects or special consultancies, in a wide range of management aspects—logistics, in Bangladesh, for example; management information systems; management training in Bangladesh and China; and systems analysis in India, Nepal, Pakistan and Sri Lanka. UNFPA also encourages countries to undertake programme research related to operations as a means of identifying and responding to problems in programme design and implementation.

Management issues have been a concern to the Fund not only within country-level family planning programmes but also within some of the regional teams it uses to execute projects. The independent evaluations sponsored by UNFPA of the Pan American Health Organization (PAHO), WHO/AFRO and the Regional Office for Southeast Asia (SEARO) found that the teams had been less successful than anticipated in helping Governments institutionalize family planning services within their health care systems. Lack of co-ordination between UNFPA and the teams and the lack of full understanding of UNFPA policies and procedures often delayed project implementation. These findings prompted UNFPA and the teams to undertake joint reviews of new work plans. Closer collaboration and a more precise and realistic definition of functions are expected to enable the teams to serve the countries of the region more thoroughly and systematically. UNFPA and WHO have held joint workshops for their staffs to learn more about policies for implementing family planning projects.

UNFPA evaluations have further documented that increasing the availability of quality services is correlated with higher levels of family planning acceptance. In Thailand, by using village health workers to deliver contraceptives and setting up mobile and special weekend sterilization clinics, the Government increased the number of service delivery points from about 5,400 in 1976 to about 29,000 in 1981. The evaluation of Costa Rica's family planning programme attributed the high level of contraceptive prevalence to the establishment of many new health facilities offering family planning services. Between 1973 and 1977, the number of health facilities more than trebled, from 117 to 431, and 263 centres were set up in rural areas. It was estimated that by 1977, 76 per cent of women in Costa Rica actually at risk of pregnancy were practising contraception. The evaluation also noted the effectiveness of the programme's information campaign; about 65 per cent of the women indicated they had received information on sex education and family planning availability over the radio. In view of these findings, UNFPA has been working with Governments to devise ways of increasing the availability of, and access to, quality family planning services. Delivery systems that minimize the costs — physical, psychological and social as well as monetary — of using family planning usually result in increased practice of family planning. Greater emphasis on community participation and wider use of private sector approaches, such as social marketing schemes, appear to be promising alternatives.

Extending services to the hard to reach will continue to be a goal of national family planning programmes. UNFPA has called attention to the needs of particular target groups — rural populations, urban marginal groups and adolescents—and has urged countries to respond to their particular needs. Most evaluation missions, however, have reported that rural populations are still underserved and that the needs of adolescents have barely been addressed. The assessment of the Thai programme noted the difficulties of providing delivery services in an urban setting. UNFPA had assisted a project for increasing the density of service points in the Bangkok Metropolis; when it became clear that the endeavour had little effect on service coverage, the project was suspended. After revamping some of the administrative arrangements for implementation, the Government of Thailand reinstituted the project with UNFPA assistance. UNFPA approved a project in Colombia executed by Profamilia, whose purpose is to intensify family planning information and services in rural areas and urban marginal areas. To respond to the needs of adolescents, UNFPA is supporting with WHO an interregional research project to design strategies and service delivery systems specially geared to the needs of young adults.

As programmes "mature", there is a tendency for the level of family planning acceptance to reach a plateau. Innovative efforts will have to be pursued in order to influence those potential users who remain unresponsive to the usual information and motivation campaigns.

Perhaps the most basic lesson of the Fund's 15 years of experience in family planning is that a successful family planning programme must be consonant with the socio-cultural setting in which it operates. Programmes must be designed with users' needs and cultural background in mind, and services must be delivered in a way that places a minimal burden on the acceptor. At present, several countries in Sub-Saharan Africa and many countries in the Middle East and Mediterranean region continue to need technical assistance in defining and implementing population policies and programmes compatible with their cultural and political settings and the needs of potential users.

In the coming decades, primary emphasis will be on action programmes. Such programmes must be buttressed by adequate research. Work continues to be needed at the country level on how particular development policies—for example, for meeting basic needs, or for improving the position of women, or for promoting better health—influence trends in fertility and the use of family planning. With the expansion of family planning services, programme research takes on increased importance. Research related to various aspects of integration and community participation is needed. Although both of these concepts have been talked about since the days of the 1974 World Population Conference at Bucharest, questions remain as to how they can best be put into operation and how their impact can be assessed. Certainly,

continued work is needed to develop new, safe and acceptable contraceptive methods, as well as adaptation of existing techniques. Better
documentation is needed on experience with the introduction and management of contraceptive technology, in order to mitigate side-effects
and to provide socially and medically appropriate combinations of
methods for different target groups. UNFPA will continue to assist
countries in all aspects of family planning research. It will also continue
to fund interregional research efforts to provide safe, more efficient and
more acceptable techniques of fertility regulation.

Although considerable success has been realized in the family planning sector, much remains to be done. According to reports of the
World Fertility Survey, half of the currently married fecund women in
15 countries stated they wanted no more children. In seven of eight
countries where data are available, more than 25 per cent of currently
married women with at least one child or currently pregnant stated that
their last pregnancy was unwanted. It has been estimated that, between
now and the year 2000, approximately 500 million couples will need
family planning services. Moreover, even though contraceptive prevalence may be increasing in some countries, the persisting desire of many
couples for large families could continue to blunt the demographic effects of contraceptive use. Continued donor assistance coupled with intensified efforts by developing countries to mobilize local technical and
financial resources will be needed to meet this challenge.

8. INFORMATION, POPULATION EDUCATION AND COMMUNICATION

SCOPE OF THE SECTOR

UNFPA uses a three-pronged approach to the creation of awareness of population issues. The first is public information, which is designed to keep the general public and its leaders, in particular, informed of population trends and important developments in the population field. A second category in this broad approach is population education, through which population issues and their individual and societal implications are studied and discussed over a period of time. Learners may range in age from very young children to elderly adults, and content will vary accordingly, the aims being to increase understanding and the ability to make informed decisions. The third category is termed population communication. This refers to the mobilization of support for population-related activities such as the creation of demand for family planning services. Communication strategies for creating such demand involve not only the channelling of messages to appropriate target groups but also provision for eliciting and using feedback from these targets so as to best meet community and individual needs.

Public information

In fulfilling its mandate to promote awareness of population issues, UNFPA has developed or supported a wide range of public information activities. The regular publications of UNFPA are essential reading for administrators and academics concerned with population. Through its annual *State of World Population* report, which has become a standard feature of the news calendar, its magazine *Populi* and through contributions to newspapers and magazines, radio, television and film, UNFPA has reached out to a wider audience. In addition, the Fund's annual *Inventory of Population Projects in Developing Countries Around the World* and *Guide to Sources of International Population Assistance*, published triennially, are valuable sources of data for countries and for donors in the population field.

As the largest international source of assistance for popul-- ''le UNFPA has a responsibility to provide information ab operations. Its *Annual Report* provides a comp-

Fund's activities. The newsletter *Population* provides a regular flow of up-to-date news about UNFPA. This is supplemented by information packages in print or on film giving brief introductions to UNFPA work.

UNFPA also supports the publication and distribution of significant technical reports and papers on population isssues developed by other organizations such as The Population Council.

Among the Fund's most far-reaching endeavours in promoting a global awareness of population were the activities undertaken in support of World Population Year, 1974. Having been designated as the secretariat for World Population Year, the Fund mounted a programme comprising activities at local, national and international levels. At the local level, it supported information and education campaigns to acquaint individuals with population problems and various policies for dealing with them. At the national level, the Fund encouraged Governments to build up the necessary infrastructure for implementing population programmes. One of the Fund's priorities for World Population Year was to involve youth, women and religious groups in population activities. Internationally, the Fund sought to promote effective international exchange of ideas. To inaugurate World Population Year, an information dossier on population was issued to media outlets throughout the world, and during 1973 and 1974 monthly bulletins were issued by the World Population Year Secretariat in English, French and Spanish, with special editions in other languages, to gain the widest possible coverage.

The culmination of the year was the World Population Conference held in Bucharest, Romania. UNFPA was one of the principal supporters of the Conference and its preparatory activities. The World Population Plan of Action, which emerged from the Bucharest meeting and which has served as the basic policy instrument in the population field over the past 10 years, underscored the importance of continued promotional activity as a means of broadening the base of support for population concerns. It stated:

"International organizations, both governmental and non-governmental, should strengthen their efforts to distribute information on population and related matters, particularly through periodic publications on the world population situation, prospects and policies, the utilization of audio-visual and other aids to communication, the publication of non-technical digests and reports, and the production and wide distribution of newsletters on population activities. Consideration should also be given to strengthening the publication of international professional journals and ʼvs in the field of population" (paragraph 91).

As part of the efforts to broaden opinion leaders' interest in population, the Fund has worked extensively with parliamentarians, believing that the increased participation of parliamentarians in population and development matters would reinforce and strengthen the work being done by other parts of governmental and non-governmental machinery. With the Inter-Parliamentary Union, the Fund co-sponsored the International Conference of Parliamentarians on Population and Development, held in Colombo, Sri Lanka, in 1979. The 58 legislators attending this first United Nations-sponsored global conference of parliamentarians acknowledged the increasing need for international assistance for population. The 22 NGOs that also participated pledged their support especially for work at the grass-roots level, complementing efforts by parliamentarians at the national level. As a follow-up to the Colombo Conference, UNFPA supported several regional meetings of parliamentarians—the African Parliamentarians Conference on Population and Development in Nairobi, the Asian Conference in Beijing, the Latin American and Caribbean Conference in Brazilia and the European Conference in Strasbourg, France.

Concerned by the rapid rates of urban growth in the developing countries, the Fund sponsored an International Conference on Population and the Urban Future (Rome, 1980). Urban planners and mayors from 41 cities whose populations are projected to reach 5 million or more by the year 2000 participated in this meeting. The dialogue between urban specialists, municipal leaders and population experts fostered an exchange of information and led to the articulation of strategies for dealing with dislocations attendant on urbanization.

In 1981, the Fund, along with the International Planned Parenthood Federation (IPPF) and The Population Council, co-sponsored the first international meeting on the global family planning situation since 1965. The meeting, in Jakarta, was attended by 133 leaders in the family planning field from 63 countries, including representatives from Governments, NGOs and major international agencies. They reviewed developments in the area of family planning over the past decade and assessed the situation in the 1980s and beyond. The Conference, identifying opportunities and challenges facing those engaged in this field, called attention to the need to reinforce the role of family planning as an essential element in development policies.

Some groups which operate through or as part of the mass media have a considerable interest in population. UNFPA has stimulated them to increase the flow of population-related news and to train staff and associates in techniques of effective news-gathering and dissemination for population work.

Population education

Population education, which may take place either in school programmes or through non-formal channels, concerns awareness and understanding of the nature, causes and implications of population
processes and how they influence, and are influenced by, groups and
individuals. More than simply the provision of information, population
education encourages the investigation and the critical analysis of alternatives regarding population issues in order to promote active and informed decision-making.

Approaches to population education vary throughout the world.
Some countries prefer to deal with population issues in the context of
environmental problems, others in the context of human sexual behaviour and improvement of family life, and still others in relation to a
variety of subjects. The issues that receive the greatest attention in a
given programme are determined in each case by the culture, by the
perceived population situation in each country and, ideally, by the interests and potential for action of the learners, who vary in age and other
characteristics.

In decisions on its assistance for population education, UNFPA, as a
fundamental principle, gives preference to undertakings that encompass the broad range of population issues affecting any given society. To
include a range of population issues in the content of both school and
non-school programmes seldom costs much more than it does to focus
on a few issues, and the benefit to a country usually increases by broadening rather than by narrowing the focus.

Population communication

Population communication refers to the use of both traditional networks and mass media to mobilize support for population-related activities. Communication activities constitute the extension or outreach
as well as the feedback components of family planning and maternal
and child health delivery and census-taking.

The use of both interpersonal communication and mass media channels, sequentially or simultaneously, has facilitated the flow of information and promoted responsiveness. For example, videotape may be
used as a teaching aid in face-to-face training. Listening groups for radio
broadcasts are another example and are most effective when provision
is made for feedback from the groups to the source of the radio broadcasts. For illiterate or semi-literate audiences, the use of materials such
as flip-charts and flannelboards promotes the exchange of ideas more
effectively than does the use of materials such as posters and handouts.
Communication is essential in delineating and organizing appropriate

activities and in reconciling the plans of administrators at the central level with the perceptions and needs expressed by members of the community.

Under the rubric of population communication, UNFPA finances a wide range of endeavours including communication projects in support of censuses, family planning programmes and the activities of national planning units. It also supports advisory services, such as assigning a communication adviser to a UNFPA Deputy Representative's unit or sending a consultant to visit a country for a short time to strengthen communication efforts. In reviewing requests for assistance, UNFPA pays careful attention to the appropriateness of the medium selected to the characteristics of the target audience. In general, UNFPA emphasizes the primacy of interpersonal communication designed to elicit feedback from the target groups and the use of mass media only where feasible and, ideally, supplemented with interpersonal communication. These principles of population communication and population education are applied in the implementation of field activities supported by UNFPA in the traditional areas of agricultural extension, health education, literacy campaigns, workers' education, home economics and family planning communication.

FUNDING LEVELS

Between 1969 and 1983, UNFPA spent approximately $118 million on population education and communication, approximately 11 per cent of its total programme. In the past two years, expenditures for activities in education and communication have increased considerably in response to growing demand and as a result of the priority the Fund has assigned to this programme area.

Population issues, especially those dealing directly with family planning and fertility decline, were not popular items for incorporation in school curricula during the early years of UNFPA operations. At the beginning of 1972, ministries of education in only 4 countries in the world had UNFPA-funded population education projects; by 1984, that number had increased to 52 countries, and another 30 were waiting only for funds to begin school projects of their own. Currently, the demand from countries for further education on population issues is so heavy that it cannot be met.

UNFPA, working with the specialized agencies, has funded a number of intercountry projects to develop methodologies, materials and training programmes for this relatively new field. ILO has developed population education curricular and training materials for use in the organized sector and in vocational training programmes. FAO has devised methodologies for the introduction of population issues into training programmes for rural development specialists, home econo-mists and agriculture extension agents. Through its Development Sup-port Communication Service, it has incorporated population concepts into many of the communication activities in the regular FAO pro-gramme. Among other things, this service has been responsible for the local development of low-cost, culture-specific training materials in some 20 countries. On a smaller scale, health educators from WHO (PAHO) have developed education programmes for adolescents at risk of pregnancy. UNESCO has developed methodologies for the introduc-tion of population content at all levels of school curricula.

As interest in population education and communication activities took root, it was realized that work at the interregional level needed to be augmented by regional activities if countries were to get their pro-grammes on a firm footing. Permanent regional mobile teams were established by the specialized agencies to assist countries in designing national projects; to carry out specialized training for national person-nel; to arrange for sharing experiences through clearing-houses; to con-tinue activities to create awareness; and to provide *ad hoc* consultancy services.

TYPES OF ACTIVITIES

The types of activities UNFPA has been asked to support over the past years mirror the changes that have occurred in this sector. In the 1970s, the major emphasis of most communication and education projects was to create an awareness of population and its consequences for develop-ment. Although this remains a principal objective, the primary focus of many projects today is to increase the motivation for family planning.

Regional differences

Approaches to population education and communication differ from culture to culture and within each culture from audience to audience. The awareness in Asian countries of the serious implications of rapid population growth undoubtedly facilitated the introduction of popu-lation education and communication activities as an attempt to understand and to respond to population and development interrela-tionships. In the early 1970s, the large number of Asian countries inter-ested in developing population education and communication projects kept the regional specialists, fielded by ILO, FAO and UNESCO, fully occupied.

They developed resource materials that served as prototypes for the countries, and trained educators and communicators in regional and country workshops. As the country projects progressed to the stage that they could receive visitors, internships and study tour programmes were organized by the regional teams to facilitate the exchange of experience between countries.

The Population Education Clearinghouse, based in the UNESCO office in Bangkok, has served as an important centre for disseminating information. It receives and distributes publications relating to population education and communication work in Asia, and it links the various sectors involved in non-formal education. A number of agricultural colleges and universities in Asia have become interested and involved in population education through the Asian Association of Agricultural Colleges and Universities, with technical assistance from FAO.

African approaches to population education and communication have usually emphasized cultural diversity, education for development, environmental issues and family life or sex education.

Although the subject of population is still sensitive, the tide is shifting. Today there is hardly an African country with a development plan that does not have a reference to population. UNFPA and the specialized agencies it works with (ILO, FAO, UNESCO and WHO) can claim some credit for the recognition and understanding of population issues that are now evident in the African region. Most population programmes in Africa have included education or communication activities or both. In order to design effective communication programmes to reach groups down to the family unit, considerable experimentation has been required. UNFPA, therefore, has supported a wide range of activities, using different channels of communication—from folk theatre to radio broadcasts—aimed at a variety of target groups.

In Latin America, the focus of population education and communication has evolved from concern principally with family issues to concern with a spectrum of population issues ranging from human sexuality and family life through population ecology. Several innovative activities undertaken by regional advisers have paved the way for recognition by individual Governments of population education's potential contribution to national development. For instance, advisers have assisted countries in planning and carrying out national seminars designed to lay the groundwork for the substantive orientation of projects and to encourage local political support for activities. A regional post-graduate studies programme received technical support for providing academic and field training to national project personnel from several Latin

American countries, thereby strengthening the technical resource base in countries. Another accomplishment in Latin America has been the regional advisers' pioneering work in developing mechanisms for implementing Technical Co-operation Among Developing Countries (TCDC).

Like their counterparts elsewhere, regional advisers in Latin America compiled a resource manual on population concerns, which provides educators with information on educational techniques and population issues specifically within the context of Latin America. The aim of the manual is to facilitate curriculum development. To ensure that its purpose was served, regional advisers hand-carried the new book to country seminars, where the purpose and relevance of the document was explained and its uses explored with national curriculum development experts and with those university faculties of education responsible for introducing innovations into national school curricula.

In countries where national projects were under way, this "sourcebook discussion" approach served to strengthen the school curriculum and to ensure the collaboration of university scholars who might otherwise have remained distant from the project. Where no projects were under way or foreseen, this approach introduced population issues as relevant concerns for the key educators responsible for designing and upgrading school curricula. Once knowledgeable about population and appreciative of its relevance to their own work, such specialists will be likely to ensure that appropriate contents and methodologies find their way into the national education system. This may be especially important in countries that can afford to effect innovations without undue demands on international funding.

The diverse approaches to population education in the Arab world have elicited broad support. In a regional seminar on Population Education and Curriculum Development held in Rabat, Morocco, in 1981, 37 educators from 21 Arab nations reached a consensus that population education can contribute to the renewal of education in Arab states as innovations are introduced in curricula, teacher training, teaching methods and the use of audio-visual aids. It was also agreed that population education should be integrated into all existing educational programmes, both formal and non-formal. Most countries of the region direct their efforts in population education and communication to address overall development concerns.

The regional programmes funded by UNFPA have assisted Governments of the Middle East and Mediterranean in such activities as formulating population education and communication projects, as well as setting up training courses and national seminars, incorporating population information in publications, organizing study tours and providing advice to countries on curriculum revision. The regional advisers, some of whom have been periodically based at agency headquarters, maintain communication with Governments in the region as well as with special organizations such as the Arab States Broadcasting Union and the International Confederation of Trade Unions in the Arab World. This communication facilitates the development and implementation of programmes on a regional as well as a national level. Initially, regional projects directed attention to the lack of basic data and the need for incorporation of population dynamics into education structures. In recent years, more attention has been given to curriculum development at the country level, and one volume of a regional source-book about population in Arab countries has been prepared and distributed.

Studies carried out in the region by the UNESCO Regional Population Communication Unit for the Arab States dealing with communication as a social process led to suggestions that folk and traditional media as well as radio should be mobilized in view of the low rate of literacy. By the end of 1981, the project had trained about 50 Arab broadcasters in topics such as family planning, nutrition, illiteracy and rural development.

In-school projects

In each region, a number of countries have incorporated population education programmes into the regular school curriculum. Every effort is made to persuade teachers that the "new" content is neither foreign nor totally new. The stress is on clarifying relationships, underlining the role of population change in development problems and emphasizing the importance of child spacing.

In India, the national population education programme in schools began with UNFPA assistance in 1980. Since then, 18 state governments and union territories representing 98.5 per cent of India's total population have become involved in it.

Actually, it took a long time for the population education programme to get under way. After initially encountering resistance from teachers and administrators, the central project staff managed to convince the somewhat reticent educators that population education content deals with issues concerning the quality of life, rather than being limited to issues that were, in their view, more delicate, and that they, as teachers, could have an impact on these population and development issues. Approximately 12,000 educators had been trained by mid-1982, and existing curricula were being revised to incorporate population content.

In Bangladesh, a project to introduce population education content into mathematics, environmental studies and social science curriculum materials has been developed for grades 4 through 7 of the school system. Funded by UNFPA, the project began in 1975 and will conclude in 1985. At first, in Bangladesh, as in India, teachers and officials considered population education a euphemism for family planning and objected to its introduction in schools. Now, population education has been accepted as an important discipline, and about 44,000 trained teachers and other educational workers are supporting the national programme. A variety of workshops served to bring about this change in attitude. Because religion plays such an important role in people's daily lives in Bangladesh, materials have been developed for Madrastas or religious institutions. During the second phase (1980–1985) of the population education programme, some 6,000 teachers in religious schools are being trained.

Within the framework of its general development strategy, the Philippines initiated a population education programme in 1972. The school activities funded by UNFPA have covered curriculum and materials development, teacher training, research and evaluation. Among the major achievements of the first phase (1972–1977) was the training of 262 supervisory teams who spread throughout the country to train teachers and school principals. An evaluation conducted in 1977 found that more effective training was needed to reach people in remote areas. Consequently, the second phase of the project, begun in 1981, aims at the regionalization of population education. Activities include regional seminars to tailor the course content to the needs and socio-cultural milieu of the more isolated rural population. UNFPA has also funded a population education programme focusing on teenagers. This pilot programme, undertaken by the National Capital Region in co-operation with the Population Center Foundation, instructs school counsellors on how to work with adolescents on sexual matters. This approach is now being tried out in 16 public and private high schools.

In 1974, the Republic of Korea, with the assistance of UNESCO, drew up a master plan for the institutionalization of population education as an integral part of the curriculum at all school levels. A unique feature of this programme was the mobile teaching team, which travelled throughout the country in vehicles equipped with television monitors to present population education to teachers who were being trained in other education programmes. New approaches to population education were demonstrated through such formats as discussions and dramas. Approximately 3,000 teachers a year participated in the team programmes.

In Indonesia, UNFPA has funded the subsidiary school system, which serves as an umbrella for five projects aimed at diverse audiences. Population education is brought into the programmes of the schools of the Council of Churches of Indonesia, the schools of Muhammadiya (Muslim schools), training programmes of the armed forces, schools and institutes of Islamic education, and population and family life education for workers. UNFPA assistance has been used for designing and producing motivational and instructional materials as well as for the training of trainers in the various government agencies and ministries involved in these programmes.

In Upper Volta, the Government has placed emphasis on the human sexuality aspects of population education. Subjects such as family life, family planning and human reproduction have figured prominently. The project has included training seminars for professionals in education, health, information, economics and rural development. A group of sex educators was established to conduct formal instruction sessions in sex education for the higher classes in primary and secondary schools. At present, this instructional programme is limited to selected urban areas.

In the Middle East and Mediterranean region, Egypt, Tunisia and Somalia (see feature page 128) have the most advanced in-school projects. Both Egypt and Tunisia have integrated population education into primary, preparatory and secondary schools, as well as into non-formal education, and have trained administrators, communicators, opinion leaders, social workers and others. In both countries, the programmes are administered by an office for population education located within the Ministry of Education.

In the early days of the Egyptian project, the staff devised an innovative and cost-effective means of identifying interested and capable teachers to participate in population education activities. All teachers who expressed an interest in learning about population education were asked to review by mail a collection of readings on the subject. If they chose to continue, they were instructed to conduct a population survey in their own communities in order to acquaint themselves with the use and application of basic demographic tools in their own situation. Those who successfully completed these learning exercises via correspondence were invited to participate in face-to-face training sessions in Alexandria.

Several countries in Latin America—Honduras, Mexico (funded through a multi-bi arrangement with Sweden), Nicaragua and Peru—have begun projects that combine formal and non-formal approaches to population education (see feature page 61 on Mexico's programme).

SOMALIA: AN INNOVATIVE POPULATION
EDUCATION PROJECT

In 1981, a UNFPA-funded population education project was launched in Somalia. The project, with technical assistance from UNESCO, has developed several innovations in population education which are contributing not only to the country's development but also to the field of population education in general.

In a departure from the almost universal tradition of locating population education projects in curriculum development centres or divisions, the project was placed in the strategically located Planning Division of the Ministry of Education, where it enjoys the full support of the Division's Director, the Director General, two Vice Ministers and the Minister.

Although it began as a school project, it has since been merged with an earlier communication project and now embraces both formal and non-formal education audiences. One step in this direction occurred when the adviser and the project staff became technical resource persons to an ILO-executed project on workers' population education. This provided the opportunity to ensure consistency in content for different audiences and to strengthen the skills of the project staff to include the teaching of adults. This collaboration also had a multiplier effect, as many of the adults trained were nutrition and health field-workers. The sharing of international and national technical resources occurs in other aspects of the project as well and is contributing to a cohesive development programme.

The approach taken by the staff to introducing population education has been to build upon existing elements in the school curriculum. Every effort is made to demonstrate to teachers that the content is neither foreign nor totally new. The stress is on clarifying relationships, underlining the role of population change in development problems and taking every opportunity with a number of different target groups to emphasize the importance of child spacing.

The question of family size is dealt with only after the interrelationships between child spacing, maternal and child health and nutrition practices have been examined. At the same time, larger societal concerns, such as the pressures of urban concentrations on the supply of utilities as well as problems of desertification and land pollution can be explored.

A formal evaluation in 1984 of the teacher training activities will determine the impact of the programme on attitudes; preliminary investigation already indicates a significant impact in favour of child spacing and of small family size.

At an early stage in the development of the project, a minor crisis was experienced when the staff realized that available data were totally inadequate for their purposes. They dealt with the problem by organizing a national meeting of representatives from all of the development ministries, for which each one was expected to prepare a background paper. This required that data be collected and organized around population issues of concern to each ministry. Population education staff worked closely with ministry officials in preparing this background documentation. The result was the most valuable compendium of population and development data on the country. The collected papers became a national source-book, which has been distributed to all ministries and to most embassies and foreign or international development missions to the country.

Among the cost-effective measures developed by the project was the production of 20 charts for classroom walls as an alternative to much more expensive student handbooks. Written materials prepared as guides for teachers accompanied the charts, each of which focuses on a population theme around which a lesson can be taught. Thus, teachers can use the chart as a springboard for discussion, encouraging thinking and analysis rather than rote learning. The classrooms are used by adult learners in the evenings, so the charts are serving more than one group of learners. The teachers are also taught how to use readily available materials, such as piles of sand, sticks, stones, bags of beans, leaves, mud models, matchboxes and simple posters using words and illustrations from magazines.

The project includes intensive teacher training for two weeks to prepare a large nucleus of master teachers. Periodic follow-up contacts are made by central staff over a period of 18 months to monitor progress with their own training activities. The master teachers train five teachers each, sometimes for only an hour or so per day, over a period of about 40 days, not necessarily consecutively. The Secondary Teachers College at Somalia University became so interested in the project that it asked for technical assistance for designing a core course in population studies to be given to all students in their final year. This undertaking will help make population education an integral part of the curricula in Somalia.

El Salvador began one of the world's first national population education projects in 1971. Titled "Family Education" because of cultural constraints on the use of the word "population" at the outset, the project later expanded its content to include a broad range of population issues and has developed interesting classroom materials, for example, on population and ecological concerns. In addition, there is some indication that the activities to help create awareness among community leaders and parents of schoolchildren paved the way for widespread acceptance of a new national population policy introduced in the mid-1970s.

Colombia was the scene of an early experimental school project, organized in 1971 by the Universidad del Valle in Cali. This pilot project has served as a reference point for many subsequent activities in countries throughout the region. Although it does not have a full-scale population education project, Colombia has been able to incorporate population education content into its national school curricula in health, biology and social studies, and population education became an important part of the national teacher training programme in the late 1970s. Both major accomplishments benefited from the early experiment and from continued technical support from the regional level.

The organized sector

In keeping with the recommendation of the World Population Plan of Action to extend training in population to labour leaders to help them better identify problems and frame policies, UNFPA has provided approximately $23 million over the past decade to ILO or directly to Governments to implement population education activities for members of the labour force and their employers. About 44 per cent of this amount has been spent for regional and country projects in Asia and the Pacific.

The provision of population education and information together with access to family planning services through the organized sector has, on the whole, been an extremely satisfactory approach. Such interventions have succeeded in changing attitudes of both employers and workers; population education classes have been conducted on plant sites during company time and, in some instances, companies have provided incentives to those who accept family planning. Moreover, population education projects in the organized sector have a potentially great multiplier effect. As a result of such endeavours, a large cadre of trained worker-motivators in many industrial establishments have the potential to influence fellow workers as well as other members of the community.

The Workers' Education Branch of the Department of Labour in Sri Lanka initiated an urban-based workers' population and family planning education project in 1973. This undertaking, an example of combining general population issues with an emphasis on family planning, strengthened the understanding of these subjects among trade union leaders and supervisory staff at various levels. With their support, activities were organized in concert with the country's family planning programme. As a result, workers who were motivated to practise family planning through the project found services readily available at their place of employment. Similar projects for workers in the plantation sector of the rural areas have also been highly successful, so much so that the demand for family planning services has exceeded the supply. In India and Pakistan, UNFPA is supporting ILO-executed projects designed to bring population issues and family planning information to the attention of managers as well as workers.

The organized sector in Jordan has been mobilized to promote family welfare. Employers are encouraged to provide family planning services for their employees as part of their regular health and welfare efforts. Through a UNFPA-assisted project, a population education unit was established in the Workers' Education Department of the Ministry of Labour so that educational programmes in population and family welfare could be provided to manufacturing units on a regular basis. In Bahrain and Democratic Yemen, workers' education programmes seek to raise awareness of the consequences of demographic trends for the well-being of the household.

In Zambia, UNFPA has supported a family life education project designed to assist members of the organized sector in understanding the broader aspects of population as they relate to family welfare, working conditions and the quality of life. One result of these activities is that the Government has undertaken the formulation of a national population policy.

A project for population and family welfare education in Sierra Leone has sought to improve understanding of population issues and their consequences by incorporating a population component into the education programme for members of co-operatives and their families.

Other non-formal education and communication projects

With UNFPA assistance, Mexico has fielded a number of innovative communication activities. The project for research and training in population communication, launched in 1974 in support of the National Population Council (CONAPO), is an effort to formulate a national population communication and family planning programme. The project structured its activities around three interrelated areas: production of materials, training and research. Mass communication—radio, television and films—was used to reach the target group. Materials production was accompanied by a training programme on communication strategies and techniques for the personnel of the Communication Unit of CONAPO (see feature page 61).

In Mexico and the Philippines, PIACT has developed printed family planning materials for illiterate groups, using pictures and conducting extensive research on visual perception.

In Afghanistan, family health and family life education have been incorporated into the functional literacy materials of the General Agency for Literacy Campaign, Ministry of Education. Adult rural women form the largest audience. The traditional midwives and health workers serve as important agents of population education and communication. UNFPA has provided assistance for the training of trainers and the production of simple visual aids and educational materials.

In 1978, a communication programme was launched in support of Afghanistan's first census to promote the participation of heads of households who were traditionally reluctant to share information about their families. Without their co-operation, it would have been impossible to achieve an accurate count of the population and to collect the data necessary for national planning. The communication campaign was based on research and used a number of channels. The messages included an explanation, first, of what a census is, then why it is needed, a description of how it would be conducted and, finally, how people could help. Subsequently, other countries in the region began to design similar census communication activities. In Bangladesh, projects have been initiated to build the communication training capacity of ministries and improve the communication skills of family planning fieldworkers. In addition, a population information facility has been designed to collect and disseminate population information to concerned agencies in the country. In Sri Lanka, a film produced by UNFPA about the census helped to widen public awareness of its importance in the nation's future.

UNFPA has always encouraged Governments to incorporate population activities in their development schemes. It has supported, for example, non-formal population activities within the context of Malaysia's Federal Land Development Authority (FELDA) programme. Field officers in FELDA, which is basically a population redistribution programme to bring settlers into underdeveloped areas, undergo training in conducting non-formal education sessions for settlers to help them raise their standards of living. Population education elements are integrated into the training programme as well as into the social development programme for settlers. The content focuses on the relationships between such factors as family size, growth and welfare.

Some countries in the Middle East have made extensive use of the mass media. The Egyptian High Committee for Population Communication, formed in 1979, is in charge of the national population information programme and has worked on the design and co-ordination of a national mass media campaign. In Jordan, a national population communication project is aiming at the creation of a cadre of radio and television professionals capable of providing the necessary support communication services for population activities in all sectors.

A number of African countries are experimenting with centralized, multisectoral population communication units because such arrangements could considerably enhance the impact of limited human and financial resources. In the Gambia, the unit has supported activities in population data collection and family planning by developing and producing training materials and publicity messages to support each activity. In Kenya, the Government has assigned population education and communication responsibilities to the established National Population and Development Council, the members of which include Government and concerned private-sector representatives. The Ministry of Education in Mali has set up a videotape recording centre where trained nationals produce videotapes on population topics to support functional literacy programmes and maternal and child health services. A population communication co-ordinating unit for Senegal is in the early stages of operation.

In the Caribbean, health educators have designed educational and service programmes in an attempt to meet needs of adolescents. In other regions, health education has become an important component of MCH/FP programmes.

UNFPA also supports communication training organizations such as the Development Communication Training Programme in Bangkok and the Asian Institute for Broadcast Development in Kuala Lumpur, which provide training for national project staff.

FUTURE DIRECTIONS

In extending assistance for information, education and communication, as for other areas, UNFPA has been concerned principally with the development and strengthening of country resources and programmes, basically to improve local capacity, experience and structures for long-term national action.

From the outset, UNFPA recognized the need for flexibility in its approach to population education and population communication. Countries themselves had to determine the content and emphasis of programmes and had to select methodologies that would be most appropriate in responding to locally perceived problems. The Fund's flexibility has been accompanied by technical orientation for individual countries, drawing upon international experience shared with the United Nations system. The accumulated experience over the years has been applied in the field to help countries that are just now initiating population education and communication activities to avoid mistakes made by the pioneers in these technical areas. Mechanisms for sharing this experience include clearing-houses, regional advisory missions and global projects that have collected, organized and distributed data important to project implementation.

Although there was little interest in the late 1960s and early 1970s, population information and communication projects are now under way in all regions of the world and requests are being received faster than UNFPA can provide resources to fund them. Those projects referred to in the preceding pages are only indicative of the many approaches taken and do not represent all projects funded by UNFPA in this field. There has been a gradual evolution in the types of projects called for over the years. Today, there is far less emphasis than there was originally on creation of awareness, but because some countries in each region still have not fully recognized the importance of population issues for their own socio-economic development, the need for awareness activities will continue, although on a smaller scale, for some time. In most countries, though, the next decade will see education and communication principles and methodologies become more a part of the management of family planning services and other population activities.

Although countries have already developed and, in some cases, completed projects and valuable experience has been gained, there remains a great need for continued development and monitoring of population education and communication, including some modest financial support. The population education field should not be allowed to stagnate. Continued financial and technical support will be needed for institutionalizing population education, that is, for making population education as much a part of the standard curriculum for adults and children as any other component. This may require establishing a permanent unit, however small, in the appropriate ministry, making population content a permanent part of pre-service teacher training programmes, and finding ways to channel new population data and findings into curricula as they are developed or revised. This process of institutionalization includes both the school and non-school sectors.

Population education in schools has contributed directly to national development through its impact on education systems. A great deal of experimentation has been required to formulate the most suitable approaches in each instance, with emphasis on helping learners develop intellectually, rather than simply on transmitting messages one way or telling children what to think. Encouraging the development of investigation, critical analysis and problem-solving skills in the context of socially relevant population issues has produced enthusiastic responses not only from children but also from teachers, whose morale is visibly improved when children become enthusiastic learners, inspired by relevant content coupled with interesting methods of teaching. Teachers of population education are also sharing their newly acquired skills with colleagues. These country experiences have been aided through regional support and shared through intercountry research and distribution activities.

Continued attention to school audiences will be needed despite their small numbers compared with the vast numbers of people who have never been exposed to formal education or who have dropped out of school after only a few years. The reason is that the educated portion of the population will be the vanguard of any given country's development, the leaders of today and tomorrow. It is thus important that they set good examples as community leaders and that they make careful and informed decisions. This does not, however, negate the need for an approach that goes beyond the schools. What the future demands is a broad educational approach, covering as many segments of society as possible so that the interests and needs of the whole community and individual families are taken into account when population decisions are made.

In the past, UNFPA devoted modest resources to the strengthening of traditional communication systems. It funded family planning communication projects using both folk and mass media in Bangladesh, Haiti, Mexico and the Philippines. Future needs in the population communication field call for more community organization and better planning of the uses of mass media, not necessarily more of these media. Both objectives will be difficult to meet because of growing population, which makes organization difficult, and the temptation to adopt modern gadgetry as an apparently easy way to meet all needs in the area of population communication.

Electronic media continue to grow rapidly in both volume and sophistication (coupled with ease of operation), but facilities for maintenance and repair lag behind in developing countries. This, coupled with financial constraints, will serve to postpone the day when poor countries can rely heavily on such media. Limited use can be made of selected electronic media, of course, but decisions as to appropriateness of the particular medium for a particular use and in a particular setting must be made judiciously. In the meantime, communicators have yet to discover a more effective means of communicating than face to face. It is this type of communication, and efforts to enhance it, that will need the most attention in the years to come.

9. Basic Population Data Collection

Basic population data are indispensable for effective economic and social development planning, including the formulation of population plans and policies. Population data and forecasts are also necessary for the design of programmes to address population problems. Governments, international intergovernmental organizations, bilateral agencies and private institutions that are involved in population programmes—all need current information on population size, structure, composition, distribution and change, as reflected by the three principal population determinants: fertility, mortality and migration.

Recognizing the varied and vast needs for population data and the scarce resources available, the World Population Plan of Action adopted by the World Population Conference of 1974 urged developing countries to tabulate and analyse census results and other population data and to make this information available to national policy planners to assist them in the formulation, implementation and evaluation of population and development policies. Countries were also encouraged to establish a continuing capacity for taking household sample surveys and for regularly collecting demographic and socio-economic data. They were also urged to participate in the World Fertility Survey (see feature page 143). In addition, the World Population Plan of Action drew attention to the World Programme for the Improvement of Vital Statistics and encouraged countries to enact appropriate legislation and, as a long-term objective, to establish or improve their vital registration and civil registration systems.

Data collection, perhaps more than any other activity, best illustrates the interrelatedness of the facets of the Fund's programme. Information amassed from censuses, surveys and civil registration systems provides the initial input for macro-level planning, programme design and, ultimately, project evaluation. Furthermore, data collection often constitutes a country's first involvement with any activity in the population sector. Endeavours in this area frequently raise Governments' awareness of the urgency of the population issue, thus prompting them to deal more actively with population and development interactions.

TYPES OF ACTIVITIES AND FUNDING LEVELS

In accordance with its mandate, UNFPA gives special attention to creating and strengthening the national capability to collect, analyse and use basic population data. Special emphasis is placed on the training of local personnel at national and international levels and on the provision of appropriate equipment. The combination of training and equipment helps to ensure the development of an institutional base for gathering and using population data. UNFPA has developed specific guidelines for support to population censuses, demographic surveys and other population-related surveys, and civil registration and vital statistics programmes. Between 1969 and 1983, the Fund spent $163.5 million in the area of basic data collection; of this amount approximately 70 per cent has gone for censuses, 20 per cent for demographic surveys and 10 per cent for civil registration and vital statistics systems and related statistical activities.

In financing the three principal activities in basic data collection—censuses, surveys, and vital statistics and civil registration systems—UNFPA has supported technical advisory services, including regional advisers, long-term and short-term consultancies in such fields as census organization, cartography, sampling, data processing and demographic analysis; local personnel; training, including fellowships, seminars and workshops; and equipment, including vehicles and data processing, office, cartographic and printing equipment and supplies.

Technical advisory services bridge the gaps in national expertise and help develop the base for training replacement personnel. UNFPA assistance is intended to strengthen regional and subregional advisory services. Technical assistance is also provided regularly by organizations of the United Nations system such as the United Nations Statistical Office and the Department of Technical Co-operation for Development (DTCD).

Basic data collection activities sometimes require additional staffing by local personnel. To address this need, UNFPA furnishes funds for salaries and allowances for personnel who are required on a temporary basis for cartographic work, data processing and analysis necessary for the proper implementation of project activities. Although, in principle, the cost of field staff should be borne by Governments, UNFPA may consider partial support for such personnel in exceptional cases. In all cases of support to national personnel, remuneration must be at standard national levels.

For censuses and surveys, UNFPA may support training in methodology and procedures, data processing, computer programming, cartography, demography and socio-economic analysis. In the case of civil registration programmes, training in the legal, administrative and methodological aspects of this area may be funded. Training may take the form of in-service training, workshops, seminars, courses (offered locally or at the regional level) and fellowships. Because of the frequent turnover of national personnel, training is usually required for a significant number of local staff on a continual basis.

Often the success of basic data collection depends upon the availability of equipment and supplies. Because developing countries frequently lack both the necessary equipment items and the foreign exchange resources with which to acquire them, UNFPA may provide funds for the acquisition of a range of equipment and supplies.

Censuses

Between 1969 and 1983, UNFPA financed 109 national population censuses totalling approximately $120 million. One of the most ambitious undertakings that the Fund supported was the African Census Programme, which covered 22 countries and lasted from 1970 to 1977. Many newly independent African countries had never had a complete enumeration, and reliable demographic data were urgently needed as a basis for socio-economic planning. In co-operation with the United Nations and the Economic Commission for Africa, UNFPA financed a wide range of components totalling more than $16 million by the time the project was completed.

As might be expected with an operation of such magnitude, a number of difficulties were encountered. An in-depth evaluation conducted by UNFPA in 1979 in 8 participating countries revealed that delays in posting experts and in the delivery of equipment often resulted in deviations from the initial work plan. Original goals for meeting training needs meshed poorly with actual operational conditions. In many cases, Governments were not sufficiently staffed for these undertakings and hence government inputs were not at the levels originally anticipated. The immediacy of project needs frequently prevented local staff from participating in training opportunities, and study tours and fellowships were not fully utilized. On balance, however, the evaluation concluded that in the countries studied, which were chosen as representative both geographically and in terms of the status of the project, the primary objectives of the project had been accomplished. Countries did carry out censuses (18 of the 22 countries completed their enumerations), and the technical foundations for similar exercises had been put in place successfully.

The Fund was the principal source of external assistance for the 1982 population census in China. This first modern enumeration entailed recruiting and training 4 million enumerators and 1 million supervisors. UNFPA support included funding for the pilot census, equipment and the training of personnel. Given the large scope of the operation, the tabulation proceeded with few setbacks. The results of the 10 per cent sample were published in July 1983 (see feature page 141).

Haiti undertook its first comprehensive census in 1983 with UNFPA support, a large proportion of which was used to defray local costs. Convinced of the soundness of this project, the Inter-American Development Bank furnished a grant to cover the cost of an international expert in data processing.

In extending support for censuses, UNFPA has given preference to those countries undertaking their first census. It has also given limited support to countries conducting subsequent censuses if the need for such funding has been demonstrated. In several countries, UNFPA has helped to upgrade computer equipment, as in Egypt and Yemen; in others, it has given assistance to specific facets of the census, as in its support to Morocco for updating cartographic work in preparation for the 1982 census. In the English-speaking Caribbean, UNFPA supported preliminary data processing and tabulation in the 11 countries that carried out censuses in 1980–1981. Further processing of the data from these enumerations is being done at the Barbados Statistical Office with some minimal assistance from UNFPA. Barbados has absorbed a considerable share of the local costs in this operation, thus making it a good example of TCDC.

Surveys

It is often the case that countries cannot undertake a census according to the 10-year cycle prescribed by the United Nations. In such instances, demographic surveys to ascertain fertility, mortality and migration trends are productive alternatives. Moreover, even countries that conduct regular enumerations find that surveys are useful vehicles for updating decennial census data. In addition to financing numerous country-level surveys, UNFPA has supported significant intercountry projects in this area. It has worked with the United Nations Population Division and ILO in devising suitable survey instruments and in drawing up methodological manuals for subsequent use at the country level. The Fund has co-operated with the United Nations Statistical Office in the development of the National Household Survey Capability Programme, which seeks to augment the institutional capacity of developing countries for carrying out surveys on socio-economic development issues. It is anticipated that countries participating in this programme

CHINA: A MODERN CENSUS

UNFPA provided support to China for its 1982 census, a massive under-taking in a nation that includes one quarter of the world's population.

Lengthy planning went into the enumeration. In 1980, 1981 and 1982, pilot censuses were carried out in provinces, municipalities and autono-mous regions. Computers were installed, computer technicians and field census workers selected and trained, census forms printed, and publicity campaigns undertaken.

Actual census enumeration took place in July 1982, preceded by a mammoth publicity campaign using posters, banners, loudspeakers, radio spot announcements, TV programmes, films, pamphlets, picture-books, theatrical performances, billboards—all types of media—to encourage participation and instruct people in the census procedures.

- Approximately 4,000,000 enumerators and 1,000,000 supervisors conducted the enumeration.
- 1,000,000 staff worked in census offices at various levels.
- 1,000 computer technicians, 4,000 data entry personnel and 100,000 coders worked on processing the results.

The 1982 census was the first in China to employ electronic data pro-cessing for national statistical work. (The two previous population cen-suses—in 1953 and 1964—had relied on the abacus for tabulating counts.) Data processing is scheduled throughout 1984.

By October 1982 the preliminary census results had been reported:

- The population totalled 1,031,880,000.
- Males were 51.5 per cent of the population; females, 48.5 per cent.
- There were 20,689,704 births in 1981, and 6,290,103 deaths.
- The population had increased by 45.1 per cent since 1964, with an annual increase rate of 2.1 per cent.
- The urban population constituted 20.6 per cent of the total: Shang-hai was the largest city, with 11,859,748 people, followed by Beijing, with 9,230,687.

UNFPA support totalled $15.6 million and included assistance for preparations and publicity, census-taking, data processing, printing, analysis and dissemination of findings. The Norwegian Government's support ($755,000) for paper and equipment contributed to the print-ing of results. UNFPA support provided for 21 computers, installed throughout the country, data entry stations, advisory services, and scholarships abroad as well as in-country training.

will request assistance from UNFPA for appropriate national-level components. In this connection, UNFPA is funding a project in Morocco, comprising five surveys dealing, *inter alia*, with household expenditures and consumption patterns, nutrition, employment, fertility and mortality.

UNFPA has extended support to the International Statistical Institute, which was responsible for the World Fertility Survey (WFS), which perhaps can be characterized as the major demographic endeavour of the past decade. WFS aimed at the collection of reliable data on fertility, particularly in developing countries, to enable countries to interpret their patterns and trends in reproduction; to ensure the international comparability of the data collected; and to build national institutional capability for fertility research and analysis through the use of survey methods. A UNFPA evaluation held in 1980 reported that the programme had accomplished these goals (see feature page 143).

Civil registration and vital statistics systems

Civil registration and vital statistics systems are important sources of information for development planning. Few countries, however, possess nation-wide registration systems, and the establishment of such systems usually takes years. Countries that have passed civil registration laws and established national civil registration offices may request UNFPA assistance for small-scale experimental registration projects. Because of the expense involved, the Fund does not support the setting up of full-scale national civil registration systems. The Fund has extended considerable assistance to several African countries—Burundi, Congo, Kenya, Sierra Leone, Swaziland and United Republic of Tanzania—for civil registration activities. One important aspect of these programmes has been the creation of public awareness of the usefulness of registering vital events. In Kenya, a civil registration enlightenment campaign was carried out. In the United Republic of Tanzania, along with training for village leaders and health personnel, special publicity campaigns were undertaken. The Fund has supported training and equipment components in civil registration systems elsewhere: in Burma, Nepal and Viet Nam in Asia; in Democratic Yemen in the Middle East; and in Chile, Colombia and Uruguay in Latin America, to list but a few.

Impact of UNFPA support

UNFPA assistance for basic data collection has had a major impact in increasing the availability and improving the quality of population statistics required for the planning, implementation and evaluation of

WORLD FERTILITY SURVEY

"The World Fertility Survey (WFS) is the world's largest social science research project, encompassing 42 developing countries and 20 developed countries representing 39 percent of the world's population. By the [middle of 1984, when the project ends, more than] 350,000 women throughout the world will have been interviewed in surveys conducted under WFS auspices. Their answers will provide the most complete picture to date of women's childbearing behavior and aspirations and will furnish policymakers with clues regarding policies and programs most likely to influence fertility. . . .

"Founded in 1972 as a project of the International Statistical Institute (ISI), the WFS was designed to meet the need for reliable, up-to-date information on human fertility. Its main objective was described as 'carrying out nationally representative, internationally comparable, and scientifically designed and conducted surveys of human fertility behavior.' Other primary objectives were: to provide data needed by government planners in the social, economic, health and population fields; to advance scientific understanding of fertility behavior by providing comparable data for a large number of countries; and to increase the capability of countries to undertake demographic and other types of surveys.

"The WFS was started at a time when fertility had begun to fall in many developing countries, after centuries of uniformly high fertility in most cultures. The WFS was in a unique position to document these profound changes in fertility at an important point in the history of the world.

"Initial funding for WFS was provided by the United Nations Fund for Population Activities (UNFPA). Other major donors have included the United States Agency for International Development (USAID) and the Overseas Development Administration of the United Kingdom. . . .

"WFS-sponsored surveys are carried out mostly by government statistical bureaus and other research organizations in the participating countries. For all developing countries except Iran, WFS provided technical and financial assistance, while the participating countries were responsible for collecting and analyzing the data. . . . All WFS-supported surveys . . . utilize a 'core questionnaire' developed by WFS. This can be supplemented by 'modules' covering additional areas related to fertility. All questionnaires are translated into local languages and dialects and administered by trained interviewers, predominantly females, whose work is closely monitored by field supervisors. . . .

"The 42 developing countries participating in the WFS represent some 30 percent of the Third World's population. . . . Many of them had never before had a national fertility survey. . . .

[A large number of publications have already emerged from the WFS project: 32 First Country Reports, usually published by the country concerned; 43 scientific reports, 11 technical bulletins; 23 comparative studies; and 39 summaries were available from WFS as of the end of 1983.]

"Among the major conclusions to emerge from . . . surveys . . . are:

- "Substantial fertility declines (of at least one child per woman) have been recorded in Asia, Latin America and the Middle East, although the present average fertility of some 4.6 to 6.3 children per woman in those regions is still at least double the average of about two children in developed countries.

- "No fertility decline was found in sub-Saharan African countries, where fertility ranged up to 8 children per woman (in Kenya).

- "Nearly half of the married women surveyed in 27 developing countries said they wanted no more children. If all unwanted births were prevented, birth rates in these countries would fall by between 1.4 and 15.3 points (i.e., births per 1,000 population).

- "Preferred family size in the 29 developing countries ranges from 3.0 children in Turkey to 8.9 in Senegal, with an overall average of 4.7. These levels are far above the average 2.2–2.5 children per woman needed in these countries to achieve a no-growth population in the long run.

- "Only about one-third of the currently married, fecund women interviewed in the 29 developing countries were using contraception, compared with an average of 72 percent in 16 developed countries. . . .

"In some countries, WFS findings have corroborated information gleaned from vital statistics registration systems and earlier surveys; in others the findings were completely unexpected, in terms of fertility rates that were both higher and lower than anticipated. WFS surveys have documented for the first time the extent and duration of breastfeeding in the developing world. Policymakers have been concerned by the evidence that the practice of breastfeeding is declining, since this may adversely affect infant health and may contribute to an increase in fertility if not compensated for by gains in contraceptive use.

"Overall guidance for WFS' program is provided by a Program Steering Committee, consisting of representatives of the U.N. Population Division, the U.N. Statistical Office, UNFPA, USAID and the United Kingdom Overseas Development Administration, as well as four leading demographers as individual members. In addition to laying down operational principles for the WFS, the Program Steering

Committee has guided many facets of WFS' work: the system of depository libraries, plans for 'archiving' data, dissemination of findings within countries, translation of basic documents, publication of an annual report, access to data by international researchers, and the need to publicize WFS findings as widely as possible. The Committee also examines criteria for enrollment of new countries, reviews the progress of work in participating countries, and reviews questionnaires, modules and other basic documents. . . . A second committee, the Technical Advisory Committee, met between 1973 and 1977 to advise on all technical aspects of WFS surveys. The 12-member Committee consisted of internationally recognized demographers and statisticians who were nominated jointly by the ISI and IUSSP [International Union for the Scientific Study of Population] and served in their individual capacities. During 1973 and 1974, the Technical Advisory Committee reviewed all basic WFS documents, including the draft core questionnaire. The Committee also established the basic sampling requirements and suggested important modifications to the editing and coding manual and the core questionnaire. . . . The Committee completed its work in 1977, having laid the groundwork for WFS' research and analysis procedures. . . .

"The WFS was a highly ambitious undertaking that succeeded beyond the expectation of its founders. Many other fertility surveys, both prior to the WFS and contemporary with it, have been terminated without publishing results—victims of bureaucratic inertia, difficult field conditions, erratic coders and computers, political sensitivities, and numerous other problems. The WFS is extraordinary, not only in its scope and detail, but also in its ability to overcome seemingly insurmountable obstacles to produce high-quality published reports. As one indication of WFS' ability to develop solutions to complex statistical problems, its technical manuals and reports are widely used in graduate-level statistics courses. . . . "

*   *   *

By the end of June 1984, UNFPA funding to the operations of the central organization of WFS had reached $15 million. In addition, UNFPA has financed 24 country survey projects requiring almost $5 million as well as technical advisers in the United Nations Population Division, Economic Commission for Europe, Economic and Social Commission for Asia and the Pacific and the Latin American Demographic Centre. WFS works closely with the major international demographic research organizations, including the United Nations Population Division and

IUSSP. The United Nations Population Division, with UNFPA funding, is carrying out comparative analyses of WFS results and has completed many reports and studies, of which the most recent are *The Impact of Population Structure on Crude Fertility Measures, Fertility Levels and Trends as Assessed from Twenty World Fertility Surveys* and *Marital Status and Fertility*. The Fund has also supported other United Nations organizations in analysing WFS data. With UNFPA assistance, ILO has prepared "A Cross-Cultural Analysis of Interactions Between Population and Labour Using the World Fertility Survey" and WHO has issued "Analysis of World Fertility Survey Data, Health Aspects".

UNFPA involvement with WFS illustrates how funding for one project can have an impact far beyond the project itself. In addition to the acquisition of much-needed data, the WFS project has been a vehicle for strengthening countries' capacities to undertake social science research and for training human resources. UNFPA has always emphasized that enhancing these aspects is essential if a country is to become self-reliant in the population sector. Hundreds of technical staff who have participated in the country-level surveys have received excellent training in survey techniques, data processing and analysis, and in project management. Participating countries have increased their data bases as well as their supply of trained personnel.

Source: The description of the World Fertility Survey is excerpted from Robert Lightbourne Jr. and Susheela Singh, with Cynthia P. Green, "The World Fertility Survey: Charting Global Childbearing," *Population Bulletin* Vol. 37, No. 1 (Population Reference Bureau, Inc., Washington, D.C., 1982).

national population programmes, including family planning programmes. This has been particularly important in those countries where population data were either unavailable or of extremely poor quality.

The Fund's support, by assisting Governments in undertaking censuses and establishing civil registration systems, not only has generated urgently needed data but has also contributed to the long-term development of national capabilities in the collection, processing, evaluation and dissemination of population data. The number of national personnel involved in basic data collection has increased substantially, and their performance has been improved through fellowships, seminars, training courses and on-the-job training. Governments have been urged to establish and maintain, on a permanent basis, census offices, cartographic and sampling units, etc. The capabilities of national statistical offices have been upgraded by the provision of cartographic, printing, data processing and office equipment and supplies, and vehicles. In addition, the electronic data processing and dissemination of census results have been accelerated. Cartographic materials at all levels have been improved to provide Governments with important tools for the planning of statistical and non-statistical activities in the population field. All this support has also resulted in better evaluation and use of the data collected.

FUTURE DIRECTIONS

UNFPA support for the collection of basic data has considerably broadened the base of knowledge in the population sector. In view of the vast amounts of material that have been amassed and the greatly expanded capacity of countries to undertake such endeavours, the Fund intends to help countries consolidate, analyse and utilize already existing data. UNFPA will support countries' special data needs and will continue to finance censuses, surveys and civil registration systems. UNFPA will also emphasize the need for countries to utilize data that are collected. It is likely that greater attention will be given to periodic surveys that yield data relevant to population concerns. There appears to be a consensus among countries that regular surveys addressing such demographic phenomena as fertility, mortality and migration are relatively low-cost ways of obtaining information essential for incorporating population into development planning as well as clarifying changes in demographic behaviour. For activities in civil registration, the Fund will continue to support methodological studies at the global level for eventual utilization in country-level projects and limited action programmes at the country level which will serve largely as demonstration or pilot projects.

In the coming years, the Fund will encourage Governments to collect the data needed for the design, implementation, monitoring and evaluation of action programmes, particularly family planning programmes. UNFPA is already working with a number of countries to strengthen the service statistics component of their family planning programmes. The Fund has encouraged, and will continue to encourage, countries to undertake contraceptive prevalence surveys to obtain a better idea of the magnitude of unmet needs and to launch appropriate initiatives. It will also assist countries undertaking surveys for information on infant and maternal mortality. Although it is widely acknowledged that family planning programmes have played a key role in the observed reduction in fertility, more extensive documentation would be useful. The Fund will thus support country efforts to collect those data that can be used for assessing the demographic impact of family planning programmes as well as for monitoring programme performance.

Among the most notable developments in data collection during the past 10 years has been the progress in microcomputers and the development of computer software packages for the tabulation and analysis of demographic data. These inroads not only accelerate data processing but also make data available in a form that can be readily utilized by development planners. The Fund has been concerned that the utilization of data has been less extensive than envisaged. It will, therefore, assist countries in taking advantage of these technical improvements as a means of promoting data utilization.

10. DEMOGRAPHIC RESEARCH, TRAINING AND POPULATION POLICY

The Fund has always defined population policy in the broadest sense, to address all the demographic variables—fertility, mortality and migration—as well as the interrelationship between population and overall socio-economic development. Moreover, it has worked extensively with Governments, urging them to resolve population concerns in the context of their total development framework. This holistic perspective was endorsed at the 1974 World Population Conference. The World Population Plan of Action, noting the relationship between population and development factors, called on Governments to set up population units to facilitate the incorporation of population variables into development planning.

The experience of the last decade, however, illustrates some of the difficulties encountered in attempting to integrate population into development planning on a regular basis. Some of the problems can be explained by the lack of personnel conversant with demography and development planning, the dearth of precise knowledge of the interactions of demographic and socio-economic factors and the absence of a model strategy easily adaptable to country needs. Recognizing these deficiencies, the Fund has supported numerous projects in demographic training, research and support communication, as well as action programmes, to enable countries to integrate population considerations into their development planning.

FUNDING LEVELS

The substantive areas dealt with in this chapter encompass a wide variety of activities. These include, *inter alia*, demographic projections, analysis of demographic data and research on the determinants and consequences of fertility, mortality and migration; on the interrelationships between population, environment, resources and development; and on how to integrate population factors into national development strategies. They also encompass action programmes and training in all categories.

Of the $161.5 million that UNFPA has spent for these purposes, in most regions more was expended at the regional than at the country level, and almost 30 per cent was expended at the interregional level. In the early 1970s, most countries, with the exception of several in Asia, lacked the capacity for training nationals and the research capability necessary for carrying out complex demographic and development studies. Moreover, the generic nature of many of the issues to be addressed—methodological questions, basic conceptual frameworks and training curricula—made it more cost-effective to pursue such training and research at a global level. Support for regional and interregional training institutes was a first and crucial step towards the long-term goal of helping countries achieve national self-reliance in these areas.

Research has absorbed the preponderant share of UNFPA funds in the categories of assistance. Regional variations are apparent, however. The major share of funding for Asia, 46 per cent, was channelled into action programmes. Asia took an early lead in population activities and, by the mid-1970s, most Asian countries were implementing population and development initiatives. Also, in many countries of the region, the educational infrastructure was such that much training in population could be conducted at the national level. In the interregional/global category, research accounted for a large share, 47 per cent, of UNFPA expenditures. Because of the fairly universal nature of research on population policy, it was appropriately undertaken at the global level and through comparative studies embracing several regions. In view of the nature of the issues and the dearth of capacity at the country level, the Fund worked extensively with United Nations agencies and organizations to develop general approaches that could subsequently be modified for use at the country level. For example, the Fund supported ILO in the development of the BACHUE model, a mathematical tool for development planning which incorporates population variables in equations. This model has been put into use in Brazil, Kenya and Yugoslavia. UNFPA has also supported FAO research to investigate land-carrying capacity vis-à-vis expected population growth (see feature page 155).

TYPES OF ACTIVITIES

Training and research

The shortage of skilled manpower was one of the principal problems countries faced as they embarked on activities in the population sector. Recognizing this constraint, UNFPA channelled extensive support for training to the United Nations demographic research and training centres and, on a lesser scale, to universities in both developing and developed countries.

The Fund provided approximately $26 million to the four regional and three interregional demographic training and research centres between 1969 and 1983 (see feature page 152 for brief descriptions). Basically, these centres have the same objectives: to serve as training and research institutes in demography and related fields for their regions or for students from developing countries in various parts of the world; to serve as research centres for the United Nations regional commissions and to undertake research in such fields as basic data collection, fertility, mortality, morbidity, migration, urbanization, census data evaluation and adjustment, labour force and family planning; to provide sources of intensive classroom training or guided research in demography and related fields; to provide *ad hoc* courses, in-service training and special courses; and to publish and make available technical and other research studies on population trends and their relationship to socio-economic factors within the regions.

In addition to training courses, most of the centres provide consultancy services to the countries in their regions and to United Nations and other agencies, and most provide bibliographic and reference services to libraries, organizations and researchers both within and outside the region. The Cairo Demographic Centre (CDC), IIPS and CELADE were in operation before the Fund was established, but have received significant funding since. CEDOR, IFORD and RIPS were funded from their beginning by UNFPA.

In 1977, UNFPA carried out an evaluation of the six centres sponsored by the United Nations and a UNFPA task force assessed all seven programmes in 1982. The overall conclusion was that the training centres had contributed significantly to meeting the needs for trained demographers in developing countries. Between 1969, when UNFPA support was first given, through the 1981/82 academic year, almost 4,000 persons participated in the programmes. In general, the evaluation found that the programmes had been responsive to country needs. It found that all of the centres encountered difficulties in finding the appropriate level for core courses because students' backgrounds in the prerequisites vary widely. Also, research activities had been less extensive than anticipated because of the heavy teaching loads and scarcity of resources.

UNFPA has also supported the strengthening of demographic training at the national level. It has financed demographic training at the University of Indonesia and is assisting the Government of China in building up demographic research and training capacities in various universities and at the Chinese Academy of Social Sciences. UNFPA has financed demographic training in Arabic in Morocco, and, since 1972,

DEMOGRAPHIC TRAINING AND RESEARCH CENTRES

Regional centres

International Institute for Population Studies. The International Institute for Population Studies (IIPS), located in Bombay, India, was established in 1956. A national institution largely supported by the Government of India, IIPS provides training in demography and in the relationships between population and development. Trainees are nationals of Member States of the United Nations Economic and Social Commission for Asia and the Pacific. From 1956 to 1982, a total of 800 persons, including 300 regional fellows, were trained in formal demography at IIPS. The Fund's cumulative assistance to IIPS from 1969 to 1983 amounted to $1.6 million.

Centro Latinoamericano de Demografía. The Latin American Demographic Centre (CELADE), located in Santiago, Chile, was established in 1957. In 1975, it became a part of the United Nations Economic Commission for Latin America (ECLA). CELADE offers courses of various types and degrees of complexity and provides five levels of training: a course of study leading to a master's degree; an intensive regional course on demographic techniques; intensive national courses; seminars; and a programme of research fellowships. About 1,500 students from the countries of Latin America and the Caribbean have been trained at CELADE. The Fund's cumulative assistance to CELADE from 1969 to 1983 was approximately $4 million.

Regional Institute for Population Studies. The Regional Institute for Population Studies (RIPS), located in Accra, Ghana, was established in 1971. Although RIPS has an independent status, it is a part of the University of Ghana and is situated on its campus; the degrees and diplomas offered by the Institute are those of the University. RIPS trains demographers of the English-speaking Sub-Saharan African countries. It conducts two regular courses in demography leading to a diploma and a master's degree in population studies. Since its inception, RIPS has trained more than 200 students at the diploma level; 80 of these have taken the master's course. The Fund's cumulative assistance to RIPS from 1971 to 1983 amounted to $5.5 million.

Institut de Formation et de Recherche Demographiques. The Institut de Formation et de Recherche Demographiques (IFORD), located in Yaounde in the United Republic of Cameroon, was established in 1971 by agreement between the United Nations and the Government of the United

Republic of Cameroon. IFORD is an independent institution with its own governing council and advisory committee. Its purpose is to train demographers for 25 francophone countries of Africa. The two-year training course conducted by IFORD leads to the degree of Diploma d'Etudes Demographiques. From 1974 to 1982, IFORD trained 120 graduate students. In addition to its regular training programme, IFORD organizes seminars, carries out research and provides consultancy services. The Fund's cumulative assistance to IFORD from 1971 to 1983 amounted to about $6 million.

Interregional centres

Cairo Demographic Centre. The Cairo Demographic Centre (CDC) was established in 1963 under the joint auspices of the United Nations and the Government of Egypt. CDC is an independent institution with its own governing council and advisory committee. It conducts training courses in demography at four levels: general diploma in demography; special diploma in demography; master of philosophy (M.Phil) in demography; and doctor of philosophy (Ph.D) with specialization in demography. The CDC training and research programme focuses on population trends and socio-economic relationships. About 800 students from Arab countries as well as from Sub-Saharan Africa and Asia have received training at CDC. The Fund's cumulative assistance to CDC from 1969 to 1983 amounted to $5 million.

Centre Demographique ONU-Roumanie. The Demographic Training and Research Centre (CEDOR) was established in Bucharest, Romania, in 1974, under the auspices of the United Nations and the Government of Romania. The Centre conducts a nine-month programme in French for participants from many developing countries. Since 1975, 166 students from 35 French-speaking countries have participated in the courses conducted by CEDOR. From 1975 to 1983, UNFPA provided approximately $3 million in assistance to CEDOR.

Moscow State University, Centre for Population Studies. The demographic training programme of the Centre for Population Studies at Moscow State University was initiated in 1977. It provides training in an annual three-month teaching seminar to 25 planners from English-speaking developing countries. From 1977 to 1983, the Fund's assistance totalled nearly $350,000.

has supported the International Islamic Centre for Population Studies and Research at Al-Azhar University (Cairo). ILO, in co-operation with the University of Michigan (of the U.S.), has developed a training programme to assist middle-level personnel from planning and labour ministries in implementing population and development planning. Most of the participants have been from UNFPA-funded country programmes.

Analysis and utilization of data

Most countries of the world have conducted at least one census during the last 15 years. Many have also participated in WFS (see feature page 143) and a number have conducted national demographic surveys (see chapter 9). In view of these accomplishments, the Fund has been assisting countries in analysing existing data and undertaking research that can serve as the foundation of integrated population and development planning. Countries need to utilize existing data, wherever possible, before undertaking new data collection activities.

Through the interregional programmes, the Fund has supported substantial and varied research projects. These include, *inter alia*, a series of comparative analyses of World Fertility Survey data; research on the determinants of mortality; and an FAO research project on land resources for the population of the future (see feature page 155).

In recent years, in response to growing interest in the interrelationship between migration and development, UNFPA has supported a number of intercountry and country projects. A comparative study of the relationship of migration and urbanization to development has been completed by ESCAP in co-operation with Indonesia, Malaysia, the Republic of Korea, Sri Lanka, Thailand and several countries in the South Pacific. The results have assisted planners in formulating policies and programmes on population distribution. Particular attention has been paid to the analysis of census data.

Studies are also being undertaken in Indonesia, Malaysia, the Philippines and Thailand under the auspices of an ASEAN project specifically on migration in relation to rural development. These country projects are exploring the questions of population distribution and rural development through the collection and analysis of data on settlement schemes and are developing methodologies for evaluating the effectiveness of resettlement programmes as a means of adjusting patterns of population distribution. The findings of this research will assist policy makers in the development and implemention of population distribution policies and programmes. In Pakistan, with ILO assistance, the Fund has supported research on the interrelationship between migra-

LAND RESOURCES FOR FUTURE POPULATIONS

UNFPA commissioned a study by the Food and Agriculture Organization of the United Nations (FAO) to assess the potential of land in 117 developing nations for supporting their projected populations. The project is being carried out with the collaboration of the International Institute for Applied Systems Analysis.

The study concentrates on the physical potential of the land for food production; it does not examine the many factors limiting that potential such as requirements for non-food crops or demands for diets above the minimum requirements. Because fertilizers, improved seeds and conservation measures greatly influence yields, the study has projected land potential for three levels of input: low (subsistence farming); intermediate (with some fertilizers, improved seeds, and improved cropping patterns); and high (with full use of all measures and products to achieve high yields).

By the end of this century, according to the study:

- The lands of developing countries as a whole will produce barely enough to feed projected populations if traditional methods of farming are used.
- 64 countries—29 in Africa—will be unable to feed their projected populations from their own land resources.
- Two fifths of the land area—with 60 per cent of the total population —will be carrying more people than can be supported.
- Moreover, if no long-term conservation measures are taken, land degradation may reduce food production; as land is increasingly brought under cultivation and tree cover is removed, erosion, flooding and silting will lead to soil deterioration and lower productivity.
- Even with intermediate and high levels of inputs such as pesticides, fertilizers and improved varieties of crops, and even with the movement of potential food surpluses within regions, not all these countries will be able to meet projected food needs.

The widespread malnourishment in developing countries is thus likely to continue, contributing to high mortality rates and continued high birth rates. The study's findings have made it clear to policy makers that planning must begin now for balancing population with food production or food importation. Such measures as increased inputs and increased availability of inputs to small farmers, institutional changes, land distribution, changing crop patterns and conservation, and the slowing of rates of population growth, as well as regional co-operation can help forestall the shortfalls.

tion, urbanization and development. Several African countries have also begun to focus on the migration issue. For example, in Senegal, the results of research on labour force migration are being used as an important aspect of the country's development planning. (For further information on UNFPA assistance for policy formulation regarding migration and population distribution, see feature page 160.)

A number of developing countries in Europe have received UNFPA assistance for research on demographic and development issues of special concern to that region. Bulgaria has launched a series of studies focusing on labour force needs. In the Mediterranean, Cyprus also undertook a research project dealing with the interrelationship of population, labour force mobility and employment planning.

Formulation, evaluation and implementation of population policies

As countries have become more aware of the implications of demographic trends for the realization of development objectives, interest has increased in setting up procedures and mechanisms that take account of such interactions. The integration of population with development planning in its simplest formulation involves two separate, but obviously related, aspects. The first entails the use of demographic data to enhance the accuracy of sectoral planning. Although almost all countries use some demographic data in planning, national plans do not always use the range of available data in ways that would be most useful for understanding their present situations, as well as trends. The second aspect relates to assessing the impact of development policies and programmes on demographic processes and trends. The aim is to ensure, as far as possible, that population policies and programmes and development policies and programmes are mutually supportive. UNFPA has committed considerable resources for creating and sustaining institutional arrangements to achieve integration. On the regional level, UNFPA funds regional demographic advisers who, upon request from Governments, assist in the analysis of census and other population-related data and their utilization in the formulation and revision of population policies; evaluation of the demographic effects of family planning programmes; and the preparation of project proposals related to the above-mentioned areas. The long-range objective of providing regional population advisers is to help strengthen national capabilities, thereby fostering self-reliance in the analysis of population data and in the formulation, implementation and evaluation of population policies and programmes.

Latin American and Caribbean government officials are keenly aware of the need to integrate population with development planning and also of the importance of having adequate administrative and institutional arrangements to formulate and implement population policies within the larger context of development. Benefiting from a comparatively long experience with development planning, which started during the 1950s, many countries in the region have formed population units within their ministries of planning, entrusting them with conducting policy-relevant research, providing technical support to other governmental agencies and organizing training and awareness-creation activities.

In 1979, UNFPA sponsored a Latin American Conference on Population and Development Planning in Cartagena, Colombia. Participants —ministers of planning and representatives of 23 Latin American and Caribbean countries—discussed experiences and needs in the field of population and development, especially in relation to the units dedicated to this matter in the planning offices of the region. The Conference maintained that population policies cannot and should not be considered in isolation from problems of development and emphasized the need to incorporate these policies into mechanisms for advancing towards overall development of the countries.

In Brazil, UNFPA funded a project with the Planning Secretariat of the State of Maranhao to strengthen the technical and institutional capacities of the state's planning system so that population variables could be incorporated into planning for socio-economic development at the sub-national level. The project, which completed activities in early 1983, served to collect the most reliable demographic data ever available to the state, to train technical personnel in the handling and analysis of demographic data and to create awareness of the importance of population considerations for the attainment of overall development objectives. In Costa Rica, UNFPA is funding a project on research and training on population and its interrelationship with economic and social development policy. Implemented by the Population Department of the Office for National Planning and Economic Policy, this project has permitted an assessment of the implications of current demographic trends for development. The National Planning Council of Ecuador, the government body responsible for the formulation of a population policy, has obtained UNFPA support for a project to strengthen its institutional capacity for the integration of population with development planning.

Since 1980, UNFPA has been collaborating with the National Population Council (CONAPO) of Mexico in a project to design the institutional mechanisms needed to implement the country's demographic policy at the regional and sectoral level. Mexico is the only country in Latin America with a population policy that explicitly includes demographic targets (growth and distribution) disaggregated to the sub-national level. CONAPO has been entrusted with the task of monitoring and co-ordinating activities leading to the attainment of those targets. The purpose of the project is to adapt and develop the methodological and conceptual tools required for the effective integration of population variables into all levels of development planning in Mexico; to analyse available demographic data and to facilitate their use by state and federal planning agencies; to establish appropriate institutional and co-ordinating mechanisms; and to strengthen the capacity of the national planning system to formulate population and development policies that are consistent and reinforcing. The project has led to policy-relevant studies, usually with the participation of national research centres; a vigorous programme of staff training through courses, workshops and seminars; and technical support provided to sectoral and regional planning offices.

Projects for the formulation and implementation of population policy constitute an important component of population programmes in Africa. Through these activities, policy makers become aware of the importance of population variables in overall development planning. UNFPA has received a number of requests from Governments seeking assistance in establishing projects that would enable them to incorporate population considerations into their overall development planning process. The Fund has supported the establishment of population planning units in Mali, Rwanda, Senegal, Sierra Leone, the United Republic of Cameroon and the Upper Volta, to promote a better understanding of population factors in the articulation of development programmes. Regional advisory services have been invaluable in carrying out activities in this area. The ECA Population Division and the ILO Regional Team have participated in numerous missions to assist countries in developing both sectoral and multisectoral integrated population policies and in promoting the integration of population factors into national development planning.

To emphasize the importance of integrated population and development planning, UNFPA has supported a number of regional seminars and meetings, as well as grants to institutions for the dissemination of information on population trends and activities in Africa. At the regional level, the most outstanding achievement was the convening of the Parliamentarians Conference on Population and Development in Africa in mid-1981. The Fund also supported the first African Population Conference in 1971 and subsequent subregional conferences as well as the Second African Population Conference held in Arusha, the United Republic of Tanzania, in January 1984.

Many Asian countries have made considerable strides in integrating population concerns into development planning, and UNFPA has assisted several of them in this endeavour. In Bangladesh, a project has been launched to assist the Government's Ministry of Planning in ensuring that population factors and policies are brought into the development planning process, through improving demographic data and broadening the understanding of relationships between population and development. Efforts are under way in Indonesia to enhance the capacity of the National Family Planning Co-ordinating Board to formulate population policies for the country. A population policy unit is being developed in the Board to serve as a focus for activities in the formulation of population policy. In the Philippines, UNFPA has supported the National Economic and Development Authority in stimulating the integration of population and development planning at national and regional levels, including the establishment and strengthening of institutional capability, the setting up of a system for using research on population and development and the development of a system of related training.

The Fund has financed similar undertakings in the Middle East and Europe. In the Middle East, projects have been undertaken in Egypt, Iraq, Jordan, Somalia and Sudan, among others. The Iraq project focused on the improvement and co-ordination of demographic activities and research to meet development planning needs. The Sudan project, unlike the others which were nation-wide, was centred in the southern region and concentrated on human resource development and planning in what is the poorest and least accessible part of the country.

In response to the Government of Romania's concern with the formulation and evaluation of population policies and programmes, the Romanian National Commission on Demography, a body composed of deputy ministers of all ministries concerned with population matters, as well as demographers, psychologists, sociologists and lawyers, has, since 1974, been conducting studies on the interrelationships between socio-economic growth and population law. These have been published, in French, with UNFPA support. In Yugoslavia, a demographic-economic planning model (BACHUE) developed by ILO is being used for devising development policies and programmes. UNFPA has financed the testing of this computer model as well as the training of local personnel to operate it.

At the interregional level, UNFPA has financed considerable work on the formulation and evaluation of population policy. In 1972, it initiated the Law and Population Programme, which led to the convening of an International Symposium on Law and Population (1974), a workshop

ASSISTANCE FOR POLICY-MAKING REGARDING MIGRATION AND POPULATION DISTRIBUTION

In response to the five Population Inquiries conducted by the United Nations Population Division since 1974, most countries have indicated that population distribution and migration are integral parts of their population policies and are important concerns in their development planning.

It is within this context that UNFPA has provided support for research, information exchanges and planning concerning internal migration and population distribution. Projects at the intercountry level have focused on conceptual and methodological issues and the development of handbooks for use at country levels. Projects at the country level, making use of intercountry findings, have focused on the particular country's needs.

To meet the needs expressed by planners and policy makers in developing countries to improve their capacity to deal with population distribution problems, the United Nations Population Division and UNFPA organized the 1979 Workshop on Population Distribution Policies in Development Planning. Following a review of the goals and rationale for population distribution policies, the workshop assessed the efforts of Governments to intervene in population distribution. The group also reviewed institutional requirements and information needs for formulating, implementing and evaluating population distribution policies. The resulting publication has been used in training programmes and has served as a guide to planners working at the national level.

Governments need information for policy formulation. They will be greatly assisted by a manual, developed by the ILO, of techniques for migration surveys. Based upon reviews of the literature, as well as experimental work at country levels, the survey instruments in the manual can be adapted to the particular situations in different countries.

ILO studies have focused on such important policy issues as the labour, employment and income effects of rural-urban migration and the extent to which migration policies can be effective. In collaboration with national researchers, the ILO has carried on research on labour mobility—in particular the consequences of short-term migration—and on the viability of land settlement schemes. The products of these and other studies are made available to Governments through training programmes and through the participation of regional advisers in activities at the country level.

A number of countries have requested and received UNFPA assistance for work in migration and population distribution. In Senegal and

Mali, migration and labour force surveys have been supported to collect data for population and manpower planning. Support was provided to Nigeria to determine the causes and consequences of rural-urban migration. Regional symposia, such as that held in Zaire in 1978, have assisted in the dissemination of information among the Governments of Africa and among Governments in Asia as well.

To assist the Government of Thailand in formulating guidelines for rural settlement schemes as one means of improving the country's population distribution, UNFPA has supported an analysis of the relationships between migration and rural settlement. In the Philippines, as part of a large project on the integration of population factors in development planning, a study of urbanization policies has been undertaken as a contribution to a national urbanization strategy for the 1980s. UNFPA has also provided support to the South Pacific Commission to collect and analyse migration data to assist countries in the subregion in formulating appropriate migration-related policies.

In Mexico, migrants' needs for information are being met through radio broadcasts to rural groups, supported in experimental stages by UNFPA. Broadcasts focus on migrants' problems and on the opportunities for work. To assist in the revitalization of the countryside, the Government of Colombia has received funds from UNFPA to study approaches to economic activity geared to curbing migration by maintaining populations in their areas of origin. Regional activities of the Latin American Demographic Centre (CELADE), ILO Regional Programmes of Employment for Latin America and the Caribbean, and the Programme of Social Research on Population in Latin America, supported by UNFPA, have further developed the knowledge base concerning rural-urban migration and urbanization. These agencies have also provided technical assistance to countries in the formulation, implementation and evaluation of population distribution and migration policies.

In Egypt, research on migration, supported by UNFPA, is directed at meeting the information needs of policy makers and planners. In Jordan, studies of the socio-economic and demographic implications of population growth and movement in urban areas have also been useful for planning. The Economic Commission for Western Asia has held a number of seminars and workshops on urbanization to assist decision makers in the region.

on the teaching of population issues in law schools, research projects in 29 countries and the publication of the *Annual Review of Population Law,* which summarizes laws, judicial decisions and international agreements having implications for population. UNFPA supported research on the ethical and value aspects of population policies at the country level. To further the understanding of population/development issues among decision makers, the Fund convened two major international meetings, the International Conference on Population and the Urban Future and the International Conference of Parliamentarians on Population and Development.

Much interregional support for the implementation of policies has focused on research concerning morbidity and mortality. Substantial funding has gone to WHO for work on the promotion of breast-feeding and on strategies to improve the health of adolescents. ILO has also received assistance for a programme of research and technical support for population mobility, employment and policy design.

FUTURE DIRECTIONS

Knowledge of the dynamics of population change and its consequences has increased enormously in the last decade and a half. Although reports of research often end with a call for additional research, at present, there is probably much more substantial knowledge available to apply to the problems of integrating population and development planning than is actually utilized. UNFPA, through its support at intercountry and country levels, has made a significant impact on the growth of knowledge in this field.

As a result of the Fund's support of a variety of efforts—the United Nations fellowship programme, interregional and regional demographic training centres, interregional activities to develop training modules for integration with other training in planning, national activities to develop and strengthen university-based demographic training centres, and national fellowships through projects—almost all countries now have some nationals able to undertake research and related activities for policy making and planning. Also, many short-term seminars and workshops have provided specialized training to particular audiences to meet particular needs, at both country and intercountry levels. A great deal of effort is still needed for countries to become self-reliant in training in population studies. At present, such capacities exist only in some Asian and Latin American countries. The lack of an institutional training capability is especially critical in many African countries.

In view of such needs, the Fund will continue to support training activities at national and intercountry levels. As in the past, UNFPA will work with countries to devise effective training strategies delineating what types of training should be undertaken at the national level and what aspects are best retained at regional or interregional centres. The Fund will continue to review curricular content at the institutions it supports to gauge whether course offerings are in step with emerging needs in the population and development sector. The UNFPA assessment of the United Nations demographic training and research centres suggests that the orientation of the curricula has not kept pace with new directions in the field and with the demand for persons skilled in population/development planning. The Fund is now exploring with the United Nations specialized agencies how population modules could be built into the regular training activities the agencies offer to policy makers and planners.

During the past 15 years, extensive research has been undertaken on the principal population variables and on the interaction of demographic and development factors. The expert group meetings held during 1983 in preparation for the International Conference on Population reviewed work in each of the major fields—fertility and the family; population distribution, migration and development; population, resources, environment and development; and mortality and health policy—and identified gaps in knowledge that need to be addressed. In its future funding, UNFPA will emphasize research that is essential for policy-making and that is likely to be of operational value. It will also stress the importance of disseminating the results of research endeavours as the first step in promoting the utilization of findings. Given the state of the art as well as the specific country needs for research to undergird planning, the Fund will channel its resources to population policy research at the country level rather than at regional or global levels.

The 1974 World Population Conference at Bucharest underscored the importance of systematically considering population factors in the development planning process. Despite the concerted activity on this front over the past 10 years and, in some countries, even before the Bucharest meeting, considerable confusion persists as to how to bring about the desired integration. Methodological, technical and organizational issues have proved formidable stumbling blocks. The evaluation of the Senegal project, Integration of Demographic Variables into Regional Planning, has pointed out how difficult it is to formulate a project in this field. The evaluation also emphasized the necessity of having appropriately trained personnel who are knowledgeable about demography and development planning in order to make integration a workable notion.

UNFPA convened a seminar in late 1983 to review experience and to draw up a strategy for activities in the field of population and development planning. The group observed that to date integration efforts have focused mainly on delineating the numerical implications of current and projected population levels and trends in terms of socio-economic needs; that is, population variables have been treated exogenously in making projections of consumption, production, employment and other socio-economic variables. However, the trends and characteristics of population are, at the same time, also affected by socio-economic factors: a feedback between population and development exists. The treatment of population variables as endogenous would, of course, depend very much on the extent of knowledge of the determinants and consequences of such variables as well as on the feasibility of translating them as inputs in development planning. The group also pointed out the political dimension of development planning and recommended attention to a country's policy-making process and how this operates on a national, regional and local level.

The seminar recognized that there was no model institutional arrangement that would be valid for all national settings. Many developing countries have set up (some with UNFPA assistance) population units in national planning ministries, others have established national population commissions and still others have formed population cells in sectoral ministries. The group concluded that training remains a critical consideration. It was suggested that, as a first step, an assessment of training needs to foster better integration of population into development planning should be undertaken. These needs would be primarily country-specific, determined to a large extent by the nature of the country's population policies and development priorities. The development of a multidisciplinary training programme, including a component in management training, should be pursued. The objectives of such a programme should include, *inter alia*, improving the capacity of planners to make better use of the tools for integration; enabling the staff of planning units in sectoral ministries to recognize implications of demographic factors for their strategies and vice versa; and strengthening the ability of the staff of the population unit, if one exists, to make demographic concerns understandable to those in other disciplines.

The Fund will continue to pursue the issues raised in this seminar in its programming as well as in its dialogues with countries and international donors in the population field.

11. WOMEN, POPULATION AND DEVELOPMENT

UNFPA has long recognized the close correlation between women's status and the achievement of population objectives. Speaking at the 1975 World Conference of the International Women's Year in Mexico City, the Executive Director of UNFPA underscored the critical connection between women's status, population issues and development concerns:

"Equality [between men and women] does more than contribute to development. Equality *is* development. Nowhere is this clearer than in the area of development in which I work, population... [and in particular in the matter of control over fertility]. For many women the power of decision over this one basic function would represent a major step towards equality." ("Women and Population: The Freedom to Choose")

Recognizing the interrelationships between various demographic and socio-cultural variables, the 1974 World Population Plan of Action called on Governments to formulate population and development policies that would respond to women's needs, particularly those in education, employment, working conditions and age at marriage. These same concerns were the focus of attention at the International Women's Year Conference in Mexico City in 1975, and the Mid-Decade Conference in Copenhagen in 1980.

UNFPA POLICIES ON WOMEN AND DEVELOPMENT

Immediately after the 1975 Mexico Conference, UNFPA issued "Guidelines on Women, Population and Development" (revised and expanded in 1980). The "Guidelines", which were distributed throughout UNFPA as well as to all United Nations organizations and other groups and individuals preparing and implementing UNFPA-supported projects, recommend support for the following types of activities:

1. Formal as well as non-formal education programmes for women, including functional literacy, family life education and programmes to promote educational and vocational aspirations of women;

2. Employment programmes, including pilot projects aimed at increasing the access of women to employment, career guidance and training;
3. Programmes aimed at promoting the participation of women in decision-making in family and public life;
4. Support of institutional development at the grass-roots as well as governmental levels to ensure attention to the status and role of women in population and development activities; and
5. Efforts to improve the health of women and children as part of an integrated approach to MCH/FP in health, with special attention to the employment of women as providers of health care.

The criteria established for UNFPA support to programmes relating to women, population and development are that a proposed project or activity must be within the general framework of national population plans and policies; it should in some way help increase the effectiveness of population programmes in the country; and it should be a pilot or demonstration that would facilitate policy-making.

To ensure that women would be taken into account in the planning, designing and implementation of all UNFPA-supported programmes and projects, a chapter on women, population and development was incorporated into the *UNFPA Manual for Needs Assessment and Programme Development*.

UNFPA has also met with various United Nations agencies, government agencies and field experts and has conducted an informal opinion-survey of specialists from all the geographical regions on priorities for supporting activities to improve the condition of women in developing countries. These efforts have been summarized in a report, "Towards the Integration of Women in Population/Development Related Activities" (1 March 1979). UNFPA has also published a review of types of projects supported since 1969 in the field of women, population and development.

Within UNFPA, a section in charge of women and youth programmes was established in 1978. The purpose of this special unit is to ensure that each aspect of the entire range of UNFPA programmes is reflective of the Fund's commitment to women's full participation in development processes. The section is also responsible for acting as the focal point of contacts and co-operation with other United Nations agencies in areas of common interest, and for representing UNFPA at all relevant technical and programme-related meetings. The section maintains working relations, at governmental and non-governmental levels, with national and regional women's organizations concerned with population and development-related tasks.

FUNDING LEVELS

During the period 1969–1983, the Fund supported more than 150 projects designed for women, totalling approximately $14 million. However, the Fund's actual financial commitment on behalf of women far exceeds this figure. Almost all UNFPA activities in family planning and in population education and communication directly benefit women. Other activities—for example, data collection projects yielding information on women's status—indirectly promote women's interests. However, most of these specific projects, compared with projects in other sectors, fall in the low range of funding—less than $100,000; thus far, only three projects have budgets in the range of $500,000 to $1,000,000. There are several reasons for these relatively small amounts. Most projects in this sector are innovative pilot projects covering a small number of women in only one or two small areas of the countries. Normally, once these pilot projects are implemented successfully and prove their usefulness, the local governments are expected to take over and expand the project activities. Furthermore, women's projects rarely include the long-term services of international experts, which require considerable budgetary provisions. Rather, emphasis is on using available local expertise, and whenever this is not sufficient, priority is given to training women in the needed skills, either in their own country or abroad. Also, most of these projects do not need sophisticated, expensive equipment. Moreover, within comprehensive women's projects, UNFPA funding often covers only the population-related aspects of the project activities.

TYPES OF ACTIVITIES

UNFPA has assisted four broad types of projects for women: those commonly referred to as special women's projects to improve the status of women; components related to women in broader population/development projects; national machineries created for the integration of women in development efforts; and women's organizations/groups promoting education and training of women or providing services. Activities such as research and training constitute part of all the four major categories, and may be carried out at the national or community levels, or, in some cases, at regional or interregional levels.

Distribution by types

Most projects for women involve more than one activity. The categories discussed below are based on the most important component of the type of project reviewed.

Education and training. More than 40 per cent of UNFPA support for women's projects is for education and training. Training and skill development for women provide the occasions for giving information and advice on population-related issues in general, and on child care and family planning in particular. Training is provided either through national or regional seminars and conferences or as part of a comprehensive programme for women, including economic activities and skill development. Some projects include the training of trainers and a few employ academic educational and training programmes.

At the regional and global levels, training activities supported by UNFPA have included the United Nations/UNESCO Global Seminar on Women and the Media; a project for training women as managers of family planning and health delivery systems; and an international colloquium of experts on rural development, in which, for the first time, rural women from different parts of the world exchanged views with specialists on women's needs and on the means of improving their situation.

At the national level, UNFPA has supported training activities for family life education in Mali; the training of women in nutrition and child care in Senegal and in improving family life in Madagascar; the training of women as trainers for women's education in Morocco; the training of Muslim women and of university women in Indonesia; the training of women extension workers in Nepal and Sri Lanka; the organization of women's courses and councils in Solomon Islands; the national programme for the integration of women into development in Mexico; and the training of social workers in a family planning information project in Yugoslavia.

Research. Global and regional research projects have helped clarify conceptual issues and policy alternatives and have identified appropriate methodologies and research priorities at the country level. UNFPA has supported such projects as studies on the effects of demographic change on women; effects of women's employment on fertility; women as health-care providers; women's participation in agriculture; the interrelationship between the status of women and the practice of family planning; the impact of socio-economic changes on women in Sub-Saharan Africa; and in Latin America, the integration of women in development.

At the country level, most UNFPA-supported research projects have been operationally oriented, including such studies as women, family and social organization in integrated rural development in Bolivia; the role of women related to family planning programmes in the Republic of

Korea; women and population in Mali; attitudes and behaviour of rural people related to family planning in Portugal; rural women and demographic change in Sierra Leone; and rural fertility and women's economic activity in Bangladesh. The last two studies are part of an ILO-executed project on demographic change and women's role.

Action programmes. Action programmes aimed at women's groups account for many UNFPA activities in this sector. Some examples include projects to increase income-generation in Nepal (through cottage industry) and Sri Lanka; to increase the integration and participation of women in development in Egypt and the United Republic of Cameroon; to improve living conditions in an urban environment in Senegal; a Beyond Family Planning Programme for women in Indonesia; and the Programme for Better Family Living in Zambia.

UNFPA has supported many women's organizations at the local, national, regional, and interregional levels, helping them to mobilize women towards greater participation in the development process. Such organizations can also act as lobbying groups to bring pressure on policy-making bodies to recognize and respond to women's development-related needs. At the national and local level, UNFPA has supported Mothers' Clubs in Sri Lanka, the Women's General Union of the Syrian Arab Republic, and similar organizations in Nepal, Sri Lanka and countries of the South Pacific. UNFPA also helped the Union Nationale des Femmes du Mali to develop capacity within the country to conduct research on questions crucial to the development of a national population policy and to improve the condition of women.

At the regional level, UNFPA has assisted the African Women's Training and Research Centre in a co-operative effort to help Governments plan population communication programmes and participate in training courses; the Scientific Organization for Cultural and Development Studies on Arab Women; and the Pacific Women's Resource Centre. A UNFPA-funded project in Fiji—the Fourth Regional Conference of the South Pacific Branch of the Associated Country Women of the World— is an example of activities aimed at fostering technical co-operation among women in developing countries for research appropriate to the needs of women in the region and co-ordination of the activities of local women's groups, particularly in training.

At the interregional level, UNFPA-supported groups, in addition to those already mentioned, include the Associated Country Women of the World, the International Alliance of Women, the International Council of Women, the International Federation of University Women, and their regional affiliates. These groups received funding for semi-

nars, workshops, training programmes and action-oriented programmes at the international or regional levels, followed by similar
work conducted by local affiliates at the national or community level.
The latter activities often include action-oriented projects. All of these
activities share the objective of bringing about the full integration
of women into the population and development processes and
programmes.

Programming shifts

Although UNFPA supported women's programmes as early as 1970, its
support increased considerably following the World Population Conference in 1974 and the International Women's Year Conference in 1975. In
the early 1970s, the principal characteristic of UNFPA funding activities
was that of raising awareness among women, national authorities and
the international community of the importance of women's participation in the national population and development processes. The major
types of activities supported during this period were research, conferences and seminars aimed at identifying relationships among various
issues associated with the status of women and demographic factors.
Since 1975, UNFPA has expanded its commitment to data collection concerning the socio-economic position of women in the context of the society and within the family. UNFPA also increased its assistance to
projects that would help accelerate women's full participation and integration into national population and development processes.

Since 1975, there has also been a shift of emphasis from basic research
to action-oriented research as well as to comprehensive or "package"
concepts such as family life education or community-participation projects. Most of these projects deal with training, research and action
programmes directed at women, as well as organizational support. Assistance to IEC programmes designed for women also increased as did
support to organizations.

Research findings have found their way into programme planning
and project formulation. For example, greater awareness of the relationship between the practice of child spacing and women's educational
levels as well as their economically productive activities may have contributed to the increase in requests for assistance to training and to comprehensive projects for improving the situation of women. In recent
years, the usefulness of indirect approaches to family planning through
women's projects dealing with training, communication, information
and action (socio-economic) projects has become widely acknowledged.

In recent years, UNFPA has increased its assistance to country-level
women's projects rather than to regional and interregional projects.

Some of these projects, such as national seminars, are follow-ups to activities at regional and interregional levels. Another example is training programmes for local women, which are follow-ups to regional training programmes. A majority of these country-specific projects have taken place in countries in which needs assessment missions have been conducted. The recent concentration of efforts at the country and community level reflects the thinking in the field that development is not only a goal but a process requiring the participation of all the people—rural and urban, women and men—in population and development activities.

The focus on local development in UNFPA-funded programmes is an important parallel to the efforts at the national level to involve women in official decision-making positions in all sectors and levels of population and development planning and programme operations.

In many countries, women's groups have created excellent networks for discussion and dissemination of information, including information on family planning, generating a demand for delivery of modern methods of family planning, organizing income-generating activities, and other means of involving women in self-help programmes.

Women leaders who are part of the growing network of competent professional and political groups concerned with improving the quality of life for all are needed in national deliberations on plans for development. To this end, UNFPA has brought women leaders together in seminars where they can share and benefit from their experiences and participation in public affairs. Two regional seminars for such women have been conducted thus far, one for the Middle East and the other for the Caribbean, and similar seminars are planned for other regions.

The first seminar, Women, Family and Development, was held in Tunis in October 1983 at the invitation of the Tunisian National Women's Union, in co-operation with UNFPA. This seminar was attended by Arab and Islamic delegations from 15 countries representing several governmental and non-governmental organizations, as well as representatives of international and regional Arab organizations. Seminar discussions concentrated on the changing roles of women and men within the family and the society. The participants identified issues requiring special attention and action, including upgrading maternal and child health care, basic health services, educational and employment opportunities; intensifying the efforts of Governments and non-governmental women's organizations to enhance women's capabilities for participating in planning and implementing national population and development strategies; improving co-operation among private, regional and international agencies to strengthen their roles in promoting the status of women; and increasing the budgetary resources of Governments and of international organizations for the support of programmes addressing women, population and development.

The second gathering, A Seminar for Women Leaders: Population and Development in the English-speaking Caribbean, was held in November 1983. Sponsored by the Government of Saint Christopher and Nevis, it was attended by first ladies, ministers of Governments and members of parliaments in the English-speaking Caribbean and representatives of international and regional organizations working in population, health, family planning and women's affairs. The main objective of the Seminar was to review and to reinforce the provisions of the 1974 World Population Plan of Action with respect to the roles and status of women, family planning, family life education and the family, population and development. Participants discussed these issues within the context of the Caribbean islands' specific needs and priorities. The Seminar identified the need for recognizing the significant role of the family as the primary social unit that can influence the participation of men and women in other social institutions. Recommending that new approaches be developed for providing family planning information and services for various age groups, the Seminar underscored the importance of women's participation in all aspects of such programmes. Increasing educational and training facilities for young women in and out of school and reviewing the existing laws and legislation pertaining to women were among the Seminar's other recommendations.

Both of these seminars for women leaders recognized the importance of the presence of women in national delegations to international conferences focusing on population issues. Within this context, Governments were urged to ensure the inclusion of knowledgeable and concerned women in national delegations to the International Conference on Population.

In planning and carrying out its many activities involving women's groups, UNFPA has benefited from close working relationships and collaboration with all the organizations and agencies of the United Nations at regional and global levels. In addition, some of the projects supported by the UNFPA at national and regional levels have been implemented by the specialized agencies of the United Nations. Also, frequent and systematic consultations and co-operation on technical issues have been conducted with all those agencies as well as with the United Nations Centre for Social Development and Humanitarian Affairs in Vienna. At present, UNFPA is participating in the development of a methodology for a United Nations Interorganizational Evaluation Study on Women in Development. This study, to be carried out in

Democratic Yemen, Haiti, Indonesia and Rwanda, will cover each participating agency's programme support in each of the four countries.
The purpose is to identify the extent and the nature of women's participation in, and benefits from, each of the projects supported by various
agencies, irrespective of whether the original project objectives directly
addressed women.

In addition to the programmes described above, UNFPA has sponsored several publications that have focused attention on the central
role of women in population and development concerns. One such
publication, *Message from the Village* by Perdita Huston, explored the
thoughts of women from developing countries on how population concerns have affected their own lives and the prospects for their children.
Other monographs, such as *The Triple Struggle* by Audrey Bronstein and
the *Sisterhood of Man* by Kathleen Newland, have examined the various
socio-economic and cultural barriers that have kept women from enjoy-
ing an equal share in the progress that has accompanied development.
Through these studies and through articles and features in its regular
publications, the Fund has brought the issue of women, population and
development to a wide variety of audiences.

FUTURE DIRECTIONS

The reports on UNFPA-supported activities, the careful monitoring and
evaluation of some projects and the discussions with national authorities overseeing those activities—all have indicated progress in enhancing the participation of women in national population and development
activities. Women have begun to redefine their roles and responsibilities
within the family and the community. They have recognized the need to
control their own lives and to participate in the decision-making processes affecting their lives as well as those of their family members. Governments have become increasingly aware that, to meet the goals of
their national population and development policies and programmes,
consideration of women's situation should go beyond a few social-
welfare-type programmes.

The success of programme activities aimed directly at improving the
status of women and at influencing women's reproductive behaviour
through improving their health (as well as reducing the infant mortality
rates) has been documented at the project level and at national meetings. It has also been discussed and acknowledged at some international gatherings. At the International Conference on Family Planning
in the 80's, held in Jakarta, Indonesia, in 1981, it was indicated that the

success of such comprehensive women's programmes has resulted in changes in some Governments' policies and strategies for influencing the population growth rates.

To ascertain the actual effects and impact of UNFPA policies and practices for including women in all aspects of population and development efforts, systematic monitoring of the performance of the supported activities is needed.

UNFPA is alert to the concerns that the continuation of support to women's projects may run the risk of creating a wider separation of women from the mainstream of population and development programmes. Nevertheless, the Fund maintains that, for a time, it is necessary to provide special assistance to help redress the past inequalities and to ensure that women's issues are specifically incorporated into all facets of UNFPA programme support. Such efforts will help women to determine for themselves their roles within the family and the community, and the extent of their participation in national population and development-related activities.

Despite the evident increase in the number of proponents and the amount of rhetoric in favour of the integration of women into population and development, different interpretations of "development" as well as "integration" probably will continue. The deterioration of the international economy along with the resurgence of some religious and other traditional prejudices against women will also have to be taken into account in thinking about future programming. To bridge the gap between the awareness and the achievement of the goal of integration of women as equal partners with men in the development process, more attention will need to be given both to what has to be done and to how it should be pursued.

Knowledge of what has been learned and an analysis of how the various programme approaches have worked will contribute to future work. In the conduct of the 1984 International Conference on Population and the 1985 World Conference to Review and Appraise the Achievements of the United Nations Decade for Women, the discussions should shift from concern with ascertaining the situation of women to concern with identifying how the situation of women has changed since previous conferences and how the activities have contributed to this change.

To further the process of integration, basic research is needed so that the complex principles and interrelationships affecting the condition and roles of women in society can be investigated systematically. More policy-oriented country-specific research is also needed on the current condition of women and its impact on fertility; applied studies directed towards remedial measures will also be needed. Support to such activities will continue as will support for developing methods to facilitate monitoring the progress of activities addressed to women's roles in population and development matters.

Another area for future programme emphasis is that of disseminating research and project findings in ways that will attract the attention of policy makers, such as showing the cost-benefit advantages when women are involved as equal partners in population and development programmes.

The UNFPA policy to ensure full participation of women at all levels and stages of population-related activities is backed up by a commitment at the highest level of administration as well as staff, and by the funds made available to this end. The full integration of women as equal partners in population and development processes has to take place within the context of each country's national population and development policies, strategies and good will. Governments and non-governmental as well as public and private agencies should strive to ensure that women are not isolated from major population and development efforts. The true measure of commitment to national policies promoting women's integration will be the extent of the financial and human resources devoted to this task.

Part Three

Conclusions

12. The Programming Outlook

The preceding chapters have attempted to convey some idea of how UNFPA has assisted Governments in delineating their policies and implementing programmes essential for the achievement of their population and development objectives. UNFPA financing of advisory services, training, action programmes and research in all areas of population has often been the catalyst in helping countries move closer to national self-reliance in this field. To date, UNFPA has supported more than 3,500 projects in almost all countries and territories of the developing world, thus attesting to the broad acceptability of multilateral funding in the field of population. A look at the record of the past 15 years shows that notable inroads have been made on several fronts. Many countries have come to realize that addressing population concerns is one of the surest ways of improving the overall well-being of their people. Progress has been made in reducing both fertility and mortality rates; indeed, in a number of developing countries the declines in mortality have been considerable, so that, despite reductions in fertility, overall growth rates have not significantly decreased. International organizations, NGOs and donor and recipient countries—all have acquired considerable knowledge of how to work in the population sector.

One of the objectives in undertaking this review of the Fund's programming experience was to draw on the considerable knowledge that has been accumulated as a point of departure for future activities. Population is no longer an uncharted sector, and UNFPA seeks to utilize what is already known and adapt it to present and future circumstances. In putting together its agenda for the future, UNFPA has examined the population sector from three perspectives: the regional, the substantive and the operational.

REGIONAL PERSPECTIVES

Progress on the population front has not been uniform either across or within regions. In view of the considerable differences that still exist, the Fund is convinced that greater efforts will have to be made to gauge needs accurately and to respond appropriately. Some countries—for example, those in East and South-East Asia and in Latin America—may require simply a modicum of technical assistance, whereas others will require extensive funding for a broad range of activities.

Sub-Saharan Africa will need considerable and sustained international assistance for the coming two decades if gains are to be made on the population front. All aspects of the population question will have to be addressed—how to lower fertility and mortality levels; how to deal with high rates of urbanization, large-scale internal and international migration and the influx of refugees; how to manage the environmental consequences of rapid population growth; and how to provide for the basic needs—food, shelter, health and education—of a population that is expected to grow by more than 380 million people during the next 20 years. Africa still needs to build up a corps of professionals in the fields of demography and family planning, and thus assistance for training will have to continue for some time.

In the region stretching from North Africa to South Asia, most countries will need fairly intensive population assistance during the coming years. Although some of these countries have a long history of family planning programmes—for example, Egypt, India, Nepal and Pakistan —the progress made in reducing fertility has not been commensurate with expectations, given the length of time that the programmes have been in operation and the level of support from Governments and external sources. In other countries—for example, Burma and Viet Nam— the interest in population matters is just beginning to coalesce, and hence sizeable external assistance will be necessary in the years to come.

Many countries in all regions have now instituted family planning as part of maternal and child health care and need considerable assistance to meet the demand for services.

Several countries have built up institutional capacities in the population field, and thus greater use must be made of technical co-operation among developing countries. The population sector, on the whole, is especially amenable to this strategy because, despite the barriers that have come down, some of the sensitivity regarding population lingers. Countries are often more inclined to draw on the expertise and experience of other developing countries that, only recently, were in circumstances similar to their own. The attractiveness and suitability of the TCDC approach are readily recognized; what is needed is a better understanding of this concept and a more active promotion of its application. The Fund is committed to more extensive use of TCDC in its programming in all regions.

SUBSTANTIVE PERSPECTIVES

Among the substantive directions for the Fund's future programming in the geographical regions and in the specific population activities, cer-

tainly one of the most urgent concerns is the developing world's unmet
need for family planning, which, in the early 1980s, stood at about 500
million couples who did not wish any more children but did not have
access to family planning. In view of the health benefits of family planning and child spacing to women and their families, as well as the demographic impact, efforts will have to be redoubled to provide easily
accessible, affordable services in keeping with prevailing socio-cultural
norms and the preferences of potential users. Greater emphasis will
have to be given to the use of demographic data in development planning. Incorporating such information into macro-level planning is essential if adequate attention is to be given to sectors and issues such as
health, education, employment, urbanization and the status of women,
particularly their educational opportunities and employment prospects
—all of which have both direct and indirect effects on population. The
strengthening of management aspects of population programmes constitutes another priority for the coming years. Management capabilities
are crucial if developing countries are to become self-reliant in population matters.

OPERATIONAL PERSPECTIVES

To increase the efficiency of investment in population, international
organizations, donors and recipient countries must address a range of
operational issues.

Because the pool of available resources is limited, international organizations and bilateral donors must grapple with the question of where to
channel their monies. Generally, putting a small amount of additional
resources into countries on the verge of self-reliance is likely to have a
greater return than investing the same amount or even larger sums in
countries at the other end of the scale. Yet, convincing arguments can be
made about the greater needs of countries that are just starting population activities and thus have a more valid claim to the scarce resources
available. Often, however, countries that critically need population assistance do not have the infrastructure to absorb large infusions of aid.
Thus the trade-offs must be assessed and efforts made to balance the
deployment of assistance in light of such competing factors as the magnitude of needs and acceptable rates of return. In allocating assistance,
donors must also realize that a certain critical mass of assistance must
be extended if a particular activity is to have reasonable prospects of
success.

To map out a strategy for the coming years, it must be acknowledged
that the technical co-operation requirements of developing countries

are changing considerably. Many no longer need, and are no longer willing to pay for, costly foreign experts. It will be necessary to devise a system whereby countries can draw on local resources but still have access to international expertise. Greater use of short-term consultants and United Nations volunteers seems to be a viable option. UNFPA has also observed that an increasing number of countries are interested in executing their population projects directly. When a country elects to use this modality, the Fund facilitates arrangements for technical back-up either with a United Nations agency or a qualified NGO.

Donors should make some attempt to lessen the burdens that external assistance places on recipient countries. In the population sector alone, countries in which several donors are active often have to commit a sizeable portion of staff time just to handle the paperwork required by each funder. A carefully designed division of labour among donors, and even something as simple as a certain standardization of reporting procedures, could lead to greater efficiency.

Recipient countries, too, must address operational concerns. Governments should recognize that it is their responsibility to co-ordinate external assistance in order to ensure that such aid is utilized efficiently and effectively and that it furthers their development objectives. Governments should be selective with regard to external support and should accept assistance only for those projects that are in keeping with their own priorities. If countries lack such a co-ordinating capacity, then donor groups would be well advised to build up this capability for it is an essential element in the achievement of national self-reliance.

A Government's commitment of sufficient resources to an externally funded project is a key determinant of the efficiency of population assistance. Without strong government backing, the prospects for a satisfactory outcome are dim. Efforts should also be made to ascertain that priorities in other sectors mesh with population objectives. Compatibility between development projects in health, education and employment enhances the impact of investments made in each of these areas and in the population sector.

Both donors and recipient Governments will have to address the question of availability of resources. UNFPA is optimistic that donors, seeing what has been accomplished with relatively small amounts of population assistance, will increase their commitment to this sector. Seed money for activities has often encouraged Governments to commit a considerable amount of their own resources to projects. With or without additional resources, it is nevertheless incumbent on all those involved in financing population activities to explore new approaches that will make the most and best use of the monies available. More extensive collaboration with the private sector and greater use of NGOs are two possible alternatives. Such groups often have capabilities that are not found in the public sector. Moreover, they are usually less encumbered by administrative and political concerns. Also, NGOs in developing countries are closer to the grass roots and thus could be instrumental in furthering community level initiatives. Certainly, the time has come to assess how multilateral assistance could join forces with the private sector to work for the benefit of developing countries. Moreover, the possibility of setting up public corporations—entities run along the lines of commercial establishments but operated in the public interest—should be explored.

An operational issue of particular concern to UNFPA is how to increase the efficiency of United Nations channels for delivering assistance in the population sector. Population assistance from multilateral channels is especially attractive to Governments in developing countries because it comes free of political and ideological intent. Moreover, in rendering assistance, the United Nations system is in a unique position both because of its internal technical competence in the population field and its ability to enlist expertise from all over the world.

Within the United Nations, efforts are now being made to increase co-ordination in the population field. UNFPA meets periodically with other funding organizations whose activities are related to population — WHO, UNICEF, UNDP and the World Food Programme—to explore avenues for co-operation. UNFPA and the World Bank also consult regularly and often finance complementary components of country programmes. Without doubt, better co-ordination within the United Nations and a systematic division of labour between various multilateral and bilateral donors, coupled with a strong co-ordinating unit on the government side, would promote more efficient and effective utilization of resources.

When UNFPA and the countries it serves draw up a programme agenda for the future, these various regional, substantive and operational considerations will figure prominently. The Fund, in working with Governments, will seek to reconcile these priorities with existing needs and prevailing conditions in countries. From its own institutional perspective, the Fund will continue to assess its programming policies and procedures periodically so that it can respond appropriately to changing demands. As it contemplates the programming horizon, UNFPA is confident that the principles that have enabled it to work effectively in the past—its neutrality, flexibility and readiness to innovate—will be equally valid operational premises for the future.

Appendix 1
UNFPA Publications and
Audio-Visual Aids

UNFPA Publications

Annual Review of Population Law

A compendium surveying national, regional and international developments directly or indirectly affecting population issues. Coverage includes international agreements, constitutional provisions, legislation, regulations, judicial decisions and legal pronouncements.

The Arab World and Population

Brief summaries of regional programmes, country by country, in the Arab countries of the Middle East and the Mediterranean. Issued in 1979 in English; 79 pages. Also available in Arabic.

A Bibliography of United Nations Publications on Population

Publications in print in the field of population produced by the United Nations, the specialized agencies and other bodies of the United Nations system. English, French and Spanish titles are listed.

Commitment

A bimonthly news-sheet distributed among members of parliaments and parliamentary aides interested in population and development. First issued in 1978. French and Spanish as well as English.

Needs Assessment Reports

A series of reports on the results of missions to identify the requirements for assistance in individual countries to help them achieve self-reliance in formulating and implementing population policies and programmes.

Policy Development Studies

A series, co-ordinated by the Policy and Evaluation Division of UNFPA, covering a broad spectrum of population policy issues. Studies are in the form of monographs, short essays or reports of *ad hoc* technical meetings. No. 1, *On Integration of Family Planning with Rural Development* (1979); No. 2, *Population Redistribution: Patterns, Policies and Prospects,* ed. L. A. Peter Gosling and Linda Yuen Ching Lim (1979); No. 3, *Population Growth and Food Problems in Selected Asian Countries,* by Koichi Lio, Toshiki Hirooka and Susumu Kato (1979); No. 4, *The Role of Incentives in Family Planning Programmes* (1980); No. 5, *Organizational Determinants of Family Planning Clinic Performance* (1980); No. 6, *Population and Development Modelling* (1980); No. 7, *International Perspectives on Aging: Population and Policy Challenges,* ed. Robert H. Binstock, Wing-Sun Chow and James H. Shulz (1982); and No. 8, *Population and Conflict: New Dimensions of Population Dynamics,* by Nazli Choucri (1983).

Population: UNFPA Newsletter

A monthly newsletter about UNFPA and the latest developments in the population field. First issued in 1974. Arabic, French and Spanish as well as English; bimonthly in Chinese.

Population Facts at Hand

Information about population and UNFPA in a format of 143 colour-coded 4-by-6-inch cards in a flip-box.

Population Policy Compendium

Presents country-by-country information on population policy for the Member States of the United Nations and its specialized agencies. A joint United Nations-UNFPA project.

Population Profiles

A series of monographs summarizing the population situation in a given country or providing an overview of a population-related topic.

Population Programmes and Projects, 2 vols.

Volume 1: *Guide to Sources of International Population Assistance.* General information about assistance organizations and about fields in which assistance can be provided. First issued in 1976; issued every three years; occasional supplements. French and Spanish as well as English. Volume 2: *Inventory of Population Projects in Developing Countries Around the World.* Population programmes and projects that organizations and agencies are funding or executing in 135 developing countries and territories. First issued in 1973/74; issued annually.

Populi

The quarterly journal of UNFPA, reaching an audience with special interests in population issues. First issued in 1974; quarterly in English, twice yearly in Arabic.

The State of World Population

A report by the Executive Director of UNFPA on major population questions. Issued annually as a press-kit; accompanying features, charts, diagrams and photographs. Arabic, French and Spanish as well as English.

UNFPA Annual Report

A summary of UNFPA activities in the year and of plans and future programmes. First published in 1972 (covering 1969–1972); annually since 1973. Arabic, French and Spanish as well as English.

UNFPA Information Pack — *UNFPA: What It Is, What It Does*

A brief summary of the world population situation and the role, structure and operations of UNFPA; includes leaflets, charts, maps and diagrams.

UNFPA Library Acquisitions List

A list of selected additions to the UNFPA Library, each entry containing original UNFPA Library bibliographic descriptions and subject analysis. Published irregularly; computer-produced format.

UNFPA Project Publications: ABSTRACTS

Bibliographic descriptions of final reports and publications of UNFPA projects. Computerized services available from the ABSTRACTS data base are on-line searches, specialized bibliographies printed from these searches and computer-tape copies of the data base. Four issues yearly. Published by the UNFPA Library.

Major policy statements and speeches delivered by the Executive Director are published from time to time.

Selected UNFPA-sponsored publications

The books listed below were published by external publishers, with UNFPA support.

Brown, Lester R. *The Twenty-ninth Day: Accommodating Needs and Numbers to the Earth's Resources.* London and New York, W. W. Norton and Co., 1974. A Worldwatch Institute book.

Consequences of exponential growth for development prospects.

_____.*Building a Sustainable Society.* London and New York, W. W. Norton, 1981. A Worldwatch Institute book.

Survey of environmental, social and economic issues facing the world at the beginning of the 1980s.

Hauser, Philip M., ed. *World Population and Development: Challenges and Prospects.* New York, Syracuse University Press, Syracuse, New York 13210, U.S.A., 1979. xxii + 683 pages (including epilogue and index).

Seventeen chapters by international experts address the world's current population growth and economic development from theoretical and policy-making perspectives.

Huston, Perdita. *Message from the Village.* New York, The Epoch B. Foundation, P.O. Box 1972, Grand Central Station, New York, N.Y. 10017, U.S.A., 1978. xvii + 142 pages.

Attitudes about population and development expressed by a sampling of women in 130 villages in three continents.

Moraes, Dom. *A Matter of People.* New York, Praeger, 1974.

Observations and interviews on population, prepared for World Population Year.

_____, ed. *Voices for Life.* New York, Praeger, 1974.

Essays on the human condition published for World Population Year.

Omran, Abdel-Rahim. *Population in the Arab World: Problems and Prospects.* London, Croom Helm Ltd., 2-10 St. John's Road, London SW 11, U.K., 1980. xxii + 215 pages (including selected references, index and index of personal names).

Reviews population problems of the Arab world in a historical and global context.

Population and the Urban Future. New York, State University of New York, State University Plaza, Albany, New York 12246, U.S.A., 1982. x + 187 pages.

In September 1980 UNFPA sponsored the International Conference on Population and the Urban Future in Rome, Italy. Volume contains edited versions of the three background documents prepared for the Conference and the Rome Declaration, adopted at the Conference.

Salas, Rafael M. *People: An International Choice: The Multilateral Approach to Population.* U.K., Pergamon Press Ltd., Headington Hill Hall, Oxford OX3 OBW, U.K., 1976; U.S.A., Pergamon Press Inc., Maxwell House, Fairview Park, Elmsford, New York 10523, U.S.A., 1976. English version, xv + 154 pages (including appendix and indexes). Also printed in Arabic, Chinese, French, Japanese, Russian and Spanish.

History of the establishment and operations of UNFPA by the Executive Director of UNFPA.

Salas, Rafael M. *International Population Assistance: The First Decade. A Look at the Concepts and Policies Which Have Guided the UNFPA in Its First Ten Years.* U.K., Pergamon Press Ltd., Headington Hill Hall, Oxford OX3 OBW, U.K.; U.S.A., Pergamon Press Inc., Maxwell House, Fairview Park, Elmsford, New York 10523, U.S.A., 1979. English version, xxvii + 456 pages (including 6 appendices, index). Japanese version, published by Population Study Center, Nihon University, 2-3-1 Misakicho, Chiyoda-ku, Tokyo, Japan. 1980. xvi + 396 pages. Also printed in Arabic, French, and Spanish.

Principles and policies of the Fund since its establishment in 1969.

Salas, Rafael M. *Reflections on Population.* Scheduled for publication in July 1984 by Pergamon Press.

Survey of the accomplishments of the last 10 years and the implications of present population policies and programmes for the future, particularly in the context of the International Conference on Population.

The United Nations Population Division has published, with UNFPA support, a variety of monographs, reports, bulletins, manuals etc.

The Worldwatch Institute has published, with UNFPA support, 64 books and monographs in its eight-year history.

UNFPA-sponsored films and audio-visual aids

1975

The Problem of Problems. 20 minutes.

Presents a picture of UNFPA-supported activities around the world.

1978

Maragoli. Producer: Extension Media Centre, University of California. 16 mm colour and sound, 58 minutes.

Explores the interlocking problems of high fertility, food shortages, land scarcity, education, employment and migration in Maragoli, western Kenya, one of the world's most densely populated rural areas.

1979

Egypt: Commitment to Change. Producer: Craven Films, New York. 16 mm colour and sound, 28 minutes.

Contrasts old ways in Egypt with the challenges of new ideas. In English and Arabic.

Sri Lanka: Past, Present, People. Producer: Craven Films, New York. 16 mm Eastman colour and sound, 37 minutes; 16 mm (35 mm for television and theatre presentation), colour and sound, 22 minutes.

Examines how Sri Lanka is dealing with the pressing demands of population and development. In English and Sinhalese.

UNFPA: What It Is, What It Does. Producer: Craven Films, New York. 16 mm Eastman colour and sound, 15 minutes.

Discusses population problems in relation to development and illustrates UNFPA support for maternal and child health, communication and education and data collection as well as family planning.

1980

China: The One-Child Family. Producer: Barbara Pyle. 25 minutes.

A television report for Turner Broadcasting System, Atlanta, Georgia, U.S.A.

The Human City. Producers: Hans Samsom and Laura Samsom-Rous. Multimedia presentation; colour slides with synchronized sound, three screens; 22 minutes.

Shows population pressures on cities. Shifting images are reinforced by electronic music and specially recorded sound effects.

People: A Matter of Balance. Producer: Vision Habitat, Vancouver, Canada. 16 mm colour and sound, 28 minutes.

Based on the work of the late Italian director Roberto Rossellini, *People: A Matter of Balance* was awarded the 1980 Grand Prix at the Ekofilm film festival in Czechoslovakia. Photographed in Africa and the Amazon Basin, the documentary deals with the alienation of human beings from their environment.

1981

The Finite World. Producer: In co-operation with UNFPA, Barbara Pyle, Turner Broadcasting System, Atlanta, Georgia, U.S.A.

The population programmes of 10 countries and territories.

Global Report. Producer: Peter Armstrong.

A BBC documentary reporting on the year 1981 from the perspectives of three developing countries.

The People Count: Taking the Census for the 1980s in Sri Lanka. Producer: Craven Films, New York. 16 mm colour and sound, 17½ minutes.

Follows the census-taking process from preparatory stage to actual contact work by census takers, the rechecking of data and the publication of the first report; also shows how different arms of the Government will use the information collected.

World Population. Producer: Tony Hueller, Video-77 Vision. Videotape colour and sound, 28 minutes.

Ambassadors to the United Nations exchange views on population issues; moderated by Michael Littlejohns, Chief of Reuters United Nations Bureau.

1982

The Fragile Mountain. Producer: Sandra Nichols. 16 mm colour and sound, 55 minutes.

A film on the Himalayan environmental crisis.

1983

Population: The UNFPA Experience.
   A video presentation for television and general distribution.

Appendix 2
Selected Demographic Indicators
By Region and Country

APPENDIX TWO

SELECTED DEMOGRAPHIC INDICATORS BY REGION AND COUNTRY

REGION, COUNTRY OR AREA	TOTAL POPULATION (000S)		RATE OF GROWTH		CRUDE BIRTH RATE	TOTAL FERT. RATE 1980-85	CRUDE DEATH RATE 1980-85	INFANT MORT. RATE	EXPECTATION OF LIFE AT BIRTH 1980-85	
	1984	2000	1980-85	1995-00					MALE	FEMALE
1 WORLD TOTAL	4763004	6127117	1.67	1.52	27.3	3.55	10.6	81	57.5	60.3
2 MORE DEVELOPED REGIONS (*)	1165611	1279655	0.64	0.52	15.5	1.98	9.6	17	69.4	76.9
3 LESS DEVELOPED REGIONS (+)	3597393	4851462	2.02	1.79	31.2	4.09	11.0	92	55.5	57.7
4 A. AFRICA	536685	877439	3.01	3.05	46.4	6.43	16.5	114	48.2	51.3
5 1. EASTERN AFRICA (1)	155447	266238	3.23	3.39	49.1	6.79	17.0	110	47.2	56.5
6 BURUNDI	4503	6951	2.67	2.67	47.6	6.44	20.9	137	42.4	45.6
7 COMOROS	443	715	3.04	2.84	46.3	6.29	15.9	68	46.3	51.7
8 ETHIOPIA	35420	58407	2.60	3.07	49.2	6.70	21.5	143	41.3	44.5
9 KENYA	19761	38534	4.12	4.11	55.1	8.12	14.0	82	51.2	54.7
10 MADAGASCAR	9731	15552	2.80	2.97	44.4	6.09	16.5	67	46.9	50.4
11 MALAWI	6788	11669	3.23	3.40	52.1	7.00	19.9	165	43.4	46.6
12 MAURITIUS (2)	1031	1298	1.90	1.19	25.5	2.76	6.0	32	64.3	69.2
13 MOZAMBIQUE	13693	21779	3.05	2.94	44.1	6.09	16.5	110	47.8	51.1
14 REUNION	555	685	1.40	1.18	20.5	2.23	6.5	19	64.6	68.2
15 RWANDA	5903	10565	3.46	3.66	51.1	7.30	16.6	110	47.8	51.2
16 SOMALIA	5423	7079	3.71	2.54	46.5	6.09	21.3	143	41.3	44.5
17 UGANDA	15150	26774	3.50	3.51	49.9	6.90	14.7	94	50.3	53.8
18 UNITED REP. OF TANZANIA	21710	39129	3.52	3.71	50.4	7.10	15.3	98	49.3	52.7
19 ZAMBIA	6445	11237	3.31	3.52	48.1	6.76	15.1	101	49.6	53.1
20 ZIMBABWE	8461	15132	3.50	3.65	47.2	6.60	12.3	70	53.5	57.9

		60819	96072	2.70	2.92	44.8	6.03	17.9	120	45.9	49.2
21	2. MIDDLE AFRICA (3)										
22	ANGOLA	8540	13234	2.51	2.82	47.3	6.39	22.2	149	40.4	43.0
23	CENTRAL AFRICAN REPUBLIC	2508	3736	2.29	2.57	44.7	5.89	21.8	143	41.4	44.6
24	CHAD	4901	7304	2.28	2.56	44.2	5.89	21.4	143	41.4	44.6
25	CONGO	1695	2646	2.59	2.85	44.5	5.99	18.6	124	45.0	48.1
26	EQUATORIAL GUINEA	383	559	2.15	2.41	42.5	5.66	21.0	137	42.4	45.6
27	GABON	1146	1611	1.64	2.42	34.6	4.67	18.1	112	47.4	50.7
28	UNITED REP. OF CAMEROON	9467	14424	2.54	2.66	43.2	5.78	17.8	117	46.4	49.7
29	ZAIRE	32084	52410	2.94	3.12	45.2	6.09	15.8	107	48.3	51.7
30	3. NORTHERN AFRICA (4)	121386	185671	2.88	2.45	41.9	6.01	12.9	106	54.6	57.0
31	ALGERIA	21272	35194	3.28	2.86	45.1	6.97	12.3	109	56.9	58.8
32	EGYPT	45200	65200	2.52	2.02	38.4	5.23	12.5	113	56.4	56.2
33	LIBYAN ARAB JAMAHIRIYA	3471	6072	3.84	3.27	45.6	7.18	10.9	92	58.4	59.5
34	MOROCCO	22848	36325	3.26	2.63	44.0	6.44	11.5	99	56.4	59.0
35	SUDAN	20945	32926	2.86	2.74	45.9	6.59	17.4	118	46.0	49.0
36	TUNISIA	7042	9725	2.40	1.73	34.1	4.92	10.1	85	60.1	61.1
37	4. SOUTHERN AFRICA	36246	54456	2.53	2.48	39.6	5.21	14.2	94	51.3	54.7
38	BOTSWANA	1042	1865	3.45	3.68	50.0	6.50	12.7	79	52.8	56.2
39	LESOTHO	1481	2251	2.53	2.65	41.7	5.78	16.4	110	47.7	51.0
40	NAMIBIA	1507	2382	2.78	2.86	45.1	6.09	17.3	115	47.0	49.5
41	SOUTH AFRICA	31586	40916	2.48	2.40	38.7	5.07	15.9	92	51.8	55.2
42	SWAZILAND	630	1041	3.03	3.16	47.5	6.50	17.2	129	45.3	51.9
43	5. WESTERN AFRICA (5)	162787	275002	3.11	3.31	49.3	6.86	18.5	123	45.2	48.5
44	BENIN	3890	6381	2.86	3.16	51.0	7.00	22.5	149	40.9	44.1
45	CAPE VERDE	317	382	1.36	1.00	23.9	2.64	10.3	77	55.4	58.0
46	GAMBIA	630	896	1.94	2.31	48.4	6.39	29.0	193	33.5	36.5
47	GHANA	13044	21923	3.25	3.16	47.0	6.50	14.0	98	50.3	53.7
48	GUINEA	5301	7935	2.33	2.57	46.8	6.19	23.5	159	38.7	41.8
49	GUINEA-BISSAU	875	1241	1.91	2.32	40.7	5.38	21.7	143	41.4	44.6
50	IVORY COAST	9474	15581	3.44	3.01	46.0	6.70	16.0	122	45.4	48.7
51	LIBERIA	2123	3564	3.16	3.27	48.7	6.90	17.2	112	47.4	50.7
52	MALI	7825	12365	2.76	2.84	50.2	6.70	22.4	149	40.4	43.0
53	MAURITANIA	1832	2999	2.93	3.08	50.1	6.90	20.9	137	42.4	45.6

	REGION, COUNTRY OR AREA	TOTAL POPULATION (000S)		RATE OF GROWTH		CRUDE BIRTH RATE	TOTAL FERT. RATE	CRUDE DEATH RATE	INFANT MORT. RATE	EXPECTATION OF LIFE AT BIRTH 1980-85	
		1984	2000	1980-85	1995-00		1980-85	1980-85		MALE	FEMALE
54	NIGER	5940	9750	2.82	3.19	51.0	7.10	22.9	146	40.9	44.1
55	NIGERIA	92037	161930	3.34	3.57	50.4	7.10	17.1	114	40.9	50.2
56	SENEGAL	6352	10036	2.66	2.94	47.7	6.50	21.2	141	41.7	44.9
57	SIERRA LEONE	3536	4868	1.77	2.09	47.4	6.13	29.7	200	32.5	35.5
58	TOGO	2836	4599	2.86	3.05	45.4	6.09	16.9	113	47.0	50.5
59	UPPER VOLTA	6768	10542	2.34	2.84	47.8	6.50	22.2	149	40.4	43.6
60	B. AMERICAS	658258	847654	1.73	1.46	25.4	3.16	8.6	50	63.9	69.4
61	B1.LATIN AMERICA	397138	549971	2.30	1.85	31.8	4.12	8.2	63	61.8	66.5
62	6. CARIBBEAN	31364	40833	1.51	1.60	27.1	3.36	8.4	58	62.1	66.1
63	BARBADOS	262	307	0.82	0.97	19.9	2.23	8.6	23	68.9	74.5
64	CUBA	9966	11718	0.62	0.99	16.9	1.98	6.4	20	71.8	75.2
65	DOMINICAN REPUBLIC	6101	8407	2.32	1.75	33.1	4.18	8.0	64	60.7	64.6
66	GUADELOUPE	319	338	0.12	0.47	19.5	2.55	7.3	23	67.8	73.2
67	HAITI	6419	9860	2.51	2.74	41.3	5.74	14.2	108	51.2	54.4
68	JAMAICA	2290	2849	1.36	1.25	28.3	3.38	6.7	28	68.1	72.6
69	MARTINIQUE	312	338	0.02	0.72	18.8	2.35	7.6	20	68.4	73.5
70	PUERTO RICO	3404	4212	1.55	1.18	22.4	2.62	6.9	17	70.6	77.4
71	TRINIDAD AND TOBAGO	1105	1321	0.92	1.05	24.6	2.90	6.2	28	67.8	72.6
72	WINDWARD ISLANDS (6)	419	524	1.20	1.44	30.4	3.57	6.2	32	66.8	71.4
73	OTHER CARIBBEAN (7)	769	959	1.34	1.33	24.8	2.87	6.1	26	68.5	72.9
74	7. CENTRAL AMERICA (8)	102811	149557	2.68	2.14	35.1	4.76	7.4	57	62.9	67.1
75	COSTA RICA	2534	3596	2.64	1.89	30.5	3.50	4.2	20	70.5	75.7
76	EL SALVADOR	5388	8708	2.93	2.90	40.2	5.56	8.1	71	62.6	67.1
77	GUATEMALA	8165	12739	2.92	2.74	38.4	5.17	9.3	66	59.7	61.8
78	HONDURAS	4232	6978	3.39	3.18	43.9	6.50	10.1	82	58.2	61.7
79	MEXICO	77040	109180	2.59	1.92	33.9	4.61	7.1	53	63.5	68.1
80	NICARAGUA	3162	5261	3.32	2.95	44.2	5.94	9.7	85	58.7	61.0
81	PANAMA	2134	2893	2.17	1.69	28.0	3.46	5.4	26	69.2	72.9
82	8.TEMPERATE S. AMERICA (9)	44964	55496	1.55	1.17	24.3	3.21	8.6	57	65.7	72.4
83	ARGENTINA	30094	37197	1.58	1.18	24.6	3.38	8.7	36	66.4	73.1
84	CHILE	11878	14934	1.68	1.27	24.8	2.90	7.7	40	63.8	70.4
85	URUGUAY	2990	3364	0.70	0.71	19.5	2.76	10.2	38	67.1	73.7

86	9.TROPICAL S. AMERICA (10)	2177999	304085	2.39	1.87	32.4	4.13	8.5	70	60.5	65.3
87	BOLIVIA	6200	9724	2.69	2.88	44.0	6.25	15.9	124	48.6	53.0
88	BRAZIL	132648	179487	2.23	1.67	30.6	3.81	8.4	71	60.9	66.0
89	COLOMBIA	28110	37999	2.15	1.68	31.0	3.93	7.7	53	61.4	66.0
90	ECUADOR	9090	14596	3.13	2.78	40.6	6.00	8.9	77	60.6	64.7
91	GUYANA	936	1196	1.95	1.34	28.5	3.26	5.9	35	65.8	70.8
92	PARAGUAY	3576	5405	3.00	2.34	36.0	4.85	7.2	45	62.8	67.5
93	PERU	19197	27952	2.60	2.13	36.7	5.00	10.7	99	56.8	60.5
94	SURINAME	352	423	0.06	1.59	29.5	4.10	6.1	31	67.0	71.9
95	VENEZUELA	17819	27207	3.26	2.32	35.2	4.33	5.6	39	65.1	70.6
96	B2.10.NORTHERN AMERICA (11)	261120	297683	0.89	0.74	16.0	1.85	9.1	12	70.4	78.1
97	CANADA	25302	29435	1.21	0.77	16.2	1.81	7.1	11	71.2	78.8
98	UNITED STATES OF AMERICA	235681	268079	0.86	0.74	16.0	1.85	9.3	12	70.3	78.0
99	C. ASIA	2777385	3543693	1.73	1.43	27.4	3.56	10.2	87	57.2	58.7
100	C1.EAST ASIA	1238640	1470036	1.14	1.11	18.2	2.30	6.8	36	65.9	70.1
101	11. CHINA	1051551	1255656	1.17	1.17	18.5	2.33	6.8	38	65.5	69.4
102	12. JAPAN	119492	127683	0.57	0.40	12.4	1.71	6.7	8	74.0	79.4
103	13. OTHER EAST ASIA (12)	67597	86697	1.75	1.36	23.8	2.91	6.6	30	64.1	69.5
104	HONG KONG	5498	6894	2.14	0.99	17.9	2.06	5.9	12	70.4	77.7
105	KOREA	59939	76742	1.69	1.37	24.1	2.93	6.7	30	63.7	69.1
106	DEM. PEO. REP. OF KOREA	19630	27256	2.31	1.85	30.5	4.00	7.4	32	62.7	66.0
107	REPUBLIC OF KOREA	40309	49485	1.39	1.12	21.0	2.46	6.3	29	64.4	70.8
108	MONGOLIA	1851	2673	2.66	2.00	33.8	4.82	7.2	50	62.7	66.6

REGION, COUNTRY OR AREA	TOTAL POPULATION (000S)		RATE OF GROWTH		CRUDE BIRTH RATE	TOTAL FERT. RATE 1980-85	CRUDE DEATH RATE 1980-85	INFANT MORT. RATE	EXPECTATION OF LIFE AT BIRTH 1980-85	
	1984	2000	1980-85	1995-00					MALE	FEMALE
109 C2.SOUTH ASIA	1538745	2073657	2.20	1.65	34.9	4.65	12.9	109	53.5	53.8
110 14. SOUTHEASTERN ASIA (13)	393082	519707	2.06	1.56	31.7	4.11	10.9	79	55.2	58.0
111 BURMA	38513	55186	2.52	2.03	37.9	5.53	12.7	94	53.4	56.7
112 DEMOCRATIC KAMPUCHEA	7149	9918	2.89	1.40	45.5	5.13	19.6	160	42.0	44.9
113 EAST TIMOR	638	876	2.50	1.50	48.0	5.84	23.0	183	39.2	40.7
114 INDONESIA	162167	204486	1.77	1.27	30.7	3.90	13.0	87	51.2	53.9
115 LAO PEOPLE'S DEM. REP.	4315	6213	2.51	2.10	40.6	5.84	15.5	122	48.3	51.2
116 MALAYSIA	15204	20615	2.29	1.55	29.2	3.69	6.4	29	65.0	68.8
117 PHILIPPINES	53395	74810	2.48	1.83	32.3	4.20	6.9	50	62.0	66.3
118 SINGAPORE	2540	2976	1.27	0.74	18.0	1.74	5.3	11	69.1	75.5
119 THAILAND	50584	66115	2.09	1.57	28.6	3.59	7.7	51	60.8	64.8
120 VIET NAM	58307	78129	2.02	1.72	31.2	4.31	10.1	90	56.7	61.1
121 15. SOUTHERN ASIA (14)	1036011	1385652	2.19	1.59	35.8	4.78	13.9	120	52.3	51.3
122 AFGHANISTAN	14292	24180	0.04	2.15	49.6	6.90	27.3	205	30.0	37.3
123 BANGLADESH	98464	145800	2.73	2.24	44.8	6.15	17.5	133	48.3	47.3
124 BHUTAN	1388	1893	2.03	1.82	38.4	5.53	18.1	144	46.6	45.1
125 INDIA	746742	961531	1.99	1.34	33.2	4.41	13.2	118	53.0	52.0
126 IRAN	43799	65549	3.02	2.21	40.5	5.04	10.4	101	60.4	60.0
127 NEPAL	16107	23048	2.33	2.16	41.7	6.25	16.4	144	46.6	45.4
128 PAKISTAN	98971	142254	3.08	2.16	42.6	5.84	15.2	120	51.0	49.0
129 SRI LANKA	16076	20843	2.03	1.36	27.0	3.37	6.7	38	66.0	69.0
130 16. WESTERN ASIA	109651	168293	2.85	2.48	37.8	5.46	10.1	75	56.8	62.5
131 ARAB COUNTRIES (15)	55904	93095	3.39	3.03	43.8	6.70	11.3	86	50.9	60.0
132 BAHRAIN	414	688	4.32	2.59	32.3	4.63	5.3	37	66.1	70.3
133 DEMOCRATIC YEMEN	2066	3309	2.69	2.90	47.6	6.87	18.8	138	45.5	47.5
134 IRAQ	15158	24926	3.43	2.91	44.9	6.00	10.7	72	57.2	60.9
135 JORDAN	3375	6400	3.66	3.97	44.9	7.38	8.4	63	63.0	65.4
136 KUWAIT	1705	2969	5.27	2.70	36.8	6.15	3.5	30	68.9	72.7
137 LEBANON	2644	3617	-0.01	1.89	29.3	3.79	6.6	40	63.1	67.0
138 OMAN	1181	1909	4.55	2.84	47.3	7.07	15.9	122	48.5	51.0
139 QATAR	291	469	4.02	2.66	30.1	6.77	4.6	45	68.2	73.2
140 SAUDI ARABIA	10824	18864	3.94	3.23	43.0	7.07	12.1	103	54.5	57.0
141 SYRIAN ARAB REPUBLIC	10189	18102	3.69	3.31	46.5	7.18	7.2	57	65.6	68.5
142 UNITED ARAB EMIRATES	1255	1916	5.63	1.88	27.0	5.94	4.0	45	66.2	73.2
143 YEMEN	6386	9859	2.37	2.76	48.5	6.77	16.6	154	43.0	45.0

144	NON-ARAB COUNTRIES	53686	74602	2.30	1.82	31.7	4.31	8.8	104	61.6	66.0
145	CYPRUS	659	759	1.15	0.76	19.7	2.31	8.2	17	72.7	76.1
146	ISRAEL	4216	5576	2.06	1.32	23.6	3.09	6.6	15	72.1	76.1
147	TURKEY	48811	68466	2.34	1.87	32.5	4.45	9.0	110	60.8	65.3
148	D. EUROPE	490456	513110	0.33	0.26	14.0	1.90	10.7	16	70.0	76.6
149	17. EASTERN EUROPE	112339	120970	0.56	0.46	16.4	2.17	10.8	20	68.5	75.1
150	BULGARIA	9162	9713	0.47	0.33	15.4	2.25	10.7	20	69.7	75.1
151	CZECHOSLOVAKIA	15588	16776	0.44	0.56	16.1	2.20	11.8	16	68.2	75.3
152	GERMAN DEM. REP. (16)	16658	16553	-0.11	-0.01	12.5	1.65	13.7	12	69.8	75.7
153	HUNGARY	10786	10908	0.16	0.14	14.3	2.06	12.7	21	68.0	74.5
154	POLAND	37228	41391	0.95	0.58	18.5	2.25	9.0	21	68.2	76.0
155	ROMANIA	22897	25629	0.76	0.69	17.4	2.45	9.7	26	68.5	73.6
156	18. NORTHERN EUROPE (17)	82090	83410	0.09	0.09	12.8	1.76	11.9	11	70.8	77.3
157	DENMARK	5141	5126	0.08	-0.08	11.1	1.52	10.9	8	72.0	78.0
158	FINLAND	4859	4970	0.37	0.05	12.7	1.60	10.3	7	69.0	77.6
159	ICELAND	239	270	0.99	0.62	17.0	2.04	7.1	7	73.7	80.0
160	IRELAND	3555	4247	1.11	1.11	20.9	3.19	9.8	13	70.4	75.7
161	NORWAY	4140	4227	0.27	0.06	12.3	1.69	10.5	8	72.7	79.3
162	SWEDEN	8284	8065	0.00	-0.21	10.5	1.55	11.6	7	72.8	79.0
163	UNITED KINGDOM	55624	56235	-0.01	0.08	12.8	1.78	12.4	12	70.5	77.0
164	19. SOUTHERN EUROPE (18)	141814	153147	0.58	0.42	15.4	2.12	9.5	18	70.4	76.4
165	ALBANIA	2985	4102	2.21	1.75	27.7	3.60	5.8	43	69.0	73.0
166	GREECE	9884	10734	0.58	0.48	15.8	2.31	9.9	19	72.1	76.0
167	ITALY	56724	58155	0.25	0.09	12.8	1.81	10.4	14	71.1	77.8
168	MALTA	380	419	0.68	0.57	17.3	1.97	10.5	15	69.4	74.2
169	PORTUGAL	10008	10995	0.68	0.50	17.8	2.27	9.9	25	67.6	74.1
170	SPAIN	38717	43442	0.82	0.67	17.0	2.40	8.8	12	71.3	77.5
171	YUGOSLAVIA	23028	25200	0.76	0.49	16.4	2.07	8.8	29	68.5	74.0

REGION, COUNTRY OR AREA	TOTAL POPULATION (000S)		RATE OF GROWTH		CRUDE BIRTH RATE	TOTAL FERT. RATE 1980-85	CRUDE DEATH RATE 1980-85	INFANT MORT. RATE	EXPECTATION OF LIFE AT BIRTH 1980-85	
	1984	2000	1980-85	1995-00					MALE	FEMALE
172 20. WESTERN EUROPE (19)	154212	155583	0.06	0.04	11.7	1.58	11.2	11	70.5	77.9
173 AUSTRIA	7489	7498	-0.05	0.0	12.1	1.63	12.6	13	69.5	76.7
174 BELGIUM	9877	9925	0.04	0.05	12.1	1.60	12.2	11	70.1	76.7
175 FRANCE	54449	57083	0.30	0.28	13.8	1.83	10.7	10	70.6	78.7
176 GERMANY, FED. REP. OF (16)	61214	59755	-0.18	-0.17	10.2	1.42	12.0	13	70.0	76.6
177 LUXEMBOURG	363	358	-0.12	-0.06	10.1	1.38	11.9	11	69.2	76.7
178 NETHERLANDS	14456	15011	0.40	0.15	11.6	1.44	8.7	8	72.6	79.3
179 SWITZERLAND	6309	5889	-0.26	-0.47	8.0	1.33	10.7	8	72.6	79.3
180 E. OCEANIA	24460	30403	1.50	1.27	21.1	2.71	8.4	39	65.5	69.9
181 21. AUSTRALIA-NEW ZEALAND	18783	22361	1.21	1.04	16.1	1.97	7.8	11	70.9	77.7
182 AUSTRALIA (20)	15519	18668	1.31	1.10	16.2	2.00	7.7	11	71.0	77.9
183 NEW ZEALAND	3264	3693	0.75	0.72	15.6	1.85	8.1	12	70.3	76.7
184 22. MELANESIA	4831	6986	2.60	2.05	38.5	5.52	11.5	84	56.5	57.1
185 FIJI	674	821	1.66	0.96	27.2	3.18	4.1	28	70.5	74.6
186 PAPUA NEW GUINEA	3601	5292	2.69	2.16	40.4	5.99	13.6	98	53.5	53.0
187 OTHER MELANESIA (21)	556	873	3.19	2.45	39.9	5.98	6.6	41	64.7	69.1
188 23. MICRONESIA-POLYNESIA	846	1056	1.69	1.19	36.1	5.34	6.4	39	65.4	69.7
189 MICRONESIA (22)	348	437	1.70	1.26	34.9	4.98	8.5	58	60.9	64.5
190 POLYNESIA (23)	498	619	1.68	1.15	36.8	5.60	4.9	27	68.3	73.1
191 F.24. U.S.S.R.	275761	314818	0.95	0.76	18.8	2.36	9.3	25	66.5	75.4

Source: *World Population Prospects: Estimates and Projections as Assessed in 1982* (United Nations publication, forthcoming).
Data supplied through the courtesy of the United Nations Population Division, Department of International Economic and Social Affairs.

FOOTNOTES:

DATA FOR SMALL COUNTRIES OR AREAS, GENERALLY THOSE WITH POPULATION OF
300,000 OR LESS IN 1975, ARE NOT GIVEN IN THIS TABLE SEPARATELY.
THEY HAVE BEEN INCLUDED IN THEIR REGIONAL POPULATION FIGURES.

(*)   MORE DEVELOPED REGIONS INCLUDE NORTHERN AMERICA, JAPAN,
      ALL REGIONS OF EUROPE, AUSTRALIA-NEW ZEALAND AND UNION OF SOVIET
      SOCIALIST REPUBLICS.

(+)   LESS DEVELOPED REGIONS INCLUDE ALL REGIONS OF AFRICA, ALL
      REGIONS OF LATIN AMERICA, CHINA, OTHER EAST ASIA, ALL REGIONS OF
      SOUTH ASIA, MELANESIA AND MICRONESIA-POLYNESIA.

(1)   INCLUDING BRITISH INDIAN OCEAN TERRITORY, DJIBOUTI AND SEYCHELLES.
(2)   INCLUDING AGALESA, RODRIGUES AND ST. BRANDON.
(3)   INCLUDING SAO TOME AND PRINCIPE.
(4)   INCLUDING WESTERN SAHARA.
(5)   INCLUDING ST. HELENA.
(6)   INCLUDING DOMINICA, GRENADA, SAINT LUCIA AND SAINT VINCENT AND
      THE GRENADINES.
(7)   INCLUDING ANTIGUA, BAHAMAS, BRITISH VIRGIN ISLANDS, CAYMAN ISLANDS,
      MONTSERRAT, NETHERLANDS ANTILLES, ST. KITTS-NEVIS-
      ANGUILLA, TURKS AND CAICOS ISLANDS AND UNITED STATES
      VIRGIN ISLANDS.
(8)   INCLUDING BELIZE.
(9)   INCLUDING FALKLAND ISLANDS (MALVINAS).
(10) INCLUDING FRENCH GUIANA.
(11) INCLUDING BERMUDA GREENLAND AND ST. PIERRE AND MIQUELON.
(12) INCLUDING MACAU.
(13) INCLUDING BRUNEI.
(14) INCLUDING MALDIVES.
(15) INCLUDING GAZA STRIP (PALESTINE).
(16) THE DATA WHICH RELATE TO THE FEDERAL REPUBLIC OF GERMANY AND THE
      GERMAN DEMOCRATIC REPUBLIC INCLUDE THE RELEVANT DATA RELATING TO
      BERLIN FOR WHICH SEPARATE DATA HAVE NOT BEEN SUPPLIED. THIS IS
      WITHOUT PREJUDICE TO ANY QUESTION OF STATUS WHICH MAY BE INVOLVED.
(17) INCLUDING CHANNEL ISLANDS, FAEROE ISLANDS AND ISLE OF MAN.
(18) INCLUDING ANDORRA, GIBRALTAR, HOLY SEE AND SAN MARINO.
(19) INCLUDING LIECHTENSTEIN AND MONACO.
(20) INCLUDING COCOS (KEELING) ISLANDS, CHRISTMAS ISLAND, AND NORFOLK ISLAND.
(21) INCLUDING NEW CALEDONIA, SOLOMON ISLANDS AND VANUATU.
(22) INCLUDING GUAM, KIRIBATI (WHICH ALSO INCLUDES CANTON AND ENDERBURY
      ISLANDS), NAURU, PACIFIC ISLANDS (COMPRISING THE CAROLINE,
      MARIANA, AND MARSHALL ISLANDS), TUVALU, JOHNSTON ISLAND, MIDWAY
      ISLANDS, PITCAIRN, TOKELAU AND WAKE ISLANDS.
(23) INCLUDING AMERICAN SAMOA, COOK ISLANDS, FRENCH POLYNESIA, NIUE, SAMOA,
      TONGA, AND WALLIS AND FUTUNA ISLANDS

INDEX